Naari "शक्ति" Rocks!
| *Towards The Better You* |

"Dolce far niente"

"सर्वेजगतःसुप्रियंहिन्दुस्थानंहमासु"
سارے جہاں سے اچھا ہندوستان ہمارا
Наша Индия лучше всего мира.
India kita lebih baik daripada dunia ini.
Hindistan'ımız dünyadan daha iyidir.
与世界上其他地方相比，我们的印度更好。.
Nossa Índia é melhor do que o mundo inteiro.
Nuestra India es mejor que el mundo entero.
India kami lebih baik daripada seluruh dunia.
"Vårt Indien är bättre än hela världen"
Vårt India er bedre enn hele verden.
Intia on parempi kuin koko maailma.
"Ons India is beter dan de hele wereld."
"우리인도는전세계보다더나아요 "

"Nuestra India es mejor que el mundo entero"
"La nostra India è migliore del mondo intero"
Isikhathi sethu sisonke singcono kunye nomhlaba jikelele.
"Mas maganda ang aming Indya kaysa sa buong mundo."
"私たちのインドは世界よりも良いです。"
"Unser Indien ist besser als die ganze Welt."
"Notre Inde est meilleure que le monde entire"

Rahul Thakur

BLUEROSE PUBLISHERS
India | U.K.

Copyright © Rahul Thakur 2024

All rights reserved by author. No part of this publication may be reproduced, stored in a retrieval system, or transmitted in any form or by any means, electronic, mechanical, photocopying, recording or otherwise, without the prior permission of the author. Although every precaution has been taken to verify the accuracy of the information contained herein, the publisher assumes no responsibility for any errors or omissions. No liability is assumed for damages that may result from the use of information contained within.

BlueRose Publishers takes no responsibility for any damages, losses, or liabilities that may arise from the use or misuse of the information, products, or services provided in this publication.

For permissions requests or inquiries regarding this publication, please contact:

BLUEROSE PUBLISHERS
www.BlueRoseONE.com
info@bluerosepublishers.com
+91 8882 898 898
+4407342408967

ISBN: 978-93-5989-652-6

Cover design: Shivam
Typesetting: Namrata Saini

First Edition: January 2024

> *I Commit 100% of the royalty generated from this work to be dedicated for the education of girl child.*

"Education is the most powerful weapon which you can use to change the world."

Dr. B.R Ambedkar

Dedicated to

OUR COUNTRY AND OUR WOMEN FOR THEIR EXCEPTIONAL ABILITIES AND CONTRIBUTION

"Educate a man and you educate one person; educate a woman and you educate a whole family."
- First Prime Minister of India

EARLIER WORK BY RAHUL THAKUR-

The Journey To A New You – Dec 2021

Contents

Poem .... **xi**

Preface .... **xiii**

ERA 1: The Rise of Modern Bharat **1**

Zero To ISRO 2

So, what`s cooking – Impact of Space Science to the common and beyond 18

What is Space Science & Why? 33

The Green Carpet: The Enlightened Bharat | G20 & beyond 47

ERA 2: Challenge your Mindset. **65**

The Mindset Reboot 66

Decoding UCC: Uniform Civil Code - looking beyond the obvious 105

ERA 3: The Buddha Way **169**

Critical Thinking - Think Like the Budha | What would he do if he faced. 170

The Second Copy: Are we using the "The second Copy" of Education System in *Bharat*? 178

ERA 4: Are we Right? **231**

The Prakriti effects: Cost of Progress 232

Am I Really Free? 234

The Green Currency 246

ERA 5: The Shakti... 247

The Feminine Energy - Why our world can't exist without "शक्ति." 248

How to build better "tables" and "seats" for Women 250

The Gangafication | Menstruation & Periods | Purification of Perception 259

Leadership Lessons from "शक्ति." 272

ERA 6: Towards SOLUTIONS 279

Surprise for the Men, finally! Men get space here! 280

"Stimulated" Language - Top must Know languages of this era. 287

ERA – The Finale 299

Towards ACTIONS 299

1 Minute Course towards the Better You 319

About the author 321

Bibliography 326

Dear Reader,

Here is a personal note for you...and a short poem, the next.

I am glad that you stopped by to read. If you have come this far, I am sure you encountered something that could touch your heart, or you feel it has the potential to do so. If you want to get better at yourself, it is simple, be yourself.

All of the examples and stories I have introduced you to are real and firsthand experiences. Most of them have personally inspired and evolved me in my journey.

No amount of *#Reading* can make you learn if you lack *"Curiosity."* "Curiosity" is the fuel that drives learning. And why only learning. I am certain that it is one of the most efficient ways to approach everything in life. *Doing* things with a beginner's mindset and with a childlike approach, without the fear of failure is the most effective way to learn.

Reading is not a great hobby anymore, your current YOU can improve once you *act,* however minuscule it may be. I am sure you will have your "ahhaaa moments" during this journey. Do ensure to have an open mind as it may challenge your existing beliefs and what you have always believed to be true which I may put under the hammer.

Finally, I am of the genre where my focus is to help us all *"get better"* rather than *"feel better."* While writing this piece, it helped me to evolve myself and became a better version, I uncovered aspects of my own self which otherwise I would have never known. I hope it does the same for you.

Before we dive in together, please take a moment to find how you can find me, let us rock together @

Also, if you would like to connect, I am available at the above scan, where we together can discuss solutions and be growth partners for each other.

I look forward to hearing from you as you take on this journey!

Keep Learning! That is the only way to live!
Good Luck…

Poem

(English and Hindi both the versions are available)

Title: *"Where does he buy such power from?"*

Father felt weak, the first time when he had your first touch in his lap,
Let us see today, *where from he buys such power*,

Without finishing his own childhood and youth, took on the responsibility,
He was also fond of once listening to his mother, the story,
The bond with his dreams broke, ever since the *queen* came into the life,
He had a lot to do and say, but no one listened to him including his wife.

Let us see today, *where he buys such power from?*

He shouldered family, society, and many lives,
He did sweat profusely but did not hide in a hive.
He sweated a lot, saved from the soot of the coal mine,
brought the mascara, to make his little one shine,
everyone felt that the little one was decorated very well,
did not let anyone know, it required killing his dreams and diving in a well,

How graciously the almighty has created, the father said to his father -
How did you maintain so many *relations?*
The pain you underwent, did not find any mention.

Listen to the wisdom from a father now –

Being a father is a blessing, keeping all your relations.
Respect everyone, smile is your only mention,
get ready with your hard work now,
so, you marry your daughter some time from now,

Would it be wrong to ask now, *where he buys such power from?*

In a new city, fought unaware of the fight, tried his best,
There was *talk* in his hard work, blessing in from the best.
When there is honesty in action, there is a saying from the west.
Angel's sing: *Take your hard-earned aids and leave the rest.*

Would it be wrong to say,
who is alive for your loved ones and others, is called Father!
Gave courage, love, strength, fame, and wealth,
If there was no him, how would a mother be a mother?
....

……………………..read the upcoming lines the section –

ERA 6: Towards SOLUTIONS>> 19. Surprise for the Men, finally! Men get space here!

Preface

Thank **you** in the first place for deciding to pick this piece of work to sail through. I am sure that you will **read** and also **act** upon this with as much love as I have loved to write this journey.

Some questions are never answered.

Why is **"Why"** not asked?

What are the values that can make *Bharat, The India* that we dream of? What makes Indian defense forces special? Will reserving a third of seats by rotation change the male mindset? Why are we heading for space when we have burning problems at home? Why is education leading to suicidal mindset? Why are we spending a huge cache of money on events like G20?

Why is India Canada relations tasting jittery? Why is there a need for UCC (Uniform Civil code) or why not?

Why or why not to develop critical thinking? Why is it important to have the right *Mindset* and reboot it from time to time? Why was I not able to crack that last interview? Why is menstruation or periods still considered taboo talk in our society? Why is a girl raped and still the criminal is not punished? What do we want to prove by delaying justice? Why can't we be a united society? Why are Hindu & Muslim fighting and for what?

How are we paying the **"cost of progress?"** Are we paying for this in terms of massive floods, fire, and earthquakes? Why is homeland punishing the innocent? Shouldn't a woman decide for her? Why is a girl's right given more importance in divorce and why is it that no one talks about the fathers` or husbands` rights? Why is technology important? How is AI going to help or not help us?

Will the laws designed in 19th & 20th century be able to provide Justice in the 21st century? Why do all the rights of criminals pop up after committing a crime, but no one talks of victims' rights when they are being tortured. How will Israel and Hamas sort out and who is at fault? Is there any language that would help to bring harmony?

Will there ever be peace around us?

Unanswered are these questions, right? But aren't these questions? These are valid questions in every sense that is what brings my mental faculties to pen down the TRUTH as it is that looks to find actionable solutions.

What do you unpack with the book?

The book is about **You.** Yes, you heard it right! I hope the title of this piece - "Naari शक्ति Rocks!" does not make you feel that this work belongs to *feminists*. Absolutely not, it is about **YOU,** *irrespective of gender, age, profession, caste, and political orientation, and* any other demographics that differentiates us.

How to read this book?

You should read as an individual in this priority – **Human** > Indian > Daughter > Son > Siblings > Friends > Colleagues > Professionals > ~~Polarized Society~~.

Read that again! Yes, please do read with an open mind and read as a **human** instead of donning any other shoes as mentioned above. The value of **Advaita Vedanta** is enough to answer the polarizations created in our society. It is my most humble request and advice to *not be a prisoner of Polarization*.

It will make you meet yourselves at the end. "The Journey" is universal and each one of you and I are in the same boat, ferry, carriage, aircraft, rocket, space capsule and whatever you can think of. It is about creating better 'tables' & 'seats.' Oooo oo! Worried what did you read just now? Do not worry we all are not cabinet makers but yes, we are the *"crafts*women*" and craftsmen* of our expedition. Do not tax your mental faculties hard now. But yes, do keep it for later in the journey. I have used 'tables' & 'seats' metaphorically here. You will be able to connect the dots once we together have sailed through ***"The Journey To A New You."***

Co-incidentally this title happens to be my first published work recently in Dec 2021. While writing the earlier journey, I knew that I would be writing my next work that is in your hand right now, but what is more important is, the series of events that propelled me to time my next work now. I assure you that we all will be a better version of ourselves after navigating through this piece of work. And if it does not have any influence in our lives together, then…

<u>How I became interested in the subject of the book and why did I choose to write about it and that too NOW?</u>

At the rock-bottom of my career, I abruptly started authoring a book. Everyone wondered how I became interested in the subject of the book, and why to draft a book, but the answer was not simple.

I am going to just give you my dream shamelessly, because that is the thing that I can do best. You may have heard this line in one of the speeches from the great *"Maddy"* or R Mahadevan. I completely resonate with this line and have borrowed it from his inspirational journey. I will give my dream after you go through few lines here:

If you have carefully observed the beautiful cover page, there is a formula written on it. Now I know most of you will see or have seen the cover page after reading this, Hahaha! Am I right or am I right? So, what is significant enough to observe on the cover page?

Ok, I am not that bad at making you feel miserable, let me answer it for you.

$$"शक्ति" = \text{WORLD} = \text{WE}.$$

Bingo! Yes, if you got this, you were right. Now with your permission I am going to use the word "शक्ति" instead of girls, women, wonder women, females, "*papa ki Pari*" and others. I will also introduce you to a stimulating new term that I developed to signify Women.

Let us descend further. I came across overwhelming facts during my research. I consider myself so "blessed" to come across this reality.

"शक्ति" comes from a Sanskrit word meaning power or energy.

This resonates perfectly as Shri Narendra Modi, PM already termed our step on the moon as Shiv "शक्ति" Point which would have been incomplete without "*Tirangaa Point*," the steppingstone. This name represents the perfect balance of Masculine and Feminine energy.

Further, the much *hulla-bulloed*, talked about, "Naari "शक्ति" Vandan Adhiniyam Bill, 2023 also signifies how important the feminine energy is.

It is the Sanatan Dharma concept or personification of the divine feminine aspect, sometimes referred to as 'The Divine Mother'. Shakti represents the active, dynamic principles of feminine power. It refers to "Energy, ability, strength, effort, power and capability". It is the primordial cosmic energy, Woman in aspect. "शक्ति" represents the dynamic forces that are thought to move through the universe. "शक्ति" often refers to the wife of lord Shiva.

Similarly, Islam gives immense importance to mothers or in other words - "शक्ति."
The Prophet Muhammad (PBUH) said:
"Paradise lies at the feet of mothers." (An-Nasa'i, 3104)
"God has forbidden for you to be undutiful to your mothers."
(Sahih Al-Bukhari)

Not only Muslim brothers but also Muslim "शक्ति" is recommended to be obedient to their mothers. Men are not a dominating gender according to Islam. Parents have a very prestigious status in Islam.

From woman, man is born.
within woman, man is conceived; to woman he is engaged and married.
Woman becomes his friend; through woman, the future generations come.
When his woman dies, he seeks another woman; to woman he is bound.
So why call her bad? From her, kings are born.
From woman, woman is born; without woman, there would be no one at all.

— *Guru Nanak, Raag Aasaa Mehal 1, Ang 473*
From woman, man is born.

In this Shabad, from the holy Guru Granth Sahib, the Guru expresses the importance of "शक्ति." It begins with the line "From a woman, a man is born" to emphasize that all people come from a "शक्ति. This theme then continues with the Guru highlighting, in a logical sequence, the various stages of life where the importance of "शक्ति" is noted – "within woman, man is conceived," and then, " he is engaged and married" to a "शक्ति" who becomes his friend, partner, and the source for future generations.

This Shabad shows that, throughout a man's life, he is dependent on "शक्ति" at every critical stage.
There is also a proverb from holy Bible,

Proverbs 31:16-17
"She surveys a field and acquires it; from her own resources, she plants a vineyard. She works energetically; her arms are powerful."

- If a woman sets her mind on something, she will get it done — no matter what.

The Bible tells the stories of many amazing "शक्ति," including Mary of Nazareth, Eve, and Mary Magdalene, all of whom play prominent roles in the story of Christianity. Biblical passages about their journeys inspire those who follow the Lord, but these verses are not the only words which give strength to mothers, wives, daughters, and sisters. There are broader Bible verses for "शक्ति" that could empower and uplift followers of Jesus Christ who may need a boost of confidence after a hard week or a reminder that God is on their side.

One of the oldest representations of the goddess in India is in a triangular form. The Baghor stone, found in a Paleolithic context in the *Son* River valley and dating to 9,000–8,000 BCE, is considered an early example of a yantra. Kenoyer, part of the team that excavated the stone, considered that it was highly probable that the stone was associated with "शक्ति." The admiration of Shiva and Shakti was also prevalent in the Indus valley civilization.

Hey! Stop.

Before you begin to think this is turning into a history class, let me tell you we are the proudest human beings to be born to the "Motherland" "भारत माँ" - India. And what makes us proud is the unique diverse rich culture that none of the countries in the world and our elegant and able "neighbors" possess.

Fast forwarding, Imagine a world without "शक्ति" for a moment. I seriously mean it. We will all together try to be in this moment for a while. Believe me, you are going to get an astounding first-hand experience like never before if you do it honestly with me.

Are you ready? Really?

I insist on being honest to yourselves and do this with your highest "state of attention" away from distractions around you and your own self called the "mind" that does not let you focus these days.

Are we ready? If we are, let us start then.

Severely visualize the environment around as without a single Woman. No "शक्ति" around us in the office, in school and colleges. No "शक्ति" in the metros in our daily travel, none of them at home, not even on silver screens in both – Bollywood and Hollywood. No Woman anchors on our TV sets. No "शक्ति" in hospitals and no female teachers. No products for "शक्ति," none of the markets sell stuff related to "शक्ति." The Heart for shopkeepers and big brands reading this certainly would jump out of their soul with this thought. Are you with me? Let us travel furthermore together.

Ok so no Women around us now. Some questions for the moment being in this trance -

With this fact what are we supposed to call our country as we proudly refer to it as Homeland? Rivers referred to as feminine beings, what are we going to call our rivers then? What are we going to call the education goddess Saraswati? Will we be able to celebrate Navratri or Diwali for that matter? Both signify the victory of good over evil.

What would happen to the epics "Ramayana" and Bhagavad Gita? Without "शक्ति" would the history be written?

Is the world even possible without "शक्ति"?

Isn't it scary? Dull. I think the best word that can describe a world without "शक्ति" is - 'Non-existence' of the world without you my dear Shaktis. And all the men please hold on!! I know what you are thinking right now, you will get your share of worth too, hahaha! but it will be a story in the *"ERA 6: Towards Solutions"* as soon as you mind-travel there.

Special creatures get special remarks, you know, so this is the moment for all the "Shaktis" around us in different forms and relations – our mothers, wives, sisters, colleagues and for that matter, *mother-in-law, sister-in-law* as well. Why leave our better half's family! Do not ever dare to leave them otherwise you think of ways to oversee your better half *better. Hahahhaa!!*

Then our Women students, teachers, professors, principals, office colleagues, HR professionals, trainers, social media influencers, Woman writers, singers, producers, directors, actress, Woman politicians and presidents, receptionist, nurses, pilots, doctors, lawyers, judges, fashion designers, authors, medal winners and champions, entrepreneurs, bosses, team members, self-help group (SHG) member/Coordinators, farmwomen, Agricultural worker, Dairy farmer, weaving and textile Woman, Rural business owner, Anganwadi worker, the

Woman vendors, fruit sellers, metro drivers, army women. Our cousins, friends or girlfriends and live in partners too.

The list can go on and on as the entire world around us is *borne, created, and protected by* "शक्ति" as highlighted by our rich history and shastras.

Right now, this is the moment for "Shakti" – The power of Universe. Let us give it up for all the Women around us! The entire human race wants to thank 'you':

For ***empowering us***, though *we* always *'talk'* of empowering you.
For ***bearing all the pain*** to give us birth and the chance to be in this universe, though when we grow older, we do not ***care,***

For spending ***sleepless nights*** for us when *we* were in your womb, though we are reluctant to wake up a single minute as we are busy and tired,

For **protecting** us since our birth, though *we* rarely think of protecting you.
For **satiating our hunger**, though *we* never asked you about your starvation,

For always ***eating in the end***, though *we* never made you eat before others,
For ***understanding*** us, though *we* rarely tried to understand you,

For ***educating*** us, even though *we* did not offer a fair '*table*' to educate you,
For ***marrying*** us, though *we* hardly asked your consent and the will to get married,

For ***bodily pleasure,*** though we seldom offered to *understand your body, mind, and soul,*
For ***giving birth to a child***, though we questioned the "gender" of the precious gift.

For ***making us parents,*** though we hardly understood you as a parent and did not thank you,
For ***protecting our children and conditioning them,*** though we rarely taught our children to say "thanks" for your deeds,

For giving ***"Streedhan"*** when we were in dire need, though we rarely think about your needs.
For being ***selfless,*** though we have always been self-seeking,

For making the world around us ***beautiful***, though *"many among us"* have crushed your beauty,
For ***holding*** the most difficult and ever-changing *designations*, though *we* never appreciated.

Thank you for making us what we are today! And thank you is a miniscule word against what you do for us.

Our imagination itself will cease; the imagination stops working for us when we even try to think of a "शक्ति" free world.

Getting back to the promise that I will give my dream shamelessly, it is now time to Rock for Naari Shakti as evident from the title of this piece-

"I dream of giving equitable education access to each and every girl in India & the world."

And by that, I mean when we talk of dreams, we have one of our greatest scientists and philanthropists Dr. Abdul Kalam, and he said something which is interesting. He said, "Dreams are not what you have when you sleep. The true dreams are the ones that do not let you sleep." I have been experiencing this since the day I dreamt. While writing this line it was then, 2:47 AM early morning Sunday away from home, sitting in mother nature's lap in one of the most beautiful places in India. Would you like to know the place?

Let me tell you the name and how you can get there. So, the name is...

Oh wait! What? Would you just like to know the name of the place? Or if you are like me of the genre *"Yeh Pyaas hai baadi"*, *"Ye Dil mange More"* and *"Ye dil hai ki manta nai"* why not, and allow me to say - *"aao huzur tummko hawao me le chalu"* that will help you explore *"Ye hasi vadiyan ye khula aasman"* so that you can experience *"Panchin nadiyaan, pawan ke jhoke, koi sharhad na inhe roke"* and then you get a feel to sing –

> *"Ye Duniya Ek Dulhan,*
> *Ye Duniya Ek Dulhan*
> *Dulhan Ke Maathe Ki Bindiya*
> *Ye Mera India*
> *Ye Mera India*
> *I Love My India*
> *I Love My India"*

Would you like to miss this beautiful experience by knowing the name now? Of course, not I believe, right?

Interestingly, I have good news for you. In the very first chapter of this piece – "Zero To ISRO," I will personally take you along on our space journey to understand what it means for the commoners followed by four of our friends to one of the best places on the lap of mother nature that I have ever been to in India.

The better news is, it is not exceedingly difficult to reach and affordable as well. And the best news is that we have already marked our way to the moon at Shiv "शक्ति" Point which would have been incomplete without "*Tirangaa Point,*" the steppingstone. We are starting right away. Let us fasten your seatbelts now. Get ready to fly..oops!!

I think let us launch…. We are quite skilled in launching you know, and we do it with ease!

And before we launch, reinforcing my dream again about women empowerment. I do not know what "Women Empowerment" is for all but for me, it means that women in India (RURAL + URBAN INDIA both), specially, RURAL INDIA - Once they return from their fields, farms, work, study or even if they are at home, they get time and the environment to talk about art and culture.

That is what I call "women empowerment."

Why?

Because that is what makes our country unique. The rich heritage added glam to the herculean G20 Summit. It is the X-factor that is rich, original, authentic, and sets us apart from *the rest, the west, the best of the worlds,* and makes us the best of the best, *The Vishwaguru.* Culture is the thing that protects our heritage, it is the safety net that we all rely on, in this fast-paced planet to save the species.

And why rural India? Because that is the place where our culture is nurtured and protected, and they are the actual heirs of our rich culture. This is pretty evident from the fact that our culture had gripped the city as well as the venue during the G20 Summit, right from Madhubani Paintings from Bihar to the Natraj Statue from South, and from the green carpet to the shape of Baharat Mandapam.

"I dream of an empowered world for women."

Further, going back to what APJ Abdul Kalam said, "When you have that dream once it is a dream; when you have it twice it becomes a desire. And when you see it for the third time consecutively, it becomes a passion, an aim, and a goal," and that is the passion with which I want to see this fantasy that I have for the "शक्ति" in India at the first place and then of course around the world.

Abraham Lincoln also was a dreamer, and you know, but he said one thing that makes most sense in trying to achieve this goal that I have dreamed for my nation. He said, "If I have six hours to cut down a tree, then I would spend the first four hours sharpening the axe." There is a great philosophy in that.

In this era of instant gratification, we just keep thinking we can achieve all these goals by just tweaking this and that, it is not true. A missionary zeal is required to make that quantum change, which can make India what I am dreaming about right now.

Do watch out for the summary that offers *learnable* and *Key action points* at the end of every chapter.

So, we have fastened our seatbelts now. Let us get launched together!

Rock it!
Crack it!
Smack It!

And Tic Tic...

It is 6.04 PM, 23rd August 2023
Here you go.!

ERA 1:

The Rise of Modern Bharat

- **Zero to ISRO**
- **What's cooking – Impact of space Science to commoner and beyond**
- **What is Space Science & Why? | A guide for the Youth**
- **The Green Carpet | The Enlightened Bharat | G20 & more**

Zero To ISRO

'India
I reached my destination and you too!'

Wow! Do we need an introduction as to who uttered these words?

The lines that rocketed the entire world and specially *Bharat* on 23rd Aug 2023 @ 6:04 PM, which now will be celebrated and *"National Space Day"* or better called as *"Hindustan National Space Day"*. Amazing as it sounds and still my manes go berserk and goose bumps all around the body when I write this and expect the same, when you are reading the lines, yes! I can see that proud smile on your lips. A day, an event, an achievement that will inspire millions and billions of current and upcoming generations.

Do you think ISRO is more than a space organization, an emotion?

Youngsters who think and would have planned to go abroad for studies and research need to rethink the worth of leaving *"Bharat* Maa." A person born on the land that is hailed as *Vishwaguru*, need not look for any other country, as the entire world, the west and all, now looks at the best, *Bharat*, *Bharat* as their leader.

Many amongst us wondered what going to space has to do with normal people when we have burning problems at home.

Let me tell you something catchy and worth noticing.

Have you been an APPLE mobile phone fan or anything that has to do with the company? Have you used or thought of buying the latest Apple i15, recently launched at the time of writing. What interests me is neither the model nor the design, I am also not a huge fan of the APPLE series. But what caught my attention is something else. It included ISRO's regional navigation satellite system NavIC (Navigation with Indian Constellation) in the latest iPhone series. Earlier Xiaomi, POCO, Vivo, & OnePlus adopted the same technology.

It is designed with a collection of seven satellites and a network of ground stations working 24*7 for India's positioning, navigation, and timing. This is the first batch of Made in India iPhones which will see support for the indigenous GPS system. The government is keen to ask other smartphone players to integrate NavIC into their hardware by 2025. India's homegrown navigation system is going to compete with U.S.'s GPS, EU's Galileo, Russia's GLONASS and China's BeiDou.

Integration of GPS systems like the NavIC needs to be done at the hardware level. For this, smartphone makers will need to purchase chips that can support such integration. Observers argue that this may raise the input cost for smartphone brands, which are likely to pass it down to buyers.

What is NavIC?
Developed by the Indian Space Research Organization (ISRO), NavIC stands for Navigation with Indian Constellation. As stated above, It consists of a constellation of seven satellites and a network of ground stations. Three satellites of the constellation are placed in geostationary orbits, while four are placed in inclined geosynchronous orbits. The ground network consists of a control center, a precise timing facility, range and integrity monitoring stations, and two-way ranging stations, among others.

The major difference between NavIC and other global navigation systems is that NavIC maneuvers chiefly over Indian territory (and 1,500 kms beyond it) while the latter systems revolve around the earth twice, daily.

Why do we need it?
NavIC can majorly cut our dependence on navigation systems operated by other countries, which can be critical during emergencies, natural calamities, or war. As an indigenous system, NavIC is designed keeping in mind our topography and the variety of our landscapes, by Indian scientists with a better sense of understanding the country and its geographical peculiarities.

Another Feather in the cap, Amazon Web Services (AWS) India Private Limited has signed a strategic Memorandum of Understanding with the Indian Space Research Organization (ISRO) and Indian National Space Promotion and Authorization Centre (IN-SPACE) to support space-tech innovations through cloud computing.

This collaboration will give space startups, research institutes, and students access to innovative cloud technologies that accelerate the development of novel solutions in the space sector.

"Cloud computing-led innovations enable the space industry to make better decisions, faster – pushing the boundaries of possibilities, and AWS is committed to help startups identify use cases, accelerate solution development, and build a strong talent pool in India with expertise in cloud and space. "We look forward to helping customers in India build space-tech solutions to make life on Earth better," said Shalini Kapoor, Director and Chief Technologist, Public Sector, AWS India, and South Asia.

AWS said its educational programs on cloud computing in combination with ISRO's space-tech expertise will inspire future generations to pursue a career in India's growing space sector.

PM Modi has always said, "Dream Big." Currently, ISRO has given us every chance to make that happen. And why not?

India's Strides in the space sector over the past few years has been commendable and we are building them for more success. It includes the setting up of "**Bhartiya Antariksha Station**" by 2035 and sending the first Indian to the moon by 2040. The PM who heads the Department of Space (DoS), had first announced about the *Gaganyaan* program during his I-day address in 2018. Big dreams do take time and are full of challenges.

Due to the Covid pandemic, the human spaceflight program got delayed, but post-pandemic, it has gained momentum, and a series of tests has been planned in the coming session.

Would you like to have a cup of good news? Let me serve it for you.

The very first test, **TV-D1, was** already successful on 21st October 2023 after a series of holds due to technicalities and the best news was the brief time period in which the technicalities were corrected and launched a few minutes later the same day. It involves launching the crew module to outer space, bringing it back to the earth and recovering it after the touchdown in the Bay of Bengal. A diving team from the Indian Navy will use a dedicated vessel to recover the crew module.

After this successful test, three more tests **D2, D3, D4** will be conducted and later a humanoid, Vyommitra, will be conducted and if all goes well, the final staffed or ***Womanned*** mission comprising of 2-3 Indian Astronauts orbit Earth at a height of 400Km, will be launched in 2025.
Isn't that something *simply awesome*?

Moving on, **Shiv "शक्ति" Point**, so aptly named by our PM, Shri Narendra Modi, which expresses the unison, amalgamation, and balance of male and feminine energy. I was so happy after listening to his address on 26th August 2023 from Bengaluru ISRO center where he appreciated the efforts of our eminent scientist that proved that *Bharat* Indeed is a *"Vishwaguru" or "Kulapati* (A term you will get to see in upcoming chapters)". I was so glad for my own work due to the title and the topic that I had once decided to draft on as it naturally resonated with the balance of both the energies.

In Shiv there`s resolutions for humanity`s welfare and **"शक्ति"** gives us strength to fulfill those resolutions. This point also gives a sense of connection from the Himalayas to Kanyakumari, said Modi. We must recognize the contribution of Naari "Shakti" as women scientists to the moon mission, underscoring the blessings of the **"शक्ति."** In the success of our lunar mission, they have played a crucial role reaffirming the importance of gender diversity in scientific endeavors.

More than one hundred women played a direct and significant role in conceptualizing, designing, realizing testing, and executing Chandrayan-3. And how can I not name them. At least some of them. As soon as the lander module touched down and the mission's success was celebrated at ISRO, the team addressed the nation. Along with the four men who stood at the podium, was one woman.

She had a grin on her face that she couldn't contain. She was introduced as Deputy Project Director Kalpana K, and it was a "goosebump" moment. Kalpana attributed the success of the entire mission to her team and their efforts.

Speaking after the landing she said, "This will remain the most memorable and the happiest moment for all of us and for our team at Chandrayaan-3. We have achieved our goal flawlessly from the day we started rebuilding our spacecraft after the Chandrayaan-2 experience. It has been a breathe-in and breathe-out Chandrayaan-3 for our team. Starting from the reconfiguration and all the assembling we have conducted meticulously; this has only been possible because of the team's immense effort."

Kalpana, who hails from Bengaluru, is an IIT Kharagpur graduate. She joined ISRO in 2003 and has been a part of various projects. She played a vital role in designing and optimizing the lander system for Chandrayaan-3.

She was also a part of the Chandrayaan-2 mission and the Mangalyaan team for the Mars Orbiter Mission.

Let us now meet a lady who is also known as the 'Rocket Woman of India,' Dr Ritu Karidhal who has been an aerospace engineer at ISRO since 1997. She is one of the prominent figures in Indian space history. She developed the onward autonomy system of the craft that made Mangalyaan a successful mission. She is one of the senior scientists at ISRO and has been a key member of many major space missions.

She has been the operations director for many missions. She helmed the Mars mission as the deputy director of the project. She has many accolades to her name, including the ISRO Young Scientist Award in 2007 presented by the former president of India, the late Dr APJ Abdul Kalam.

Moving on, next on our list is the project director of Chandrayaan-2, without such a mission we couldn't have thought about a successful Chandrayan-3 mission. She is none other than Vanitha Muthayya. She joined ISRO as a junior engineer and went on to become the first woman project director at ISRO. She also was the deputy project director for a number of satellites including the Cartosat-1, Oceansat-2, and Megha-Tropiques.

She was also a part of the team that led Mangalyaan. In 2006, she received the Best Woman Scientist Award by the Astronomical Society of India. Next up is a rocket scientist besides being a *home scientist*, Nandini Harinath, who has worked on over fourteen space missions and contributed to many projects in the last 20 years that she has worked at ISRO.

She was the deputy operations director on the Mars Orbiter Mission (Mangalyaan), which successfully placed a spacecraft in orbit around Mars in 2014. At the time of writing, she is currently working as the project manager and mission designer. Joining her on the list is Anuradha TK, a scientist who joined ISRO in 1982, was the first woman to be a Satellite Project Director. She headed the successful launch of three communications satellites such as GSAT-9, GSAT-17, and GSAT-18. She specialized in communication satellites and retired after 34 years of working at ISRO.

Next up is a Physicist, Moumita Dutta who played an instrumental role in the Mars Orbiter Mission and has been a part of projects like HySat and Chandrayaan-1. She specializes in the development and testing of optical and IR sensors, instruments, and payloads. She was the recipient of the ISRO Team of Excellence Awards after the success of Mangalyaan.

And to conclude our list with one name is VR Lalithambika, director of Gaganyaan, who has been part of more than one hundred missions in ISRO. She was born in Thiruvananthapuram, Kerala, and before ISRO was the deputy director at the Vikram Sarabhai Space Center. For her contributions, she has received the Astronautical Society of India Award of Excellence in launch vehicle technology.

The women behind the mission and in the field of science and technology have set precedents and have set the stage for future generations to come. Their relentless pursuit and drive for the country and their simplicity have gained them heaps of praise and immense mass following.

So, What's next?
Is that all that we had to do? Or is it just the beginning where we are headed for greater heights? I have heard people say, "Why are we going to space and spending crores when we are bustling with daily life problems in all the nooks, corners, and villages. Is it worth it to spend that humongous amount on space exploration and research?

We will try to find an answer and actionable steps from here on through this chapter. Whether it is Space Science or Science, we all need to understand the role that science plays in uplifting society.

Let me give you a glimpse of what`s Next. Might be possible that by the time you are reading this piece, the mission I am going to talk about has already been achieved. I came across a beautiful article in, *The times of India*, 29th Aug 2023 in which information was sourced by none other than the champion ISRO.

After the successful Mars and Moon mission, ISRO is to launch a solar mission, Aditya-L1 to study the energy source that sustains life on earth. But what is more important is to know the **"Why"** behind the mission.

Why is that important? Let me answer it for you. This is what makes us different from the rest of the world. Let us take a closer look at the Sun:
It seeks to study:
1. Coronal heating and solar wind acceleration.

2. Initiation of coronal mass ejection, flares, and near-Earth space weather
3. Coupling and dynamics of the solar atmosphere.
4. Solar wind distribution and temperature anisotropy.

And the next question to ask should be the why behind the above *Whys*.

Why are the Bharatiya Scientists looking to study the Sun?

The sun is the nearest star and therefore can be studied in much more detail compared with other stars. It is a very dynamic star that extends much beyond what we see. It shows several eruptive phenomena and releases immense amounts of energy. If such explosive solar phenomena are directed towards the Earth, it could cause various disturbances in the near-earth space environment.

Various spacecraft and communication systems are prone to such disturbances and therefore early warning of such events is important for taking corrective measures beforehand. The sun provides a good natural lab to understand these phenomena that cannot be directly studied in the lab.

For those of you who are like me *"Yeh Pyaas hai badi and ye dil mange more,"* let us keep the locus of our focus intact and take a further plunge into the unknown.

What are Lagrange points?

These are five locations around a planet's orbit where the gravitational forces and the orbital motion of the spacecraft, sun and the planet interact to create a stable location from which to make observations. These points are known as Lagrangian points or "L" points named after the 18th century Italian astronomer and mathematician Joseph-Louis Lagrange. The L points are denoted as L1, L2, L3, L4 and L5. The distance of L1 from earth (1.5 million Km) is about 1% of the Earth-Sun distance (151 million Km).

The Aditya-L1 mission-
It is the first space-based observatory class *Bharatiya* Solar mission. The spacecraft is headed for a halo orbit around the L1 point because a satellite placed therein has the major advantage of continuously viewing the sun without any occultation or eclipse. This will provide a greater advantage of observing the solar activities continuously.

Aditya-L1 will carry seven payloads to observe the below amazing findings using electromagnetic and particle detectors:
1. The photosphere
2. Chromosphere
3. The outermost layer of the Sun (the corona)

Four payloads on board will directly view the sun and the remaining three will conduct in-situ studies of particles and fields at L1. The payloads are expected to provide information regarding the problems of:

1. Coronal Heating.
2. Coronal mass ejection.
3. Pre-flare and flare activities and their characteristics.
4. Dynamics of Space weather
5. Study of the propagation of particles and fields in the interplanetary medium

It will be interesting to note the solar missions launched by other countries:

1960 - 1969
US`s NASA launched six pioneer missions – 5, 6A, 7B, 8C, 9D, E. Of six orbiter missions, five were successful, one failed.

1974 – 1997
1. Helios A (Germany - US, 1974 - 1982)
2. Helios B (Germany - US, 1976 - 1985)

3. ISSE – 3 (Nasa, 1978 - 1982)
4. Ulysses (ESA – NASA, 1994-95)
5. WIND (NASA, 1994 - 2020)
6. SOHO (ESA – NASA, 1996, extended till 2025)
7. ACE (NASA, 1997 until 2024)

2000 to Present.
1. Ulysses (Second pass, ESA – NASA in 2000-01)
2. Genesis (NASA, from 2001 – 04)
3. STEREO A (NASA launched in 2006 and active till Sept 2021)
4. STEREO B (NASA 2006 - 2018)
5. Ulysses (third pass, ESA – NASA in 2007 – 08, partial success)
6. DSCOVR (NASA, Feb 2015, successful)
7. Parker solar probe (Launched by NASA, 2018 – Dec 2025; en route)
8. Solar Orbiter (ESA, Feb 10, 2020; en route)
9. CuSP (Launched Nov 16, 2022, but no contact now)

Where it all started and the Future of Space Science | The man Behind

How can we even think of proceeding without mentioning "The father of *Bharatiya* Space Research, Dr. Vikram Sarabhai" and "the father of the *Bharatiya* nuclear program, Homi Jehangir Bhabha." This is an opportune time to remember the man who started it all and whose name since 1974, has graced a small, bowl-shaped crater (The Sarabhai Crater) on the Mare Serenitatis in the north-east quadrant of the moon.

Before proceeding, let us hear his dream which is so sacrosanct and true to be true.

His dream was, as from the author of *"Vikram Sarabhai: Life."*

"To link technology with development serving the needs of the masses while nurturing a highly sophisticated work culture and scientific abilities."

Why is space science important? Why spend money when we have burning problems at our homes? Who has time for all this? Well! These are questions of a "fixed mindset" which you will learn about in the upcoming chapters. But if you belong to the tribe of "Growth Mindset" or even if you want to develop a mindset of your own, this is for you.

Let us first understand the "***why***" of visionary Vikram Sarabhai behind space science and what impact it has on our daily lives.

Vikram chose the path of science despite being born in a family of world's wealthiest industrialists, the Sarabhai's who were unusually political and close to Gandhi and allied themselves firmly with the anti-colonial struggle. Although, he was surrounded by luxury, spoilt for choice and yet aware of the family legacy of political activism.

In the era marked by the excitement of discoveries regarding the atom, he became a physicist. Unlike others who studied cosmic rays for the atomic particles thrown up by them, he became interested in cosmic rays as a tool to study outer space. His interest tied in with an emerging trend.

In 1961-62, against a background of a global push in space research by the International Council of Scientific Unions, the Department of Atomic Energy supported by the then PM Nehru and DAE (Department of Atomic Energy) secretary Homi Bhabha, initiated space research in *Bharat* and set up a sounding rocket programme under Vikram's leadership.

The idea of the so-called poor and newly independent country like *Bharat* entering a field requiring technology and investment such as space research seemed unimaginably audacious. And the programme was equally so, with Vikram encouraging bright young scientists and engineers such as Vasant Gowarikar and MR. APJ Abdul Kalam, beside many others, joined and set them challenging tasks with thread-bare resources on the beaches of Thumba, a fishing village in Kerala.

Henri Cartier Bresson captured the slapdash energy of the enterprise in evocative white and black photographs including an iconic one of the two scientists casually carrying a nose cone on a bicycle.

The cheekiness was counterbalanced by a highly evolved vision. In 1963, when the Soviets had about launched the first synchronous satellite, Vikram was already thinking of using satellites for communications. He envisaged applications for space in:
1. Agriculture
2. Forestry
3. Oceanography
4. Mineral Prospecting
5. Cartography (the art and science of graphically representing a geographical area, usually on a flat surface such as a map or chart.)

In a 1966 paper on "Space Activity for Developing Countries ", he hoped that space activity would stimulate growth in electronics and cybernetics and create a new culture of collaboration between countries and specializations.

One of his favorite phrases was "Leapfrogging" which referred to his faith in the power of technology to enable developing countries to circumvent the long processes followed by the West. His ideas created a big sensation internationally, according to Japanese space scientist Hideo Itokawa, and birthed ambitious schemes such as the world`s first experiment in direct broadcasting by satellite using an American ATS-6 on loan to transmit locally produced content to 2400 backward *Bharatiya* villages.

Let us hear a small snippet of what he had to say about the effects of science before we *launch* our journey.

"A person who has imbibed the ways of Science injects into a situation a new way of looking, hopefully perhaps a degree of enlightenment." So, this is what he would hope to gain from the moon mission -

"Broadening of Minds, a trigger to innovation and greater wisdom."

The greatness of space science has also proved its mettle in the film industry as an astounding film released in 2022. *Rocketry: The Nambi Effect* won the best *Bharatiya* feature film recently at the National Film Awards 2023.It was based on Nambi Narayanan's life in which Sarabhai was played by Rajit Kapur in the Hindi version and by Ravi Raghavendra in the Tamil version. A 2022 web-series Rocket Boys was based on the fictionalized lives of Sarabhai and Homi J. Bhabha, played by Ishwak Singh and Jim Sarbh, respectively.

I would strongly recommend watching both the flicks if you haven't seen them yet!

He was also honored with Padma Bhushan in 1966 and the Padma Vibhushan (posthumously) in 1972.Dr. Vikram A. Sarabhai, Chairperson of the *Bharatiya* Space Research Organization (ISRO) and head of *Bharat*'s Department of Atomic Energy and Dr. Thomas O. Paine, NASA Administrator, signed an agreement to cooperate in an unprecedented experiment using a space satellite to bring instructional television programs to some 5,000 *Bharatiya* villages.

Known as the cradle of space sciences in *Bharat*, the Physical Research Laboratory (PRL) was founded in 1947 by Vikram Sarabhai. PRL had a modest beginning at his residence, the "RETREAT", with research on cosmic rays.

The institute was formally established at the M.G. Science Institute, Ahmedabad, on 11 November 1947 with support from the Karmakshetra Educational Foundation and the Ahmedabad Education Society. Kalpathi Ramakrishna Ramanathan was the first Director of the institute. The initial focus was research on cosmic rays and the properties of the upper atmosphere. Research areas were expanded to include theoretical physics and radio physics later with grants from the Atomic Energy Commission. He led the Sarabhai family-owned business conglomerate.

His interests varied from science to sports to statistics. He set up the Operations Research Group (ORG), the first market research organization in the country. Most notable among the many institutes he helped set up are the Nehru Foundation for Development in Ahmedabad, the *Bharatiya* Institute of Management Ahmedabad (IIMA), the Ahmedabad Textile Industry's Research Association (ATIRA) and the (CEPT).

Along with his wife Mrinalini Sarabhai, he founded the Darpana Academy of Performing Arts. Other projects and institutions initiated or established by him include the Fast Breeder Test Reactor (FBTR) in Kalpakkam, Variable Energy Cyclotron Project in Calcutta, Electronics Corporation of *Bharat* Limited (ECIL) in Hyderabad and Uranium Corporation of *Bharat* Limited (UCIL) in Jaduguda, Jharkhand. Sarabhai started a project for the fabrication and launch of a Bharatiya satellite.

As a result, the first *Bharatiya* satellite, Aryabhata, was put in orbit in 1975 from a Russian cosmodrome. He was the founder of Indian Space Research Organization.

On 30 December 1971, Sarabhai was to review the SLV design before his departure for Bombay the same night. He had spoken to A. P. J. Abdul Kalam on the telephone. Within an hour of the conversation, Sarabhai died at the age of 52 due to cardiac arrest in Trivandrum (now Thiruvananthapuram). His body was cremated in Ahmedabad.

Laurels and positions that he held were:
1. President of the Physics section, *Bharatiya* Science Congress (1962)
2. President of the General Conference of the I.A.E.A., Vienna (1970)
3. Chairperson of the Atomic Energy Commission of *Bharat* (1966–1971)
4. Vice-president, Fourth UN Conference on 'Peaceful uses of Atomic Energy' (1971)
5. Founder and Chairperson (1963–1971), Space Applications Centre

The Vikram Sarabhai Space Centre, (VSSC), which is the Indian Space Research Organization's lead facility for launch vehicle development located in Thiruvananthapuram (Trivandrum), capital of Kerala state, is named in his memory. Along with other Ahmedabad-based industrialists, he played a leading role in setting up the Indian Institute of Management, Ahmedabad.

Indian Postal Department released a commemorative Postal Stamp On his first death anniversary (30 December 1972). In 1973, the International Astronomical Union decided that a lunar crater, Bessel A, in the Sea of Serenity will be known as the Sarabhai crater. The lander on *Bharat*'s Moon mission

Chandrayaan-2 which was to land near the South Pole of the Moon on Sep 20, 2019, was named Vikram in his honor.

Vikram A Sarabhai Community Science Centre (VASCSC) located in Ahmedabad; Gujarat is named after him. Vikram Sarabhai established this institute around the 1960s. Former World Quiz Champion Vikram Joshi was named after him. A Space Museum was dedicated to him at B M Birla Science Centre, Hyderabad on 26 July 2019. Pranav Sharma curated the museum.

ISRO's Vikas (rocket engine) is named after him. On his 100th birthday on 12 August 2019, the *Bharatiya* Space Research Organization (ISRO) announced an award in the name of Vikram Sarabhai. The Vikram Sarabhai Journalism award in Space Science Technology and Research will be given to those journalists who have contributed to the fields of space science, applications, and research.

On 12 August 2019, Google's Doodle for *Bharat* commemorated Sarabhai's 100th birth anniversary. On 30 September 2020, ACK Media along with ISRO released a book namely, Vikram Sarabhai: Pioneering *Bharat*'s Space Programme. It was released in Amar Chitra Katha's digital platform and merchandise, ACK Comics.

So, what`s cooking – Impact of Space Science to the common and beyond

Let us now understand how space science can benefit all of us, the commoners, beside the bigger impacts. The youth of the country should very well especially understand this so as to open new horizons to their careers as our PM, Modi has already given this to all of us as homework. This was back envisaged by Dr. Vikram Sarabhai but put into perspective with the current scenario.

And what can be a better way to learn about technology from technology, below impacts have been suggested by my dear friend ChatGPT, which I have started using, although cautiously. Technology has to be learnt ethically and also it comes with a set of banes with it, but for now let us restrict ourselves to *learning about technology by technology*.

1. **Communication and Connectivity:** when was the last time you made a video call to your dear one? How are you able to make a video call, almost free of cost?

    Satellites enable global communication through services like mobile phones, internet, and television broadcasting. These technologies have revolutionized how people communicate, access information, and stay connected with others across the world.

2. **Weather Forecasting:** One of the best examples that I can portray here is the proactive and accurate prediction about the Biparjoy Cyclone in Gujarat & Mumbai around, second week of June 2023. We have seen how it helped to minimize the impact of such vulnerable natural disasters, which assisted in saving lives as well as economic losses in millions.

    Weather satellites provide real-time data that meteorologists use to predict weather patterns and severe weather events. Accurate forecasts help people plan their activities, make informed decisions, and take necessary precautions.

3. **Navigation:** Remember the last time when you last used Google Location to find enroute to your favorite restaurant or that movie theater or that foothills to which you planned your getaway weekend?

Global Positioning System (GPS) satellites allow for accurate navigation and location tracking, assisting people in finding directions, reaching destinations, and optimizing travel routes.

4. **Emergency Services:** Satellite-based communication and location services are essential for emergency response. They enable first responders to locate and assist individuals in distress, improving emergency services' effectiveness and saving lives.

5. **Agriculture and Food Security:** Satellite imagery and data help farmers monitor crop health, predict yields, and manage irrigation. This leads to more efficient agricultural practices, increased crop yields, and better food production.

6. **Natural Disaster Management:** Space-based monitoring helps in detecting and assessing natural disasters such as earthquakes, tsunamis, and hurricanes. This information aids in disaster response, evacuation planning, and recovery efforts.

7. **Environmental Monitoring:** How do we know the AQI and how is climate changing? Satellites provide data on environmental changes, such as deforestation, pollution, and climate shifts. This information supports efforts to address environmental challenges and promote sustainable practices.

8. **Medical Research and Healthcare:** Research conducted on the International Space Station (ISS) and in microgravity environments contributes to medical advancements, including understanding bone density loss, muscle atrophy, and cardiovascular changes. These

insights have implications for improving healthcare on Earth.

9. **Education and Inspiration:** Space exploration captures the imagination of people, especially young students. It serves as a source of inspiration, encouraging interest in science, technology, engineering, and mathematics (STEM) fields, shaping future careers.

10. **Consumer Technologies:** Many consumer technologies, from wireless headphones to memory foam mattresses, have been developed as a result of space research and its focus on creating efficient and compact solutions for space travel.

11. **Resource Management:** Satellite data assists in monitoring and managing natural resources, such as water availability, forestry, and land use. This helps in making informed decisions for sustainable development.

12. **Search and Rescue Operations:** Distress beacons equipped with satellite communication capabilities aid in locating and rescuing individuals in remote or hazardous environments, such as at sea or in wilderness areas.

13. **Transportation and Logistics:** Space research has contributed to advances in transportation systems, including improved aircraft design, efficient fuel consumption, and enhanced safety measures.

14. **Energy Solutions:** Research on space-based solar power and advanced energy storage technologies could offer cleaner and more reliable energy solutions for the future.

These examples illustrate how space research touches various aspects of daily life, enhancing convenience, safety, and overall quality of life for people around the world.

Moreover, space science has far-reaching positive impacts on society, ranging from technological advancements and scientific knowledge to improvements in healthcare, disaster management, education, and more. As our understanding of space grows, so too does our ability to address global challenges and create a better future for humanity.

Where do we start from now after knowing this?

Let us build a rock-solid foundation just as *The Vikram lander* gripped the moon surface like "Angad" as was highlighted by PM, Modi ji. To make it easy for you, I have an interesting principle called HEAL (**H**istory, **E**volution, **A**cceptance, **L**ayer Removal). This is nicely described in my previous work *"The Journey To A New You,"* published recently that will help you all to optimize your learning.

Let us talk women in Space first –
The first woman to go to space was Valentina Tereshkova. She flew in 1963 but it was not until the 1980s that another woman entered space again. All astronauts were required to be military test pilots at the time and women were not able to join this career, this is one reason for the delay in allowing women to join space crews. After the rule changed, Svetlana Savitskaya became the second woman to go to space, she was also from the Soviet Union.

Sally Ride became the next woman in space and the first woman to fly to space through the United States program.

Since then, eleven other countries have allowed women astronauts. The first all-female spacewalk occurred in 2018, including Christina Koch and Jessica Meir. They had both previously participated in space walks with NASA. The first woman to go to the Moon is planned for 2024.

Despite these developments women are still underrepresented among astronauts and especially cosmonauts. Issues that block potential applicants from the programs, and limit the space missions they are able to go on, include:

1. Agencies limiting women to half as much time in space than men, arguing with unresearched potential risks for cancer.
2. A lack of space suits sized appropriately for female astronauts.

History & Evolution of Space Science & Bharat

Organization structure and facilities In *Bharat*

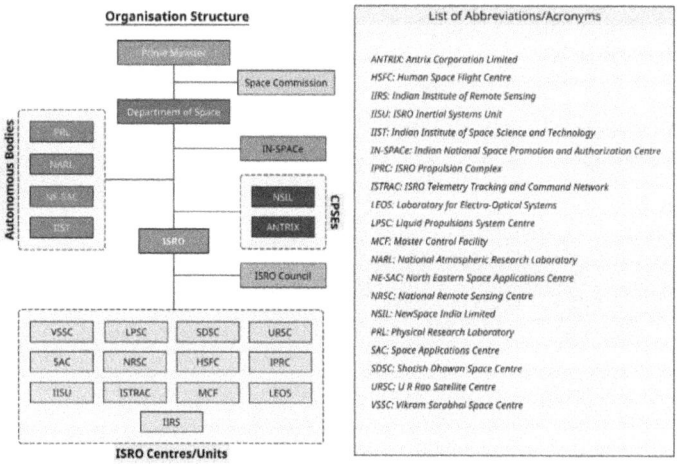

By Samuel Johnson - Own work, CC BY-SA 4.0,
https://en.wikipedia.org/w/index.php?curid=73270409

ISRO is managed by the DOS, which itself falls under the authority of the Space Commission and manages the following agencies and institutes.

1. *Bharatiya* Space Research Organisation (ISRO)
2. Antrix Corporation – The marketing arm of ISRO, Bengaluru
3. Physical Research Laboratory (PRL), Ahmedabad
4. National Atmospheric Research Laboratory (NARL), Gadanki, Andhra Pradesh
5. NewSpace *Bharat* Limited – Commercial wing, Bengaluru
6. North-Eastern Space Applications Centre (NE-SAC), Umiam
7. *Bharatiya* Institute of Space Science and Technology (IIST), Thiruvananthapuram – *Bharat's* space university

Formative years

Modern space research in *Bharat* can be traced to the 1920s, when scientist S. K. Mitra conducted a series of experiments sounding the ionosphere through ground-based radio in Kolkata. Later, *Bharatiya* scientists like C.V. Raman and Meghnad Saha contributed to scientific principles applicable in space sciences. After 1945, important developments were made in coordinated space research in *Bharat* by two scientists: Vikram Sarabhai and Homi Bhabha.

Initial experiments in space sciences included the study of cosmic radiation, high-altitude and airborne testing, deep underground experimentation at the Kolar mines—one of the deepest mining sites in the world.

Hey Stop! Where have you heard of Kolar Mines? Can you try and tax your mental faculties?

If you are reminded, kudos to you, even if you are not, I am here to bring that up.

So, one your own favorites, KGF Movie, right! Oh! Now you are interested. Come on! Let us have a look. Kolar Gold Fields (K.G.F.) is a mining region in K.G.F. taluk (township), Kolar district, Karnataka, *Bharat*. It is headquartered in Robertsonpet, where employees of *Bharat* Gold Mines Limited (BGML) and BEML Limited (formerly India Earth Movers Limited) and their families live. K.G.F. is about 30 kilometers (19 mi) from Kolar, 100 kilometers (62 mi) from Bengaluru, capital of Karnataka.

Over a century, the town has been known for gold mining. The mine closed on 28 February 2001 due to a fall in gold prices, despite gold still being present there. One of *Bharat*'s first power-generation units was built in 1889 to support mining operations. The mine complex hosted some particle physics experiments between the 1960s and 1992.

The history of the Kolar Gold Fields was compiled by Fred Goodwill, superintendent of the Police, Maldives, and Kolar Gold Fields. Goodwill's studies were published in the Quarterly Journal of the Mythic Society and elsewhere.

The Jain Western Gangas Dynasty founded Kolar in the second century CE. For as long as they were in power (1,000 years) they used the title "Kuvalala-Puravareshwara" (Lord of Kolar), even after they moved their capital to Talakadu. From Talakadu, the Western Gangas ruled Gangavadi (the southern home of the Kannada people).

Kolar came under Chola rule in 1004. Following their usual naming system, the Cholas called the district Nikarilichola-mandala. Around 1117, the Hoysalas (under Vishnuvardhana) captured Talakadu and Kolar and drove the Cholas from the

Kingdom of Mysore. Vira Someshwara divided the empire between his two sons in 1254, and Kolar was given to Ramanatha.

The Western Gangas made Kolar their capital and ruled Mysore, Coimbatore, Salem. Around the 13th century, the sage Pavananthi Munivar wrote Nannool about Tamil grammar at the Ulagamadhi cave. Under Chola rule, King Uththama Chola is said to have built the temple to Renuka. The Chola rulers Veera Chola, Vikrama Chola and Raja Nagendra Chola built stone structures with inscriptions at Avani, Mulbagal, and Sitti Betta.

Vijaynagar rule of Kolar lasted from 1336 to 1664. During the 17th century, Kolar came under Maratha rule as part of the jagir of Shahaji for fifty years before the Muslims ruled it for seventy years. In 1720, Kolar became part of the province of Sira; Fath Muhammad, the father of Hyder Ali, was faujdar of the province. Kolar was then ruled by the Marathas, the Nawab of Cuddapah, the Nizam of Hyderabad, and Hyder Ali. Ruled by the British from 1768 to 1770, it passed again to the Marathas and then to Hyder Ali. Lord Cornwallis conquered Kolar 1791, returning it to Mysore in the Treaty of Seringapatam the following year.

Inscriptions in the region indicate the reign of Mahavalis (Baanaas), Kadambas, Chalukyas, Pallava, Vaidumbaas, Rastrakutas, Cholas, Hoysalas and Mysore kings. Lewis Rice recorded 1,347 inscriptions in the district in the 10th volume of Epigraphia Carnatica.

John Taylor III acquired a number of mines in K.G.F. in 1880, and his firm (John Taylor & Sons) operated them until 1956; the Mysore Gold Mining Company was a subsidiary. In 1902, the mines were electrified with a 140-kilometre (87 mi) cable run by General Electric from the hydroelectric power plant at

Shivanasamudra Falls. The government of Mysore took over the mines in 1956.

With the growth of the gold mines requiring more labour, people from the Dharmapuri, Krishnagiri, Salem and North and South Arcot districts of Tamil Nadu and the Chittoor, Annamaya and Sri Sathya Sai districts of Andhra Pradesh settled nearby; the settlements began to form the outskirts of K.G.F. The well-to-do families of British and *Bharatiya* engineers, geologists, and mine supervisors lived in the town centre. Robertsonpet and Andersonpet townships are named after two British mine officials.

The establishment of BEML Limited expanded the city, providing employment and attracting new residents.

Rooting back to space science. It has the power to define history and the future. It also included studies of the upper atmosphere. These studies were done at research laboratories, universities, and independent locations.

In 1950, the Department of Atomic Energy (DAE) was founded with Bhabha as its secretary. It provided funding for space research throughout *Bharat*. During this time, tests continued on aspects of meteorology and the Earth's magnetic field, a topic that had been studied in *Bharat* since the establishment of the Colaba Observatory in 1823.

In 1954, the Aryabhatta Research Institute of Observational Sciences (ARIES) was established in the foothills of the Himalayas. The Rangpur Observatory was set up in 1957 at Osmania University, Hyderabad. Space research was further encouraged by the government of *Bharat*.In 1957, the Soviet Union launched Sputnik 1, opening up possibilities for the rest of the world to conduct a space launch.

The Indian National Committee for Space Research (INCOSPAR) was set up in 1962 by Prime Minister Jawaharlal Nehru at the suggestion of Dr. Vikram Sarabhai. Initially, there was no dedicated ministry for the space programme and all activities of INCOSPAR relating to space technology continued to function within the DAE. IOFS officers were drawn from the Indian Ordnance Factories to harness their knowledge of propellants and advanced light materials used to build rockets.

H.G.S. Murthy, an IOFS officer, was appointed the first director of the Thumba Equatorial Rocket Launching Station, where sounding rockets were fired, marking the start of upper atmospheric research in *Bharat*. An indigenous series of sounding rockets named Rohini was subsequently developed and started undergoing launches from 1967 onwards. Waman Dattatreya Patwardhan, another IOFS officer, developed the propellant for the rockets.

1970s and 1980s

Under the government of Indira Gandhi, INCOSPAR was superseded by ISRO. Later in 1972, a space commission and Department of Space (DoS) were set up to oversee space technology development in *Bharat* specifically. ISRO was brought under DoS, institutionalizing space research in *Bharat* and forging the *Bharatiya* space programme into its existing form. *Bharat* joined the Soviet Interkosmos programme for space cooperation and got its first satellite Aryabhatta in orbit through a Soviet rocket.

Efforts to develop an orbital launch vehicle began after mastering sounding rocket technology. The concept was to develop a launcher capable of providing sufficient velocity for a mass of 35 kg (77 lb) to enter low Earth orbit. It took 7 years for ISRO to develop a Satellite Launch Vehicle capable of putting 40 kg (88 lb) into a 400-kilometre (250 mi) orbit.

An SLV Launch Pad, ground stations, tracking networks, radars and other communications were set up for a launch campaign. The SLV's first launch in 1979 carried a Rohini technology payload but could not inject the satellite into its desired orbit. It was followed by a successful launch in 1980 carrying a Rohini Series-I satellite, making *Bharat* the seventh country to reach Earth's orbit after the USSR, the US, France, the UK, China, and Japan.

RS-1 was the third *Bharatiya* satellite to reach orbit as Bhaskara had been launched from the USSR in 1979. Efforts to develop a medium-lift launch vehicle capable of putting 600-kilogram (1,300 lb) class spacecraft into 1,000-kilometre (620 mi) Sun-synchronous orbit had already begun in 1978. They would later lead to the development of PSLV. The SLV-3 later had two more launches before discontinuation in 1983.

ISRO's Liquid Propulsion Systems Centre (LPSC) was set up in 1985 and started working on a more powerful engine, Vikas, based on the French Viking. Two years later, facilities to evaluate liquid-fueled rocket engines were established and development and testing of various rocket engine thrusters began.

At the same time, another solid-fueled rocket Augmented Satellite Launch Vehicle based upon SLV-3 was being developed, and technologies to launch satellites into geostationary orbit (GTO). ASLV had limited success and multiple launch failures; it was soon discontinued. Alongside technologies for the *Bharatiya* National Satellite System of communication satellites and the *Bharatiya* Remote Sensing Programme for earth observation satellites were developed and launched from overseas initiated.

The number of satellites eventually grew, and the systems were established as among the largest satellite constellations in the world, with multi-band communication, radar imaging, optical imaging, and meteorological satellites.

1990s

The arrival of PSLV in the 1990s became a major boost for the *Bharatiya* space programme. With the exception of its first flight in 1994 and two partial failures later, PSLV had a streak of more than 50 successful flights. PSLV enabled *Bharat* to launch all of its low Earth orbit satellites, small payloads to GTO and hundreds of foreign satellites. Along with the PSLV flights, the development of a new rocket, a Geosynchronous Satellite Launch Vehicle (GSLV) was going on.

Bharat tried to obtain upper-stage cryogenic engines from Russia's Glavkosmos but was blocked by the US from doing so. As a result, KVD-1 engines were imported from Russia under a new agreement which had limited success and a project to develop indigenous cryogenic technology was launched in 1994, taking two decades to reach fulfillment. A new agreement was signed with Russia for seven KVD-1 cryogenic stages and a ground mock-up stage with no technology transfer, instead of five cryogenic stages along with the technology and design in the earlier agreement.

These engines were used for the initial flights and were named GSLV Mk.1. ISRO was under US government sanctions between 6 May 1992 to 6 May 1994. After the United States refused to help *Bharat* with Global Positioning System (GPS) technology during the Kargil war, ISRO was prompted to develop its own satellite navigation system IRNSS which it is now expanding further.

21st century and beyond the obvious

In 2003, when China sent humans into space, Prime Minister Atal Bihari Vajpayee urged scientists to develop technologies to land humans on the Moon and programmes for lunar, planetary and crewed missions were started. ISRO launched Chandrayaan-1 in 2008, the first probe to verify the presence of water on the Moon, and the Mars Orbiter Mission in 2013, the first Asian spacecraft to enter Martian orbit, making *Bharat* the first country to succeed at this on its first attempt.

Subsequently, the cryogenic upper stage for GSLV rocket became operational, making *Bharat* the sixth country to have full launch capabilities. A new heavier-lift launcher LVM3 was introduced in 2014 for heavier satellites and future human space missions.

On 23 August 2023, *Bharat* became the first country to successfully land a spacecraft near the lunar south pole as the ISRO successfully completed its 3rd Moon mission. *Bharatiya* moon mission, Chandrayaan-3 (translated as "moon craft" in English), saw the successful soft landing of its Vikram lander at 6.04pm IST (1234 GMT) near the little-explored region of the Moon in a world's first for any space programme.

Agency logo
ISRO did not have an official logo until 2002. The one adopted consists of an orange arrow shooting upwards attached with two blue coloured satellite panels with the name of ISRO written in two sets of text, orange-coloured Devanagari on the left and blue-coloured English in the Prakrta typeface on the right.

Goals and objectives
As the national space agency of *Bharat*, ISRO's purpose is the pursuit of all space-based applications such as research, reconnaissance, and communications. It undertakes the design and development of space rockets, satellites, and explores upper atmosphere and deep space exploration missions. ISRO has also incubated technologies in *Bharat*'s private space sector, boosting its growth.

On the topic of the importance of a space programme to *Bharat* as a developing nation, Vikram Sarabhai as INSCOPAR chair said in 1969:

To us, there is no ambiguity of purpose. We do not have the fantasy of competing with the economically advanced nations in the exploration of the Moon or the planets or crewed spaceflight. But we are convinced that if we are to play a meaningful role nationally, and in the community of nations, we must be second to none in the application of advanced technologies to the real problems of man and society, which we find in our country.

And we should note that the application of sophisticated technologies and methods of analysis to our problems is not to be confused with embarking on grandiose schemes, whose primary impact is for show rather than for progress measured in tough economic and social terms.

The former president of *Bharat* and chairperson of DRDO, A. P. J. Abdul Kalam, said:

Very many individuals with myopic vision questioned the relevance of space activities in a newly independent nation which was finding it difficult to feed its population. But neither Prime Minister Nehru nor Prof. Sarabhai had any ambiguity of purpose. Their vision was noticeably clear: if Indians were to play a meaningful role in the community of nations, they must be second to none in the application of advanced technologies to their real-life problems. They had no intention of using it merely as a means of displaying our might.

Bharat's economic progress has made its space programme more visible and active as the country aims for greater self-reliance in space technology. In 2008, *Bharat* launched as many as 11 satellites, including nine from other countries, and went on to become the first nation to launch 10 satellites on one rocket. ISRO has put into operation two major satellite systems: the Indian National Satellite System (INSAT) for communication services, and the *Bharatiya* Remote Sensing Programme (IRS) satellites for management of natural resources.

What is Space Science & Why?

Space exploration is the use of astronomy and space technology to explore outer space. While the exploration of space is conducted by astronomers with telescopes, its physical exploration is conducted both by uncrewed robotic space probes and human spaceflight. Space exploration, like its classical form astronomy, is one of the main sources for space science.

While the observation of objects in space, known as astronomy, predates reliable recorded history, it was the development of large and efficient rockets during the mid-twentieth century that allowed physical space exploration to become a reality. The world's first large-scale experimental rocket program was Opel-RAK under the leadership of Fritz von Opel and Max Valier during the late 1920s leading to the first crewed rocket cars and rocket planes.

It paved the way for the Nazi era V2 program and US and Soviet activities from 1950 onwards. The Opel-RAK program and the spectacular public demonstrations of ground and air vehicles drew large crowds, as well as caused global public excitement as so-called "Rocket Rumble" and had a large long-lasting impact on later spaceflight pioneers like Wernher von Braun. Common rationales for exploring space include advancing scientific research, national prestige, uniting different nations, ensuring the future survival of humanity, and developing military and strategic advantages against other countries.

The early era of space exploration was driven by a "Space Race" between the Soviet Union and the United States. A driving force of the start of space exploration was during the Cold War. After the ability to create nuclear weapons, the narrative of defense/offense left land and the *power to control the air* became the focus. Both the Soviet and the U.S. were fighting to prove their superiority in technology through exploring the unknown: space.

In fact, the reason NASA was made was due to the response of Sputnik I. The launch of the first human-made object to orbit Earth, the Soviet Union's Sputnik 1, on 4 October 1957, and the first Moon landing by the American Apollo 11 mission on 20 July 1969 are often taken as landmarks for this initial period.

Fast forwarding, Voyager 1 became the first human-made object to leave the Solar System into interstellar space on 25 August 2012. The probe passed the heliopause at 121 AU to enter interstellar space.

The Apollo 13 flight passed the far side of the Moon at an altitude of 254 kilometers (158 miles; 137 nautical miles) above the lunar surface, and 400,171 km (248,655 mi) from Earth, marking the record for the farthest humans have ever traveled from Earth in 1970.

As of 26 November 2022, Voyager 1 was at a distance of 159 AU (23.8 billion km; 14.8 billion mi) from Earth. It is the most distant human-made object from Earth.

Targets of exploration
Starting in the mid-20th century probes and then human missions were sent into Earth orbit, and then on to the Moon. Also, probes were sent throughout the known Solar System, and into Solar orbit. Uncrewed spacecraft have been sent into orbit around Saturn, Jupiter, Mars, Venus, and Mercury by the 21st

century, and the most distance active spacecraft, Voyager 1 and 2 traveled beyond 100 times the Earth-Sun distance. The instruments were enough though that it is thought they have left the Sun's heliosphere, a sort of bubble of particles made in the Galaxy by the Sun's solar wind.

The Sun

The Sun is a major focus of space exploration. Being above the atmosphere in particular and Earth's magnetic field gives access to the solar wind and infrared and ultraviolet radiations that cannot reach Earth's surface. The Sun generates most space weather, which can affect power generation and transmission systems on Earth and interfere with, and even damage, satellites, and space probes.

Numerous spacecraft dedicated to observing the Sun, beginning with the Apollo Telescope Mount, have been launched and still others have had solar observation as a secondary objective. Parker Solar Probe, launched in 2018, will approach the Sun to within 1/9th the orbit of Mercury.

Earth

Space exploration has been used as a tool to understand Earth as a celestial object. Orbital missions can provide data for Earth that can be difficult or impossible to obtain from a purely ground-based point of reference.

For example, the existence of the Van Allen radiation belts was unknown until their discovery by the United States' first artificial satellite, Explorer 1. These belts contain radiation trapped by Earth's magnetic fields, which currently renders construction of habitable space stations above 1000 km impractical.

Following this early unexpected discovery, a large number of Earth observation satellites have been deployed specifically to explore Earth from a space-based perspective. These satellites have significantly contributed to the understanding of a variety of Earth-based phenomena. For instance, the hole in the ozone layer was found by an artificial satellite that was exploring Earth's atmosphere, and satellites have allowed for the discovery of archeological sites or geological formations that were difficult or impossible to otherwise identify.

Moon

Apollo 16 LEM Orion, the Lunar Roving Vehicle and astronaut John Young (1972). The Moon was the first celestial body to be the object of space exploration. It holds the distinction of being the first remote celestial object to be flown by, orbited, and landed upon by spacecraft, and the only remote celestial object ever to be visited by humans.

In 1959 the Soviets obtained the first images of the far side of the Moon, never previously visible to humans. The U.S. exploration of the Moon began with the Ranger 4 impactor in 1962. Starting in 1966 the Soviets successfully deployed a number of landers to the Moon which were able to obtain data directly from the Moon's surface; just four months later, Surveyor 1 marked the debut of a successful series of U.S. landers.

The Soviet uncrewed missions culminated in the Lunokhod program in the early 1970s, which included the first uncrewed rovers and also successfully brought lunar soil samples to Earth for study. This marked the first (and to date the only) automated return of extraterrestrial soil samples to Earth. Uncrewed exploration of the Moon continues with various nations periodically deploying lunar orbiters, and in 2008 the *Bharatiya* Moon Impact Probe.

Crewed exploration of the Moon began in 1968 with the Apollo 8 mission that successfully orbited the Moon, the first-time humans orbited any extraterrestrial object. In 1969, the Apollo 11 mission marked the first-time humans set foot upon another world. Crewed exploration of the Moon did not continue for long. The Apollo 17 mission in 1972 marked the sixth landing and the most recent human visit. Artemis 2 is scheduled to complete a crewed flyby of the Moon in 2024. Robotic missions are still pursued vigorously.

Mars

The exploration of Mars has been an important part of the space exploration programs of the Soviet Union (later Russia), the United States, Europe, Japan, and *Bharat*. Dozens of robotic spacecrafts, including orbiters, landers, and rovers, have been launched toward Mars since the 1960s. These missions were aimed at gathering data about current conditions and answering questions about the history of Mars.

The questions raised by the scientific community are expected to not only give a better appreciation of the Red Planet but also yield further insight into the past, and future, of Earth.

The exploration of Mars has come at a considerable financial cost with two-thirds of all spacecraft destined for Mars failing before completing their missions, with some failing before they even began. Such a high failure rate can be attributed to the complexity and substantial number of variables involved in an interplanetary journey and has led researchers to jokingly speak of The Great Galactic Ghoul which subsists on a diet of Mars probes.

This phenomenon is also informally known as the "Mars Curse". In contrast to overall high failure rates in the exploration of Mars, ***Bharat has become the first country to achieve success of its maiden attempt. Bharat's Mars Orbiter Mission (MOM) is one of the least expensive interplanetary missions ever undertaken*** *with an approximate total cost of ₹ 450 Crore (US$73 million).*

Artemis program

The Artemis program is an ongoing crewed spaceflight program conducted by NASA, U.S. commercial spaceflight companies, and international partners such as ESA, with the goal of landing *"the first woman and the next man"* on the Moon, specifically at the lunar south pole region by 2024. Artemis would be the next step towards the long-term goal of establishing a sustainable presence on the Moon, laying the foundation for private companies to build a lunar economy, and eventually sending humans to Mars.

In 2017, the lunar campaign was authorized by Space Policy Directive 1, utilizing various ongoing spacecraft programs such as Orion, the Lunar Gateway, Commercial Lunar Payload Services, and adding an undeveloped crewed lander. The Space Launch System will serve as the primary launch vehicle for Orion, while commercial launch vehicles are planned for use to launch various other elements of the campaign.

NASA requested $1.6 billion in additional funding for Artemis for fiscal year 2020, while the Senate Appropriations Committee requested from NASA a five-year budget profile which is needed for evaluation and approval by Congress.

Rationales

Astronaut Buzz Aldrin had a personal Communion service when he first arrived on the surface of the Moon. The research that is conducted by national space exploration agencies, such as NASA and Ros cosmos, is one of the reasons supporters cite to justify government expenses. Economic analyses of the NASA programs often showed ongoing economic benefits (such as NASA spin-offs), generating many times the revenue of the cost of the program.

It is also argued that space exploration would lead to the extraction of resources on other planets and especially asteroids, which contain billions of dollars' worth of minerals and metals. Such expeditions could generate a lot of revenue. In addition, it has been argued that space exploration programs help inspire youth to study in science and engineering. Space exploration also gives scientists the ability to perform experiments in other settings and expand humanity's knowledge.

Another claim is that space exploration is a necessity to humankind and that staying on Earth will lead to extinction. Some of the reasons are lack of natural resources, comets, nuclear war, and worldwide epidemic. Stephen Hawking, renowned British theoretical physicist, said that "I don't think the human race will survive the next thousand years, unless we spread into space.

There are too many accidents that can befall life on a single planet. But I'm an optimist. We will reach out to the stars. Arthur C. Clarke (1950) presented a summary of motivations for the human exploration of space in his non-fiction semi-technical monograph Interplanetary Flight.

He argued that humanity's choice is between expansion off Earth into space, versus cultural (and eventually biological) stagnation and death. These motivations could be attributed to one of the first rocket scientists in NASA, Wernher von Braun, and his vision of humans moving beyond Earth. The basis of this plan was to:

1. "Develop multi-stage rockets capable of placing satellites, animals, and humans in space.
2. Development of large, winged reusable spacecraft capable of carrying humans and equipment into Earth orbit in a way that made space access routine and cost-effective.

3. Construction of a large, permanently occupied space station to be used as a platform both to observe Earth and from which to launch deep space expeditions.
4. Launching the first human flights around the Moon, leading to the first landings of humans on the Moon, with the intent of exploring that body and establishing permanent lunar bases.
5. Assembly and fueling of spaceships in Earth orbit for the purpose of sending humans to Mars with the intent of eventually ***colonizing that planet"***.

Known as the Von Braun Paradigm, the plan was formulated to lead humans in the exploration of space. Von Braun's vision of human space exploration served as the model for efforts in space exploration well into the twenty-first century, with NASA incorporating this approach into the majority of their projects.

The steps were followed out of order, as seen by the Apollo program reaching the moon before the space shuttle program was started, which in turn was used to complete the International Space Station. Von Braun's Paradigm formed NASA's drive for human exploration, in the hopes that humans discover the far reaches of the universe.

NASA has produced a series of public service announcement videos supporting the concept of space exploration.

Overall, the public remains supportive of both crewed and uncrewed space exploration. According to an Associated Press Poll conducted in July 2003, 71% of U.S. citizens agreed with the statement that the space program is "a good investment", compared to 21% who did not.

Human nature
Delta-v's in km/s for various orbital maneuvers Spaceflight is the use of space technology to achieve the flight of spacecraft

into and through outer space. Spaceflight is used in space exploration, and also in commercial activities like space tourism and satellite telecommunications. Additional non-commercial uses of spaceflight include space observatories, reconnaissance satellites and other Earth observation satellites.

A spaceflight typically begins with a rocket launch, which provides the initial thrust to overcome the force of gravity and propels the spacecraft from the surface of Earth. Once in space, the motion of a spacecraft—both when unpropelled and when under propulsion—is covered by the area of study called *astrodynamics*. Some spacecraft remain in space indefinitely, some disintegrate during atmospheric reentry, and others reach a planetary or lunar surface for landing or impact.

Satellites
Satellites are used for a large number of purposes. Common types include military (spy) and civilian Earth observation satellites, communication satellites, navigation satellites, weather satellites, and research satellites. Space stations and human spacecraft in orbit are also satellites.

Commercialization of space
The commercialization of space first started out with the launching of private satellites by NASA or other space agencies. Current examples of the commercial satellite use of space include satellite navigation systems, satellite television and satellite radio. The next step of commercialization of space was seen as human spaceflight.

Flying humans safely to and from space had become routine to NASA. Reusable spacecraft were an entirely new engineering challenge, something only seen in novels and films like Star Trek and War of the Worlds. Great names like Buzz Aldrin supported the use of making a reusable vehicle like the space shuttle. Aldrin held that reusable spacecraft were the key in making space travel affordable, stating that the use of "passenger space travel is a huge potential market big enough to justify the creation of reusable launch vehicles".

How can the public go against the words of one of America's best-known heroes in space exploration? Exploring space is the next great expedition, following the example of Lewis and Clark. Space tourism is the next step in reusable vehicles in the commercialization of space. The purpose of this form of space travel is used by individuals for the purpose of personal pleasure.

Private spaceflight companies such as SpaceX and Blue Origin, and commercial space stations such as the Axiom Space and the Bigelow Commercial Space Station have dramatically changed the landscape of space exploration and will continue to do so in the near future.

Human spaceflight and habitation
To date, the longest human occupation of space is the International Space Station which has been in continuous use for 22 years, 298 days. Valeri Polyakov's record single spaceflight of almost 438 days aboard the Mir space station has not been surpassed. The health effects of space have been well documented through years of research conducted in the field of aerospace medicine.

However, it does not take long for the environmental dynamics of spaceflight to commence its toll on the human body; for example, space motion sickness (SMS) – a condition which affects the neurovestibular system and culminates in mild to severe signs and symptoms such as vertigo, dizziness, fatigue, nausea, and disorientation – plagues all space travelers within their first few days in orbit.

Space travel can also have a profound impact on the psyche of the crew members as delineated in anecdotal writings composed after their retirement. Space travel can adversely affect the body's natural biological clock (circadian rhythm); sleep patterns causing sleep deprivation and fatigue; and social interaction; consequently, residing in a Low Earth Orbit (LEO) environment for a prolonged amount of time can result in both mental and physical exhaustion.

Long-term stays in space reveal issues with bone and muscle loss in low gravity, immune system suppression, and radiation exposure. The lack of gravity causes fluid to rise upward which can cause pressure to build up in the eye, resulting in vision problems; the loss of bone minerals and densities; cardiovascular deconditioning; and decreased endurance and muscle mass.

Radiation is the most insidious health hazard to space travelers as it is invisible to the naked eye and can cause cancer. Space crafts are no longer protected from the sun's radiation as they are positioned above the Earth's magnetic field; the danger of radiation is even more potent when one enters deep space. The hazards of radiation can be ameliorated through protective shielding on the spacecraft, alerts, and dosimetry.

Human representation and participation
Participation and representation of humanity in space is an issue ever since the first phase of space exploration. Some rights of non-space faring countries have been mostly secured through international space law, declaring space the "province of all mankind", understanding spaceflight as its resource, though sharing of space for all humanity is still criticized as imperialist and lacking.

Additionally, to international inclusion, the inclusion of women and people of color has also been lacking. To reach a more inclusive spaceflight some organizations like the Justspace

Alliance and IAU featured Inclusive Astronomy have been formed in recent years.

Key Learnings & Action Steps decoded.

So, what's the learning?

Those are infinite if you sit and self-introspect. But I have done that for you with my analysis.

Here, I have impactful lessons which are actionable as well, from the remarkably successful Chandrayan-3 mission from the Executive director of IMF, Krishnamurthy Subramanian's perspective as he puts in an article titled "From the moon, lessons for the policy makers". But we will try and understand as it is applicable to all sorts of fields.

He starts by saying, "Success has many fathers, but failure is an orphan." But what the journey from the Chandrayan-2's failure to Chandrayan-3's success demonstrates is that a culture of leadership that doesn't treat failure as an orphan is critical for unprecedented success.

He further exclaims, watching the pall of gloom that befell ISRO scientists when Chandrayan-2 failed in 2019, then the warm glow after our PM gave a tight, long hug to an emotional ISRO chief. His words of motivation that day were, "India stands with you with pride and gratitude…the learnings from today will make us stronger and better. There will be a new dawn and a brighter tomorrow soon." And here we are.

Our scientists knew that they were not being orphaned for the failure, we need to learn two key lessons from this chronicle.

***First*, the cliché` service `celebrating failure` misses the point. We should *celebrate learning from failure*,**

not naked failure, by distinguishing between '*novel failures*' and '*incompetent failures*'.

Attempts to create novel technological, business or policy making models are riddled with several unknown unknowns. These `failures` provide valuable lessons about paths forward. But failure can also result from poorly thought-out designs, flawed analysis, lack of transparency and bad management. Tolerating such failures only breeds incompetence and sloth.

A culture of tolerance for failure requires a culture of *meritocracy*. Given ISRO`s competence, the Indian taxpayer can be confident that its failure is `novel` and not `incompetent`. Chandrayan-3`s success proved that ISRO learnt by critically analyzing every aspect of Chandrayan-2`s failure.

Can this be applied to our education system also? I would be more interested in exploring this, as of now let's restrict ourselves to the `*Spaciology*`!

But the taxpayer funds scores of research and policy institutes. Are their failures `novel` or incompetent?

A comparison of 253 laggards with IITs and DAE based on research publication per institution over two decades shows that the laggards research output is abysmally low. While IIMs and DRDO publish only eight and eleven publications per year, IITs and DAE are orders of magnitude higher at 331 and 229, respectively.

As India ranks fifth in total research publications but the lowest among top-10 countries in citations per publication, none of these laggards can claim that their appalling research productivity is offset by high quality;, citations measure how path-breaking a publication is. Unlike the taxpayer`s investment in ISRO, she seems to primarily reap `incompetent failures for her investment in these laggards`

When ISRO can rank India among the world's top four nations, why can't every public institution at least rank among the top 100 in research productivity? The taxpayer must rightfully demand *shape up, rank in the top 100, else you don't get a dime.*

Second, **Chandrayan 3`s lesson to not orphanise `novel failures` needs to be transported from space missions into the decision -making apparatus prevailing in India`s government and public sector specially education.**

You will get a glimpse of what I mean in the upcoming chapter titled, *"The Second Copy: Are we using the "The Second Copy" of the Education System in Bharat?*

Anyways, while the risks involved in a space mission are rightly celebrated, policy making by our bureaucrats and public sector officials involves a lot of peril. Yet, these are rarely even acknowledged, yet alone celebrated. Would we be celebrating the Chandrayaan 3`s success if the culture at ISRO encouraged sitting on the fence?

Of course not! In an uncertain world policymaking can throw up adverse outcomes even when policy is conceptualized and implemented with the best judgment. If you have to spend your post- retirement life running from pillar to post because the decision you made in your best judgment went kaput, will you take the risk?

A cardinal principle in economics is that decent returns cannot be generated without assuming professionally managed risk. Yet, because failure from policy making is unceremoniously orphaned, our government and public sector officials suffer huge personal losses if the risks they take end up delivering unfavorable outcomes.

To create a system where failure in policy making is not offended, the system of investigation prosecution needs to recognize hindsight bias. Officials must make decisions with the information available at that time. Overtime, of course more information becomes available.

However, such information was not available to the official when making the decision. Investigating as if the official must have foreseen that information creates huge hindsight bias and scares off risk- taking.

Chandrayaan-3`s success must teach us two lessons-

1. **Do not tolerate incompetence.**
2. **Tolerate novel failures.**

Be it in space missions or in mundane policy making, Uniform Civil Code, or education system which you are going to have a good insight in upcoming chapters.

The Green Carpet: The Enlightened Bharat | G20 & beyond

It is the time to unfurl *The Green Carpet* now and for whom? We are a country who believes in **The Green**, we believe in **Advaita Vedanta** *(we will discuss in detail in upcoming chapters), and of course* **Vasudev Kutumbakam** a Sanskrit phrase found in texts the such as Maha Upanishad, which means "The World Is One Family".

After the amazing Moon and the star Mission, let me bring you the *Real Star* here.

Any guesses?

Let me jump in with that, as I just can't stop myself from revealing it.

It is the **rich culture**, and the diversification, the strength of our country, which is the real star. While I was talking and discussing with my angel mother, she uttered "Why do you talk politics with me, I don't like politics."

This statement made me think my favorite question, **Why**? Why would a person not like politics? Well! I will answer that as why or why not shortly, but the most critical point to underscore here is that we after being ruled for more than 200 years, after being a victim of uncountable invasions and numerous attacks, we stand tall and the ***Tirangaa***, smiles proudly like never before, shining brightly across the sky representing the entire nations faith.

How are we able to do that? Through keeping our roots alive, the culture that teaches us ***One Earth, One Family***.

However, not everything is on the brighter side. There are numerous challenges that require immediate attention not only from the policy makers and government but also from **You** and **Me**. Once we are aware of the challenges, we will try to forge actionable changes that we all together can think of taking to make our country brighter than ever and be a part of history in the making.

In this chapter we are trying to navigate amazing insights in the fields of Indian Culture and Art, Politics, political divide - polarization, and ways of depolarization.

Let us start with a place that saw our Constitution in the making, a great speech called "At the stroke of Midnight, bombing by Bhagat Singh to retaliate against Britishers, it saw our independence and what not." So, let us start from where it all started and witness history in the making that marks the new era for us.

"If the old Parliament House gave direction to post-independence India, the new building would become a witness to the creation of - Atma Nirbhar Bharat."

Shri Narendra Modi,
Hon'ble Prime Minister
The New Parliament

We have been eyewitnesses of the history in the making, the new parliament building and the day 1 on 19th September 2023, Tuesday. A day to be marked in golden words. The day chosen was an amazingly auspicious day, Ganesh Chaturthi, a day also when I got an offer letter from the new company that I would have joined by the time you would read this. It is auspicious indeed!

The construction started with once again my favorite question. Why is it needed, and that too NOW? Well! The second part of the question I would love to answer right away.

Is there a particular time to progress? Shall we wait for something to progress? So, the best answer that I can give to all those who ask Why is ***Why Not?***

What should we wait for and why?

I am right or am I right?

The next part, I mean the first one now. To explore the why behind the new building we will need to have a bit of background about how and what happened that made what we see the National Capital, New Delhi today as. Let me quickly take you to few days in the past that created the current present and also bring out to you inspiring lines that should be apt here, Our PM in his speech said,

Though it was built by Britishers, we own the sweat, it was us and our ancestors who constructed it with sweat and blood, it was our money which built it, that is the legacy we carry.

Birth of the Central Vista

During the colonial era, leading British architects Edwin Lutyens and Herbert Baker envisaged the Central Vista complex as the centre of administration in India to house all facilities needed for efficient functioning of the Government. It was inaugurated in 1931 and comprised the buildings, namely Rashtra Pati Bhawan, Parliament House, North and South Blocks and the Record Office (later named as The National Archives), along with the India Gate monument and the civic gardens on either side of the Rajpath.

The plan was designed using traditional urban planning instruments, featuring a strong axis, an emphasized focal point, formation of important nodes, and a definitive termination point. At the time, it was one of the largest projects of its kind in the world, conceived and designed to reflect the spirit, progress and global importance of India.

Indian influences marked the overall design of the Central Vista. It comprised the use of red and beige sandstone, which had been used for the monumental architecture of Delhi since the 13th century; the modelling of the dome of Viceroy's House on the Great Stupa at Sanchi; ancient Indian bell capitals for the Pillars of Dominion placed between the Secretariat Blocks; and countless features of Indian architecture – jalis (pierced stone screens), chhajas (projecting overhangs), chhatris (pillared cupolas), and more.

The Capital of India moved from Calcutta to Delhi | The Delhi Durbar – December 1911

The foundation of Delhi was laid at the Coronation Durbar of 1911 by King George V and Queen Mary as the capital of British India. Prior to this, Calcutta had served as the capital of British India for a long time. Shifting of the Capital from Calcutta to Delhi was led by two major factors:

- Indian Councils Act of 1909
- The ongoing crisis caused by the Bengal partition.

Delhi was finalized as the nation's capital as it was easily accessible and closer to the summer capital, Shimla. Delhi has also been associated with the Mahabharata and the Mughal Empire. On these geographical, political, and historical grounds, Delhi was chosen as the new capital of India.

From British Raj to Indian Independence
New Delhi – The New Capital of British India. The Delhi Town Planning Committee was set up in 1912 to plan, develop and design the major buildings like the Viceroy's House, the Secretariat buildings and other structural works connected with the aesthetics of the new city. Edwin Lutyens became a member of this committee in March 1912.

The Delhi Town Planning Committee prepared a layout, which divided the new capital into three main categories. The first category focused on the buildings that the Government would provide before the new city became the seat of the government, the second focused on the buildings that the Government could add later on to the new city and the third included the buildings that were to be constructed by private agencies. Priority was given to the first category and major projects that fell under this were:

- Government House
- The Secretariats
- Residence of his Excellency the Commander in Chief
- Residence of the Council Members
- Residence for clerks
- Construction of roads, water supply, drainage, parks, public gardens, open spaces, including arboriculture, railways.

At its inauguration in 1931, New Delhi comprised the Viceroy's House, the Secretariats, Council House, Records Office, All India War Memorial, the ceremonial avenue, gardens, and a few bungalows. The new capital was carved out from undivided Punjab province.

The power of the Indian democratic system manifests in our Parliament, which weathered the Indian freedom struggle from colonial rule and witnessed many historical milestones. The old building served as independent India's first Parliament and witnessed the adoption of the Constitution of India. Thus, conserving and rejuvenating the rich heritage of the Parliament building is a matter of national importance.

And this is the answer to *why* a new parliament building.

An icon of India's democratic spirit, the Parliament building sits at the heart of the Central Vista. India's previous Parliament House was a colonial-era building designed by British architects Sir Edwin Lutyens and Herbert Baker, which took six years to construct (1921-1927). Originally called the Council House, the building housed the Imperial Legislative Council.

The Parliament building witnessed the addition of two floors in 1956 to address the demand for more space. In 2006, the Parliament Museum was added to highlight the 2,500 years of rich democratic heritage of India. The building had to be modified to suit the purpose of a modern Parliament.

After initial deliberations about the shape of the building, a circular shape was finalized by both the architects, Herbert Baker, and Sir Edwin Lutyens as that would give the feel of a colosseum design for the Council House. It is popularly believed that the **unique circular shape of the Chausath Yogini temple in Morena, (Madhya Pradesh)** had inspired the design of the Council House, though there are no historical proofs for this.

The old Parliament House, currently renamed as **Samvidhan Sadan,** has served as the 'The Temple of National Discussions' in the world's largest democracy. The two houses of the Parliament have been the pillars that have supported the socioeconomic growth of the country since independence.

Hon'ble Prime Minister, Shri Narendra Modi laid the foundation stone of the new Parliament Building on 10th December 2020

Why New Parliament Building, The Need:

The old Parliament House building construction was started in 1921 and commissioned in 1927. It is almost 100 years old and a Heritage Grade-I building. Over the years, the parliamentary activities and the number of people working therein, and visitors have increased manifold. There is no record or document of the original design of the building. Therefore, the new constructions and modifications have been done in an ad-hoc manner. For example, two new floors constructed in 1956 over the outer circular part of the building hid the dome of the Central Hall and changed the facade of the original building.

Further, the coverings of Jaali windows have reduced the natural light in the halls of two houses of the Parliament. Therefore, it is showing signs of distress and over-utilization and is not able to meet the current requirements in terms of space, amenities, and technology. Below mentioned marks the concrete reasons:

- Narrow Seating Space
- Distressed Infrastructure
- Obsolete Communication Structures
- Safety Concerns

- Inadequate workspace

Fast forwarding, the very first day and the first bill is that blew me off, the name coincides with the name of the work that is in your hand right now, Naari "शक्ति" Vandan Adhiniyam bill, 2023, the historic 128th Constitution Amendment Bill to provide 1/3rd reservation for women in the House of the People and state legislatures. It was first attempted in 1996. So, 23 years in the making and a lot of stuff in between these years and still a lot!

I came across a thought intriguing quote by Florentina Gomez Miranda,

"When a woman enters politics, it changes her. When many women do, it is the politics that change."

There has been much *hooting* around this bill, which seeks to empower women. I, along with my mother, have been glued to television for the last couple of days, and she, though being least interested in politics, has been the one discussing it the most. That means there is something that is catching the attention of household females.

With different political parties fighting to take the credit of *Who's the owner*, some parties are so greatly skilled that they demanded quota within quota and introduced polarization even in women empowerment. And you know what's more interesting to me. It is the women who are fighting against women for this bill. Isn't women empowerment something that belongs to all the women, and men, then how is there a political divide and why?

Although it was voted as 454-2 in the Lok Sabha, and then 214-0 in Rajya Sabha as a clear winner, the ruckus among parties, hats-off to the political faculties.

But there is an important question that interestingly my mother asked me and was also reported Times of India dated 21st Sept 2023 –

Will reserving a third of seats by rotation change the male mindset?

Noting how much women have been empowered since 1947 or 1996, cannot hide how much discrimination still persists and how much it is costing *Bharat* in wealth and wellbeing.

First, given the rotational reservations, Male MP's will have to give their seats if the seats become a reserved one. This could mean that women proxies or the "bahu-Beti" brigade take the place of sitting MP If he happens to be a male.

Second, women who contest from reserved seats may not be able to nurture their constituencies because they will lose them in the next election, and importantly, the bill will pit women against women in reserved constituencies and reduce political contest in those seats into *"a battle in a ladies compartment."*

For sure more women need to enter politics, but as equal mainstream players based on leadership qualities and political intelligence. A reserved seat could marginalize women politicians even further.

Mahatma Gandhi said. "Those who obstruct the rise of free independent women, also obstruct the rise of free independent men." Gender justice is not about special concessions for women but an overall democratization of public life that makes politics safe enough without having to endure violence and persecution from money or muscle power.

My mother's concern – what about a great disincentive for women - the crimes against them that show no signs of abating.

Also, parties play politics over crimes against women. When violence against women in Manipur became the talk of the town, BJP was asked why it is silent, but opposition parties kept quiet when violence against women was reported from states like Bengal. Women legislators also keep quiet in these situations. There's so much to do. We need to go beyond tokenism and political gestures. A law mandating quota for women legislators may be a beginning but is it really going to empower?

Let me present ***solutions***.

1. **Understanding Polarization**
2. **Knowing how not to be a victim.**
3. **Practicing our deep ingrained value.**
4. **Knowing Stimulated language.**

While the third and the fourth will be dealt with in upcoming chapters, let us straightway start with the first two now.

Understanding Polarization and taking steps to depolarize. By not being a victim of Polarization.

So, what is polarization and how does it affect us all?

Well, it is pretty simple. You might have heard the *divide and rule* policy by the Britishers. The intention was to take advantage of division in the society on the basis of certain factors that people fall prey to. And it has not ended yet. The Divide and rule policy still finds a place in our society as polarization. In fact, it will not be wrong to say that it never ended, and we still are victims.

Recently we have seen how the bill for women, gave rise to quota within quota, and then a huge uproar about caste census ahead of the 2024 elections in India. Thanks to the Social media platforms which magically amplifies polarization by creating echo chambers where individuals are only exposed to like-minded opinions.

Polarization is practiced mainly on the basis of:

1. Origin
2. Gender
3. Age
4. Education (Surprisingly)
5. Reservation System
6. Polity
7. Class

8. **Cultural and Religious Differences:** A deep-rooted and the most vulnerable disparities contribute to polarization. Cultural identity politics worsens divisions, leading to "us versus them" mentalities. We may hear a lot of noise around OBC, Muslims, caste within caste. It is the easiest way I believe to ignite a clash as Manipur has been a life witness of a culture clash.

9. Economic Disparities: This has been existing since ages, the elites as we call them vs the common person vs our friends who find it difficult to make both ends meet. Disparities in access to opportunities and resources can contribute to a sense of unfairness.

10. **Social Issues:** Debates around social issues such as abortion, Manipur violence as stated above, LGBTQ+ rights, and immigration is highly polarizing. For example, Canada has been topping the charts of every newspaper and media channels since Mr. Trudeau had something to say that is not acceptable. It may be an international issue, but our communities were deeply hurt because of his naïve argument that was too unsupported by any evidence against

our country, and to be precise our lovely Sikh community who is known for bravery and whole-heartedness.

11. **Polarized Institutions:** Institutions such as education, media, and even religious organizations, when perceived as biased or polarized, can contribute to societal divisions.

12. **Historical Grievances:** Lingering historical grievances and unresolved conflicts can fuel polarization by shaping group identities and fostering resentment.

13. **Globalization and Technological Change:** The effects of globalization, economic shifts, and technological advancements can create winners and losers, contributing to societal polarization.

It's important to note that these factors often interact and reinforce each other, creating a complex web of influences that contribute to polarization in society. Addressing polarization often requires a nuanced understanding of these dynamics and the development of strategies that promote dialogue, understanding, and inclusivity.

Knowing and understanding polarization is one part of the solution and not the eureka moment. The key lies in the effective action from YOU & US and in knowing how not to be a victim. I am going to present what I feel in addition to how it can be executed and practiced.

But first, can you identify yourself as a victim of any or multiple causes as listed above?

I am sure there will be multiple for you as it has been for me as we are the passengers on the same boat and space capsule. Especially, when I came to Delhi in 2006, hailing from a small town in Jharkhand, I found myself on the receiving end of polarization on the basis of origin. I went through comments like *"why do people like him come to our school for admission to up the headcount and increase the capital`s population further."*

What I did after that is a story for another time.

G20 & More

First thing first, was G20 just an event for us or an emotion?

Let me bring out ground level tales that should make our heart pumping with emotion and pride. Why not start with some *Naari* things as they are ruling.

As reported in times of India, dated 24th September 2023 while I was enjoying my Sunday special tea with my family talking over national and international politics, I came across amazing insights, Sub-inspector Pinky Rani, a native of Gochi village in Haryana and posted at Mukherjee Nagar police station found herself in a tricky situation as she escorted Türkiye first Lady Emine Erdogan for shopping in Dilli Haat as wives of G20 leaders tried to explore the city, away from the serious Summit deliberations. Yeah! Women for women and shopping. Inevitable, Hahahhaa!

The interesting fact here is how she dealt with the language barrier. The first lady didn't know Hindi and Pinky didn't know her fellow lady`s language. The lady wanted to purchase a hand-woven fabric. The challenge was overcome by the G20 App when it came handy. She exclaimed recently at Bharat Mandapam during her interaction with our PM, "We took Madam (Emine) to Dilli Haat. She wanted to know about a certain fabric.

I didn't know the Turkish language and madam couldn't speak in Hindi, so we used a translation facility on the G20 App and explained to the shopkeeper what madam wanted."

Whether the First lady bargained or not is something I am concerned about! O yeah!

Then we have Suresh Kumar, who accounts for his three-day duty. He explained, "I was posted near the L1 room at Bharat Mandapam which was earmarked for bilateral meetings. While on duty on September 9, I got information that my mother was admitted to hospital after suffering a heart attack, I wanted to be by my mother's side but then I felt that I should continue with my duty for the sake of country's pride.". Pheww!!

Hats off to the dedication, G20 was just not an event it was an emotion all together that binds us. An emotion towards the country. Putting our country first. It is not easy, but it requires a great amount of courage to keep the country first. A salute to the mother of such brave hearts. Interest of the country is the first priority.

It is not bound by a word called *Bharat* or *India* as is the *hullabaloo* these days.

Our dedication and feeling towards the country are **not a prisoner of words**. In fact, the feeling that we have towards our country doesn't even require a word. This can only be felt. You call it Bharat, Hindustan, Aryavrat, Jambudwip, India or whatever, no one can toxify our feelings nor de-purify it.

The micro-level planning during G20 was evident from the account of Himachal Pradesh`s Akshar Singh, constable-driver from 44th CRPF battalion. He was among dozens of drivers who learnt to use left-hand drive vehicles.

He says "we were entrusted with the security of global leaders, we received 2-months training. I was attached as a driver for leaders from Mexico for three days."

Pravin Kumar who was among those responsible for beautification of 41 roads which were designated for VIP movement, put up as, "once I reached home at 3 AM, as I knocked the door, I received a call that due to an accident, some flowerpots got damaged on the stretch near Leela Hotel where the LG was supposed to come for inspection. As I left for the spot again, my mother said, `Don't let your country down and work as hard as possible. Go now and if needed stay there for two-three days if needed`."

Ravinder Tyagi shared how his wife felt proud that he was a part of the G20 team when he told her that for three days he would be out from early morning till late at night.

So, allow me to say that it was not just the jobs and the designated persons, it was all together a family-effort more than a team effort. We all made it happen. Right from the PM to a tea seller at roadside, a sweeper to the IPS officer, a female to a transgender person, Muslims to Sikhs and Christians to Hindus, before all these designation and words there is a word that is more comfortable and soothing to our ears,

Our Country, Bharat! India! Hindustan!

We rolled out the green carpet for the world at one of the prestigious events of history, The G20 or shall I say B20 as it was this time in *Bharat* at a great site named Baharat Mandapam.

We shall try to understand what is G20, *the Why behind* this gigantic group, presidency for Bharat along with what it means for the common person. We have just witnessed the ***Historical Present of the future past.***

Wondering what bouncer was that? Haha! Please read that again for the sake of it!

Yes, it was indeed historical in nature that will be remembered in the future even as a green past. For *The Green carpet* that was laid down, the beautified fountains, the great greens in terms of potted plants and parks, the gigantic Natraj Statue made of 8 different metals (Ashtadhatu) at Bharat Mandapam, the ethnic rich culture and engrossed the city New Delhi like a bride. Even the lights at night pleased our eyes and souls so much like never before. It was more than the feeling I had, when we together had won the Cricket world cups.

It was certainly more than that, much more than that or shall I say it was an entirely unique experience and sets the tone in becoming the ***Vishwaguru*** as it is rightly said.

Let us understand the insights from the insider about this event, the expert mind himself, by none other than Bharat's G20 Sherpa and ex-CEO Niti Aayog, Mr. Amitabh Kant.

In July 2022, PM Modi appointed him as his Sherpa to the G20. The quiet G20 secretariat housed in Sushma Swaraj Bhawan was a far cry from the bustling environment of Niti Aayog that he was accustomed to. In those initial weeks he shared that "I felt that this was not a job with much content or scope for implementation." However, then he admits that his perception changed rapidly.

A team of energetic young officers soon began to throng his new office; what he had initially deemed as uninspiring turned into the most challenging and fascinating experience of his life. The mandate from the PM himself was clear. This has to be an ambitious and inclusive presidency, with the interest of the Global South at the heart of every discussion. Working under PM`s directive, he converted hurdles into opportunities and delivered a 100% consensus on all the priorities, bringing all countries to the same page.

Our G20 presidency was not contained within the four walls of meeting rooms. The rich democratic and cultural elements of India infused life and brightened the aura into the presidency, across 220 meetings held in 60 cities covering every state and UT. With over 100,000 delegates and participants across these meetings, this truly became a presidency representative of diversity.

In the 21st Century, what I love to call the *Bharatiya Era*, Bharat is a sturdy multilateral player and will help solve the biggest problems for the world. This summit has scripted a new narrative of global cooperation in a heavily polarized world and the credit lies completely with PM Modi and the team. His global stature and standing enabled us to *Be Bold | Be Transparent |Be more*, and to take courageous risks in negotiations, which helped us to unlock a historic consensus.

Looking at his steep learning curve, Mr. Amitabh Kant says," it has truly been an honor for me to be his Sherpa to the G20."

Don't you think pondering over the G20 a bit more can put us in a much more apt situation? Let us get set!

ERA 2:

Challenge your Mindset.

- **The Mindset Reboot: Growth Mindset**
- **Decoding UCC: Uniform Civil Code, looking beyond the obvious | The Ifs and the Buts**
- **Indian Defense Forces | Values that make our defense forces special.**
- **Values that Make INDIA, The Vishwaguru, The Mother of Democracy.**

The Mindset Reboot

"This is your captain Sid (Siddharth) speaking, it is 6 15 AM serene Saturday morning, the outside temperature is pleasant 22 degrees. We are about to take off and will cover our journey in about eight hours from now and good news to share - when we reach the destination, the temperature will be less than awesomely cool below 5 degrees with hot n happening bonfire. The better news is there will be nature all around and the best news – you may get chilled beers and if you have done some virtuous deeds then some beautiful girlfriends too, but that I don't promise.

What I assure you is an unreal beautifully serene heavenly natural place that will reboot the mindset."

Seems like an announcement from a pilot, and yes, it is. The pilot is none other than Siddharth, who is driving his gray colored, beautifully maintained car. He is brutally skilled in speaking and known for living his life to the fullest, enjoying every single moment. He has learnt the art of living in the present and acknowledging life, what I called as **"Dolce Far Niente,"** at the very first page of this piece, an Italian concept.

He makes the environment lively, with his other three simply awesome friends Nimboooz (Ambuj), MG47 (Seems like the name of a gun, but this is the nickname for Manoj Gupta,) and our favorite musical person named Abhi (Abhinav).

Abhi's only job in the journey is to keep playing quality songs otherwise he gets threats from Sid and Nimbooz. To Sid's announcement which he personified as a pilot, Nimbooz answered "Aap gaadi chalane pr dhyan de, jyada bakwas na kren, vnra emergency dwaar kholkr bahar phenk die janege" "You focus on driving, and don't talk rubbish otherwise we will open the emergency gate and throw you out."

MG47, who is so mad at taking photographs, is not bothered about what kind of dialogue is going on as he is glued on to the pay meter of fuel station in stress and anger, because he is the one who is supposed to pay this time for tanking up the fuel in Sid`s car. He right now dreams of some superpower that would allow him to limit the pay meter but unfortunately, he is yet to get those powers. Hahahaha!

And Abhi, as usual playing some beautiful tracks for them who keep him threatening to play excellent quality songs otherwise "emergency dwar aapke pas bhi hai jisse aapko sadak ko chumne ka mauka mil skta hai" – "Emergency door is close to you even that can offer to kiss the road." Nimbooz said who keeps sitting on his head to play songs. Nimbooz does this work efficiently to keep the quality high; you know why?

As he is a manager in one of the renowned MNC`s in Delhi NCR. And this is the reason he has been given the task of improving the quality of songs that Abhi plays otherwise, you know, the emergency exit.

Sid has been friends with Nimbooz for more than 10 years and they know each other like a person who knows their own pocket. Their fight throughout the never-ending journey in 10 years and this mindset reboot journey reminds us of Tom & Jerry. They both are friends for lifetime, but the adorable part is that Nimbooz respects Sid as he is the one who has helped him to rise from a simple executive job to a position where he has become so skilled in delegating his work to his team that he feels he should retain some work for himself as he is not very skilled in sitting idle for the entire shift.

All the four friends have one thing in common **"The Mindset, The Growth Mindset"** which has propelled them to decide to take on this journey so that they all four can preserve their minds and work to the best of their abilities. That is what keeps them glued together. All four of them are currently going through life's "special moments" that I will reveal soon that has so much to offer us to learn.

What David Mitchell said holds true for all of us-

"Travel far enough, you meet yourself."

Only a true travel enthusiast can understand this phrase. Because traveling is not just about visiting one place after another. Travelling is all about collecting memories as well as associating yourself with the places you visit. A true travel devotee does not only travel to explore novel places but according to them traveling is a way to meet themselves.
The key thing that contributes to planning a trip is *travel motivation.*

The more you are motivated to travel far enough, the more are the chances you can meet your *inner self.* It helps you discover yourself in the best way possible. You get to spend more time with yourself and do stuff for yourself.

Does that call for planning a trip? Let me ask you a question to all of you out here –

What was the last time you met yourselves? Or when was the last time you travelled? I want you to remember as clearly and vividly as possible.

Wherever it was, it is not the point here. What is more important here is – did it help you to reboot and recharge yourselves?

Or you also resemble MG47's personality of being busy in clicking photographs with the intention of collecting *good moments*. The irony is we are busy clicking the moments and scenery to upload on social media, that we wish to experience as "second-hand travel" later when we are back from the actual trip. This also resonates with one of our chapters titled as *"The Second Copy: Are we using the "The second Copy" of the Education System in Bharat?"*

Moving on, I wonder how people say that they click pictures so that they can see the photographs later to *relive* the moments. Now, the interesting fact for me here is I wonder how can they *relive* the moment when they have actually not *lived in the moment* in the first place? Why are we bothered about a secondhand experience when we can have a firsthand involvement?

Why don't we just soak ourselves in nature instead of clicking and clicking. This signifies that even if we are travelling, we are not able to meet ourselves truly. The gadgets are not as good as you are.

That is the reason when this trip was planned among the four friends, a rule was set – *no photographs*, or else the *emergency door!* But even then MG47 was ready to listen to the ridicule from his friends but could never soak himself in for firsthand experience.

This calls for a restricting of our thoughts to effectively travel and extract the sweet fruits of Nature. So, how, and how often should one plan a trip? Well! That is a personal call, but I must tell you if you are not able to travel even once a year to meet yourselves, then you must think about what kind of life you are leading. This is something you do, or you don't like. But why? I am sure you will believe me that nature has amazing insights to offer.

I have been a die-hard fan of Bollywood movies. I remember when I was recently watching the movie "Uunchai" directed by Sooraj Barjatya. A film to celebrate friendship and linked emotions which is a treat to watch. If I have not navigated through this movie yet, I would suggest watching it ASAP. Starring the great Amitabh Bachchan, the veteran Boman Irani, the versatile Anupam Kher and smart Dany Denzonpa. The story of the movie is based on four friends, among which one of them dies, the other friends take Bhupen's (Dany) ashes and go to Everest to immerse him, which was Bhupen's favorite place where he wanted to go but could not.

Bhupen when he was alive, he said, "pahado me har sawal ka jawab hota hai." *"Mountains offer answers to all the questions."*

But this holds true when your soul is present in nature instead of being glued to gadgets. That calls for a ***Digital detoxification.***

Everyone must plan a trip once a year at least to travel to such a place where there will be no external distraction. It is the best opportunity to focus on yourself without any distraction. But people ask how traveling helps meeting yourself? Is it even possible that you can meet yourself while you are on the trip? The answer to all these questions is *yes*, traveling helps you meet yourself. The next question is how? It is possible because when you travel to such a place that is quite far from your location it brings your fast-paced lifestyle to a slower pace.

Planning a trip to Nature is the best treat you can give to yourself that can help you meet a fantastic person like YOU. Traveling and soaking in scenery is so peaceful and brings peace to your mind. To calm yourself, traveling to the peaks is an ideal option. Foothills are far from your current location, so you can focus more on yourself. What helps you discover yourself by traveling to such a place is you are only concerned about yourself. Your thoughts, feelings, and activities are just limited to yourself.

You do not focus on anything else in the world and there will be no distraction. Traveling far away can also help you to be more productive and active. You get to spend high-quality time with your soul. You can enjoy your solitude and peace by sticking around yourself. The best thing you can do here is to meditate or do yoga, which will help you focus on yourself by giving clarity to your mind. Sounds boring?

Honestly speaking, no! This is not boring at all. Instead, the most interesting thing that you will find to do in nature is to sit quietly and soak in nature and allow the ever-active mind to observe what is going on inside the head without acting on it. Just you and your thoughts so that you can keep the best ones and throw away the harmful ones. This activity is so seductive that you won't need any other activity or even a person to seduce you and your thoughts towards peace.

Meditation and yoga allow us to focus on ourselves by removing all the negative thoughts from our mind. It declutters our mind as well as heals our soul too. So that you can focus on things that are present.

Other than that, there are some more activities you can also perform that can help you discover yourself. Such as waking up for the sunrise or meditating on the sunrise. The two of these activities are also highly effective in allowing you to meet yourself. It brings calmness to your mind and makes your life easier.

Oh, you have already started to feel the seduction. Oh wait!! We will begin the journey gradually and you will be glad to know that such a place exists. I will reveal it too in a short while during the expedition, but now let us allow nature to seduce us with its beauty and peace.

With what soaking in nature offers us, we can make better decisions for the future that will make our life beautiful. Not only waking up to the sunrise, if you are not a morning person then you can still do something to meet yourself.

You can sit still under the stars during the nighttime, the way these four friends sat till 3: 15 AM on a raised platform around 10 feet above the ground with the help of four round wooden pillars over which rested a rectangular wooden platform. The night offered the sight of a moon never seen before – bigger, brighter, and better, as I say *seductive* in its own sense. It is also one of the practices that bring calmness to your life. During such moments of stillness, it helps you hear your heart and what your soul wants. Thus, you can make a better decision by listening to your heart and mind.

Also, deep breathing practice is another important thing you can do in complete silence. Traveling far away from your usual environment, you train your mind in the best way possible. It will make the vision clear by bringing clarity to your mind. You just need to get travel motivation for such a place like this, this way you can help yourself and meet your inner personality. Although it is a bit challenging for some people a little motivation can help to make this life-changing experience.

Let us go back to the journey of four friends together and they are not the only ones travelling. We all are together drifting to the "Unrealistically beautiful" place through their experience. This might be a secondhand experience, but I will try my best to seduce you to plan a trip soon as this journey has a lot to offer to learn."

As I was saying that the four friends were experiencing "special moments of life," let me reveal it right away.

1. **Siddharth**

An explorer, an enthusiast for life and a nature boy. He believes in living each moment to the fullest. He has been trying to learn this since he became a grown-up chap, but one incident propelled him to master the art of being in the moment. Presently, he was navigating through one of the hardest phases of his life. This event has the potential to drop dead the very soul and heart. It was such a psychologically, socially, and financially draining episode we will discuss in the coming sections.

Oh!! Don`t worry Sid is a *"chill kinda guy."* I am not going to portray his agony here. Although, on the other hand he is humane too, so he gets his share of emotional rain and outbursts. But even in such a situation he knows the skill to smile and make others smile. He knows the game of life, and whenever asked. He always utters this phrase –

"Every Crisis is an indication of something great."

This is what we can aim to learn as to how at such an immature age he can manage his emotions, dealing with all the adversities that too with a smile and style. So, the objective of reading and writing this chapter is to reflect on the ***"Emotional Resilience"*** from Sid`s journey. We will learn how we can develop an *emotionally resilient personality* that has magnified benefits in times of distress.

2. **Manoj Gupta:**
   A Cheerful person who believes in healthy flirting! Friends with Sid for more than 10 years, they have spent good and bad days together. Both Sid and Manoj have one thing in common, that is both are a bit spiritual that keeps them glued together.

He is navigating a crisis himself. The deteriorating medical condition of his brother and to make matters worse, unemployment. Life pressure taking toll on his head that frequently, Sid found him talking about suicides in his conversations.

3. Ambuj Purwar:

An amazingly hard-working person with an enthusiastic sense of humor. A perfect gel with Sid. They both have worked on a number of projects – different girlfriends… and how to impress them, new jobs, power points presentations, excel sheets, cans of beers, debates, and extended discussions of tough times of life.

What was bothering him was lack of purpose or what we call a mid-life crisis. Though aged around 30, it is too soon to term it as a mid-life crisis but yes that is what is true here in his case. Lack of motivation arises from lack of purpose. Recently he underwent surgery that caused him to get serious about health.

4. Abhinav

This is a gem of a person. Ambuj caught him by his collar to join them along for the trip. Why? So that the trip expense could be distributed evenly! Hahaha. Yeah, Ambuj is very calculative when it comes to money.

But jokes apart, Abhi is a close friend with Ambuj and shares common experiences which is evident from the fact that Abhi came all the way from Bengaluru to join him on this trip.

Are you wondering if next up would be about Abhi`s struggles now? Aren't the struggles of the above three more than enough. At least someone is leading a good life, let him live. *I felt a bit of jealousy while writing this!* How could someone be without problems in this world! Ahhhhhhh! Or, he had learnt the art of navigating those with a smile.

Alright! Sid declared that he would take eight hours to reach a heavenly unreal location. And hold on, I will tell you the place and guide you how to reach the place with ease. So, sit back glued and enjoy a fulfilling journey. People, now allow me to seduce you towards nature. Here you go –

The Child affects.
MG47 could not get the superpowers to stop the pay meter unfortunately, and he had to pay an amount Rs. 2520. His hard-earned money that he was so reluctant to give as if his heart would stop pumping his blood now.

So, finally the journey began with some amazing "Hanuman Ji" bhajan which they all chanted followed by "Devi Durga" & "Shani Maharaj`s" bhajan. This was one of the strongest personality traits that glued them together in friendship. After starting, soon after around an hour, Sid finally found a Hanuman Ji Temple, which he had promised MG47 that he will take him too as both were a bit spiritual and of course it was Saturday, so they had this ritual of visiting Shani & Hanuman Temple.

They had the rituals followed in the temple and the tone was set to onset the beautiful expedition towards meeting their souls. You know being spiritual attracts positive energy. And this is what happened the next moment, as Sid was driving, he saw a yellowish color bus with six children standing on the back seat and peeking out from a transparent rectangular glass window, laughing, and waving. The children aged around 5 to 12 years of age were so joyful that Sid, Nimbooz, MG47, and Abhi, lost the train of thoughts of their worries and resonated with their energy.

Sid, being a skilled pilot of his car, made sure to live this moment along with his friends. He got close to the bus not with the intention to overtake it but to be close enough so that they could communicate non-verbally. All four friends started waving their hands towards those children and in return, they responded with a pure smile and happiness, where the youngest child among them aged around 6 was the happiest wearing a white colored cotton t-shirt and she had cute curly long hair, slightly brownish in color. This is one of the moments to capture in our heart.

This exchange of waving, brightness of eyes, the happy energy was exchanged, and it was bliss to start – ***Nirvana***. Can we try to be in the moment for some time? Yes, you have to, and you would love it too!

It will not be wrong to say that the time has come to ***learn from children rather than to teach them***. They are smarter, happier, and exponentially wealthier - emotionally than most of us put together.

Why? Why is a child happier than us? What do you think?

This may be a small moment to live in, but it has much to offer to learn. Now is the time to turn on your mental faculties, flex your mental muscles.

If you are thinking hard, I am glad. A child has one skill that we should learn which can alter ourselves cognitively, our thought process and actions altogether.

A Child knows the skill of living in the moment.

"Dolce far Niente" a term that you read at the very first page in the beginning above the bell shaped 21 languages pyramid, which is an Italian concept of pausing, acknowledging life, doing nothing and being in the moment.

With that being said, it is not easy yet not that difficult. We have been living for some 30 second's rule. It is simple, right now when you are reading this journey, if your mind is making some noises like –

1. What will I do after reading this book?
2. How long should I read the book now?
3. Where will I go after this?
4. Which are the mails that you need to respond to?
5. Whom do you need to call after this task.
6. Or while reading, you are simultaneously checking the gadget's notification.

If we encounter any, some, or all of the **noises** (you may read more on noises and digital dementia in my previous work titled- *"The Journey To A New You")* in our head right now at this moment, then we need to work on the skill of living in the moment.

I came across an interesting fact about the 30 second rule explained by the great *Maddy*, R Madhavan. We are constantly thinking 30 seconds ahead of what we are doing now. For example, when you get up and brush your teeth you might be thinking about the to-do list or what you will wear for the office today.

Then when you are preparing breakfast, you might be thinking whether to have it at home or after reaching the office. When you are travelling to the office, you might be encircled with the thoughts of emails and the to-do list and the meetings that you had scheduled for today.

Now what happens is that we are never actually fully present in doing a particular activity. How many of you have really enjoyed pleasant weather? Or the first thing that you do to enjoy rain is to click a photograph? How many of us really enjoyed the last meal?

You need to think deeply about your soul, because this is the skill that brings out the excellence and happiness that is missing, living in the moment is a skill that has to be nurtured. Some are naturally happy-go-lucky people unlike me. I had to absorb hard to be able to live in the moment.

Say for Sid, who is piloting his car, such *dramebaazi* dialogues and the fun he does, despite undergoing through life`s brutal experience of "divorce" that had almost gifted him three heart attacks. One for his father, and one for his mother. And these two are enough to personally gift him a guaranteed third one, as he loves both from the deepest soul.

But on the other hand, instead of succumbing to the life-long mental and horrific injuries he has been gifted by his ex-wife and in-laws, he has mastered the skill of being in the moment. And you know if you ask him how he is, he will answer this with the greatest happiness from his soul as ***"simply awesome."*** The term Nimbooz and Sid have been coined together.

We need to be ***fully present*** from each of the cells in the body at a particular task, a hundred percent of the soul needs to be *present* to make ***"it"*** effective and full. I am sure you all will agree with me. Yes! Am I right?

And by ***"it"*** in the line above, I mean.
- Your Relationships

- Your profession
- Friendship
- Mental Health
- Upskilling
- Your Family
- Whatever activity you are doing, be it as simple as taking a shower.

By not being fully present what are you doing?

You are depriving a human's greatest desire of lifetime. You know what it is? Think through for a moment, what could be the greatest desire for a human being.

Does that come around in your mind like money, fame, a beautiful woman by our side, or good friends or travel for that matter?

Alright, let me answer. I would answer that the all-time greatest desire for human beings has been and will be:

"The desire to feel important."

You can ponder over this point deeply and think through any major problem that you are going through or have recently gone through, especially let us restrict ourselves to relationships. Doesn't matter whether personal or professional.

You will understand after deep self-introspection that whatever the problem is or was, the central core challenge revolves around *"The desire to feel important."* Don't just speed up reading from here. If you really want to benefit from this journey stop reading this right now! Close the book.

Self-introspect any existing problems in a relationship for some time alone. You will get the answer. You are the best teacher for yourselves. And if you find it difficult to find an environment of solitude and a way to self-introspect. Let me know seriously, you can connect with me over social media, we together can make this happen.

Even if you are successfully able to self-introspect, and find what I said to be true, do connect and write to me how did you feel, what did you find out by introspecting, did it help you to improve your relationships and other areas of life. Did you actually apply the learning and found it to be effective?

Furthermore, if you find this above idea of *"the desire to feel important"* not working for you and you don't want to self-introspect, do connect even to criticize me, and let me know your thoughts. I would love to learn from you and "***Grow together.***" This is the central theme of the book, right?

"To Grow Together"

So, stop the noises right now and decide to learn "**the skill of being in the moment**" along with me. "Learning is a painful process." What I strongly believe is, "**MERIT = PAIN**"

The Child Affect: | Key Take away:

- Travel far enough, you meet yourself!
- Every Crisis is an indication of something great.
- Emotional Resilience
- Nirvana.
- Learn from children rather than teaching them.
- The desire to feel important.
- The skill of being in the moment

The Age Game
While on the journey, all the four friends were finally hungry and wanted to have some quick bites, so they stopped at a roadside "Dhaba" after around 15 km from the temple. Do you know why Sid took fifteen kms or around 20 minutes to stop the car?

As Nimbooz was in a remarkable condition. He wanted to pee, yes! You read it right, and Sid being Sid, takes full advantage in these situations and his revenge on all the dialogues that Nimbooz fires with his articulate skills. Nimbooz was begging to stop the car! Hahahah! but it was the Ahaa! moment for the other three and even if Sid at a point of time wanted to stop, the other two MG47 & Abhi did not let him stop, as they also had their share of revenge from Nimbooz` s creative dialogues.

And here comes one from Abhi in return to Nimbooz' s earlier attack if you remember - "emergency dwar aapke pas bhi hai jisse aapko sadak ko chumne ka mauka mil skta hai" – "Emergency door is close to you even that can offer to kiss the road."

Abhi said, "I think somebody wants to kiss the road Sid, what shall we do."

Sid: Oh! No *kissing Vissing Yaar*, we have just been from a temple" *Mata rani paap lagaegi.* (Goddess mother will curse!)

Nimbooz: "Yes! you both are correct, but the timing is incorrect to discuss *romance with the road*, mother goddess will curse for- "ek Masoom se bacche ko susu Jaisi cheez ko tadpane ke lie." (To make it hard for an innocent boy to pee!)

Manoj: "Yes, somebody called *Massoom* (Innocent)" I am here!" Manoj exclaimed as he also was left to fire against Nimbooz' s attack in the beginning.

Nimbooz: "Somebody has correctly said - Teamwork is a dream work." You all have become a team to stop my *gun from firing, whether it's from mouth or….*" I appreciate the team's efforts.

Nimbooz: "So guys, as you are a good team by now, be ready to wash the car also because *my gun can hold it anymore. So…*"

As soon as he exclaimed about washing the car, all three others were done with the revenge and Sid finally halted the car, and for Nimbooz this was the best moment of his entire lifetime or multiple lifetimes as he could feel heavenly now. Hahahaha! You know nothing could be more relaxing than peeing at the right time at the right place.

Moving on, the place where they stopped by to grab some snacks was such a kind, they were delighted. It was a quite simple roadside stall with some old chairs, and a tin shade that offered at least some shadow, snack packets of green, yellowish, and light blue colors hanging from thin wires especially put in for this specific purpose. Some cold drink bottles at the counter and the happiness "*Kartoos*" for them. Kartoos has been used metaphorically here for cigarettes.

One of the terrible habits that they had picked during their college days. Although, you will be happy to see that later in our journey together they finally leave this awful habit that they all hated but unknowingly this had become a practice for them.

As soon as Sid & Abhi started to light their *Kartoos*, they were awestruck by the amazing, picturesque offers towards the back side of the stall. There was a huge land with lush-green plantation, and the topping on the cherry was a peacock that was wandering slowly though the lush-green land. Such a rare sight of a peacock at such a place in such a situation was surprising for them. They both were so mesmerized by the scene that they had even neglected to light the *Kartoos* that Sid was holding in his hand.

You know which power was working here that stopped them continuing with their college habits?

It is **"The power of nature."** The strongest amongst all the powers. And why I consider this as the strongest, I think events like tripping of housed in Kullu recently, amazingly strong floods in places like Delhi, Himachal & Uttarakhand, Biparjoy Cyclone in Gujarat & Mumbai around, second week of June 2023 are enough to showcase how powerful the power is and how do we pay the *"cost of progress"*, (A chapter you will find in upcoming sections) the greatest example of balance is nature, and it definitely knows how to balance itself.

Getting back to the scene, as soon as Sid, MG47 & Abhi were appreciating Mother Nature's beauty with MG47, it was time for Nimbooz, back to the section after coming from the *heavenly washroom*, with a stick in his hand meant for the other three. And he started…" Saalon…. Fu…. Y… and blah blah blah blah…." (*Friendship jingle*, you know all the abuses among friends)

While this comic scene was on display, the shopkeeper also couldn't hold his laugh on another epic dialogue by Nimbooz in conversation with the shopkeeper *"Btao bhaiya, ye aisa krte hai hamare sath, abhi to meri shaadi bhi nai hui hai, kuch ho gaya to biwi ko kya muh dikhaunga"*- *"Tell me brother, they do these things with me, I am not married yet, what face will I show my wife"*.

All four I must tell you never miss a chance to live in the moment and make fun. Do you know why this moment of nature, the fun, the stick, the *Nirvana* in friendship is possible? It is because most of them have developed the skill of *living in the moment* that we discussed in the preceding sections. They all had deliberately left their gadgets in the car, and look what they got

– a picturesque moment, the laughter that resonated with the unknown shopkeepers also.

Soon, as all this drama happened, a grey colored, wrinkled, unshaven, skinny around 52 years of old age uncle came to offer them *"garma garam aaalo Paranthe"* Hot stuffed chapati. with Curd. He was indeed very skinny with wrinkled face, was wearing a torn stylish jean. There was a hole in the jeans around the knee which explained his hardships and one more near the thighs when he came that further showed what value a cloth piece has even if it is torn. They all four observed them very closely without uttering a single word.

As soon as he kept the stuff and was walking back to his stall just five steps from the table, they observed a few more places in his jeans, rugged torn and filthy. And this was not style. It was mere challenging work and that said a lot about *the unfairness of life*. He also wore a grey colored t-shirt that was not able to serve its purpose as he was almost bare chested. And his bones were crying out of the skin. Such was the condition that still all four of them could not utter a single world.

They were so lost that Sid & Nimbooz, eyes were filled with tears as together they have been through similar pain of unfairness of life compatible with this old-aged man. The man got busy again making other chapatis for them. Once he came back to offer more chapatis, Sid asked "What is your name uncle?" To which he replied coldly "Sambhu" Period!

He looked as if he is lost, doesn't look in people's eye, his senses are working but he didn't want to project as if they are really working. He then started cleaning the space for other also.

And where are the other two by now? This was the time for MG47 & Abhi to experience the *heavenly washroom* that Nimbooz had experienced in the beginning. Yes, you are correct! They had gone now to pee.

Fast forwarding, it was time for the 4 musketeers to head on the journey to heaven. While they were on the journey, they passed through a serene place called Haridwar, a place to be and a must visit. Continuing their journey, they finally reached the foothills, and it was time to start the hill drive which Nimbooz was fearful of.

After a few kilometers climbing up the great picturesque roads which are one of its kind, hills, lush green mountains, and nature singing peaceful songs, with temperature dropping with climbing up the hill. Sid exclaimed, "passengers are now requested to have a look at their gadgets, the temperature outside has reached the *breakeven point* as it has matched the Air condition temperature of 18 degrees, so time to open the windows." And the cool breeze then! Wow! much dearer than the AC, able to touch the very deepest soul.

With another good news as AQI was matching that of Virat`s quick half century i.e., 51. It was such a clean air that they felt breathing the purest air. On their way, they stopped at another corner stall at around 3 o'clock in the afternoon on the amazing curvy roads uphill.

It was time for another snacking, but this time it was something different. Earlier it was a 52-year-old shopkeeper, now it was a young charming 12-year-old boy named *Sourav* assisted by his 11-year brother *Sunny*, who were managing the shop as if they had beaten the number game of age. At no point of time, they made the customers feel ignored and that they are too young to oversee them.

What a level of customer service they were displaying. They were at that time handling around 12 to 13 customers, cooking, serving, taking new orders, preparing *"Chhole Samosa"* &

Omlette, cleaning the table and what not. Sid asked, "What do you have in offer for us?" the elder one replied, "whatever you will like sir" with such a politeness and a smile that even Air Host will find difficult to display.

His voice touched Sid`s heart. At that moment, his younger one came to his support and exclaimed confidently, "Sir, people really love our samosa Chhole, I am sure you will love it too." Sid and his friends were more interested in how they were dealing with them rather than having their food.

All the four musketeers started conversing with the young ones seeing their confidence and simplicity. Finally, they ordered tea and then the 11-year-old applied upselling skills by saying, "Sir, if you partner tea with our famous dish, you will love your tea more." Do you think anyone could say no to such young, charming kids? And they all answered in the affirmative nodding their head feeling surprisingly happy at their demeanor.

I must highlight the best thing in the entire conversation with the young chap that has a lesson to offer. When Sid asked, "when did you cook these samosas as they seem to have been kept since long"? Sid was expecting an answer as other shopkeepers would have, like "Sir, just a few minutes back," even if it were kept for hours.

But contradicting Sid`s expectation, Sourav answered, "Sir, I have prepared it in the morning. And still it is fresh as it is kept carefully for all of you as you travel to our place from long distances, and it is with your travel that our homes are able to survive. We will not offer you anything that disturbs your digestion and creates problems in your journey. You can first taste it and I am sure you will love it as others do."

Such a strong statement by the young kid, that even Sid and Nimbooz, who are so fashioned, mouthed and overloaded with speaking skills were clueless as to what they should reply to this young champion. He was indeed a champion in dealing with customers. And the young boy won, he prepared his dish with honesty the way he chose to answer honestly about the time of cooking.

Somebody has rightly said, "Honesty is the best policy." Rare to find but as valuable as it should be. His conduct, honesty, charm, dedication to being responsible for being a bread earner for his family impressed all 4 and also other fellow travelers who were sitting beside. Further, they didn't question him anymore and wishing him good luck they continued with their journey uphill to reach around 10,000 Ft above sea level.

Finally, all the four reached their destination, a resort in the wonderland in Uttarakhand, the picturesque is jaw dropping and spell bound. Whenever Sid goes there, the first thing he does before anything else is to switch off his mobile phone and not only his, but he makes sure that the entire *jury* with him do the same.

Switching OFF the mobile phones actually *switches ON the inner self as Sid says.* I strongly believe so. When you want to meet yourselves, you need to get away from the gadgets and everything that is virtual and lost in the serene space, the peaceful environment, the purest of the pure soul i.e., YOU. Connect to yourself and charge yourself before charging anything else.

If you wonder how to do that, I have an answer to this.

Self-introspection

But this is not easy. You need to create an environment, disconnect from the outer world, and start connecting within.

Have you ever done that?

If not, then this is the moment. Even if you have done it before, let us do it more efficiently. This is the thing that you can start acting upon straight away. The next question, how do we do that? There is an interesting video on my YouTube channel to have a glimpse of the place and a detailed conversation with Mr. J.K. Akash, an eminent personality who mentored me at some good point in my life. I cannot be thankful enough for agreeing to shoot the video and also to take me to such an unreal place.

He explains in the video how to make the best of this place, how to self-introspect, question yourselves, how to function as an effective parent and what not. Link is here. (https://youtu.be/Vbu2O1C_IsA?si=jIsGPHOWNTlkHPgF) I strongly urge you to watch it before reading further.

Introspection starts by looking within and asking questions to you like:

1. How am I feeling today, at this point in time?
2. Am I passionate about something?
3. If yes, then am I doing justice to my passion?
4. If not, then am I doing enough to meet and realize my passion?
5. What is it that keeps me motivated and unmotivated?
6. Are my relations good or do I need to put more effort?
7. Am I moving up the career ladder?
8. Is the field that I have chosen to pursue the right one? Or do I need to reconsider my decisions?

These are just a glimpse of questions with which you can start, and the best news is your mind is powerful enough to answer these with precision. But you have to allow your mind to think by relaxing it, giving it an environment where it can do its magical stuff, you have to allow it a peaceful place along with decluttering it, you have to move your mind away from distractions.

This process would help you to focus on what is important and at the same time what is significant for you to focus on and put effort into. So, what are you waiting for, start it right away! Find a place or, you just close your eyes and feel the *extreme loudness of silence.*

The Agni Effect:

Moving on, finally all the four friends could feel relieved in the evening with some *"high tea"* crispy snacks and the most amazing bonfire in the chilling temperature just proved to be a heavenly place. None of the travelers could miss this moment. Whenever they tried to look far and beyond, they could see a few tiny lights glittering like silver and stars, as they were sitting at a great height.

There were around twenty-five young, old, children, friends, fathers, mothers, girlfriends, boyfriends and many comfier with jackets on and the faces lit with the yellowish light from the flame. It was absolutely dark except the flame from the significantly huge bonfire with stars twinkling above in the sky. All of them were sitting quietly and enjoying this peaceful and serene moment. With most of the couples engrossed in their romantic whispering, there was something unusual.

The cheerful jittery Sid was only physically there. Nimbooz shook him up, whispered in his ears but Sid said nothing. As Nimbooz understood him very well, he could make out that it was the time for Sid to have some ME time and he left him alone for quite some time on his own. But it left Nimbooz a bit confused!

As it was dark, with only flames allowing a narrow glimpse of face with the heat so nobody bothered to notice that Sid was crying his heart out in front of *Agni*. He was crying for more than 30 minutes with his eyes swollen and tears shining like crystals.

Why? Was it the flames that made him cry or was it the reason Sid went to such a place? But he never looked disturbed from inside during the entire journey till then. He was as jovial as others were not leaving any single moment with Nimbooz and MG47 to make the most of the trip.

Why he cried needs your most empathetic heart to understand. Are we ready? Let me bring out what had happened to Sid just a month back which devastated and broke him deeply. He was so deeply affected by an incident that he thought that he didn't deserve to live any more. His life is finished.

He recently got married a year back to a pretty girl, an arranged marriage and everything looked normal and as usual. Blessings poured down from the elders of the family. Merry-making and wish for a healthy life with chants like "Dudo Nahao, Puto Phalo"! Give us some good news soon. Imagine jokes about a child on the very first day of marriage. Hahahah! Embarrassing, right?

Some of you might have heard this if married and if not, I promise you will hear these lines as soon as you get married! But all is good if the family is happy!

Let me put up some questions here.

Imagine you came to know just after a week of marriage that your wife or for that matter husband is in a physical relationship with someone else? How would you feel if your parents were abused by your partner in the worst language possible in front of you for no reason? How would you feel if you and your parents' bank accounts were checked and accordingly the amount of respect is paid as the balance of the account.

How would you feel if you get to see nude pictures of your spouse with someone else lying on bed ***"happily?"*** How would you feel if your father's sugar level crossed the 500 marks, and he were as close to a heart-attack? How would you feel if your goddess-like mother and hero figure father's cried like thunder in your ears daily worrying about her only Son's future? How would you feel if you suddenly become purposeless in your life being robbed of all the happiness?

And cherry on the topping – the girl's family threatens dire consequences, maintenance, and alimony if you file anything like divorce. You being the only bread-earner for the family, how would you deal with the situation?

What should the old-age parents of the victim do if they face such a situation? Where should they go? What should Sid do? To make the matter worse, Sid being the only earner for the family is targeted in office as he is not able to focus on his Job resulting in mediocre performance and is asked to resign within a month. Moreover, his best guardian after his father, his elder brother who treated him like his son, sided with the girl's family on the pretext of his own wife as she didn't want Sid and his parents to progress.

Hey Stop! Aren't you wondering, we are discussing in this work about Naari Shakti and how it helps the society to progress. How is the negative portrayal of Naari? Don't worry, crimes don't have any gender. And the good news is, we have a strong and exemplary Naari coming in the next section to keep the stakes high!

That puts up an important question here. *How on one side Naari* शक्ति *is rocking the world around winning medals and piloting rockets and airplanes and on the other side the same is taking a toll on someone's life? Is crime gender specific or gender neutral?*

I asked this question to my mom about Sid and his life, and the answer that she gave me was quite convincing. She exclaimed-

"Look son! We have two shades of women in society. The ones who get you high, upwards, onwards and the other who misunderstand independence. One who misunderstands the very essence of freedom."

That was too heavy for me to understand, but the interesting part is that we will together try to navigate my mom`s statement if this existence of two shades of Naari is true and whether we can do something about it. I mean that is the sole purpose of writing this work to discuss solutions more than problems so that we can take relevant action.

Getting back to those worrying questions that Sid was confronted with, was the reason for more than half an hour of crying like anything that he couldn't control at such a heavenly place. With all the peaceful things right from bonfire to beer in his hands to his sought-after friends, mountains, soothing temperature and what not in his bucket at that moment but what was missing was his ***mental peace***!

Yes! Those made him cry. The fear of uncertainty, the pain given by Sid`s very own better half and sibling. The agony of what he was going through continuously for the last five months feeling helpless.

When he had finished the spell of loud cries through his eyes and heart, he went on to call Nimbooz, and then put up a never-ending smile on his face again and lost himself in some hot dance numbers and danced his heart out through the chilly night. But he had decided on one thing before finishing his *cry spell*.

He would make his mental peace a priority now, and he would **reboot his mindset** whenever required as the chapter titled ***"The Mindset Reboot"*** teaches. He promised himself that he will soon find a solution. He promised himself that he will be bigger than his problems, he is better than before and an immensely powerful question he asked to himself which can also be a key takeaway for us all.

"What is this situation trying to teach me?"

A powerful question indeed! Try it once if you ever find yourself in a tough situation again!

Next morning, he made sure to visit the great *Surkanda Devi Temple* enroute his return Journey to gain some spiritual strength. Sid meditated for around 20 minutes inside the temple to look within and introspect about the problems and the solutions.

Do you believe in miracles? I too never did, but what happened next makes me believe so. Miracles do happen if you **strongly want** it to happen. What happened next was absolutely *unusual and simply awesome* and Sid could get a firsthand experience of what a miracle means.

Soon within a span of a three to four month, his prayers were answered, he found himself back again @ Surkanda Devi Temple after a spell of surreal turnarounds within brief period with someone who represents what a true Naari शक्ति means. Next up..

Wondering where the *Naari* शक्ति *here?* This chapter has been talking about travelling and how one shade of female has misunderstood freedom and self-independence. So here is the good news, the next section brings the true representation of शक्ति and her energy. Same place, a different audience, a *different Sid* along with four more closest mates this time to the same place but with all together a different mindset.

The *HIGH* TEA | The Love Story begins.

Cthinnnnnn…the beautiful sound when two cups full of tea is cheered against each other, comes when Sid and *Chitra* cheered sitting at a heavenly place in a café along a Buddha Temple in Mussoorie, Uttarakhand while they were returning home from the same place.

Sitting in the 2 feet wide balcony, with hilltop mountain-view with the greenery giving a great romantic feel. The café guys going one step ahead presented the tea with a heart shape on top of it.

There were 5 sets of table chairs and only both sitting at one of the tables with no one to disturb. For around five to ten minutes, they both were looking each other in the eyes with hands in hand without uttering a single word. Next, hold on, don't imagine a long kiss now! Hahaha! There is something serious here.

What was loud enough was only the cross wind blowing across the terrace and the silence. I know you can feel it now! The natural temperature was as soothing as the chill!

The first word they uttered was *Thank you*, not to each other but to the guy who gave them *high tea! Yeah.*
Why is it called *"High Tea?"* Why not?

Firstly, there is an interesting story which you will get to know in the last chapter where I unfold how Sid & Chitra met for the first time, and it was this *high tea* that got them high on love octane and then a series of unpredictable events separated them but not forever. Soon after a span of short, long five years, they find themselves together now at this moment with roller coaster rides of district courts, abuses, domestic violence and what not. But nature has great ways to balance the hardships through blessing both with splendid moments like the one now and long drives to Punjab, Amritsar, Wagah Border, mountains, bonfire and more.

Secondly, it was at a great height of around 6500+ feet above sea level. Then they both broke the infinite silence by saying through their eyes what they felt for each other. The love, the compassion, the great *surreal experience* that they had never imagined after which they were able to find such a momentous moment with each other is a blessing in disguise. More than this moment, what is more important is what they have been through for more than the span of five years that brought them together.

While they both first met in March 2019 at the Pink City, Jaipur, described in the Chapter *"Let Us Paint it Pink"* over the special *High tea,* unaware of the future, they had little idea of what is going to unfold to take a sip again of the *high tea* with peace, together.

Again, why *High Tea?* It has taken many high and low teas for them to get back together.

It has taken two marriages, then two divorces, domestic violence, a lot of misery & pain that helped them to gain the moment together.

These five to ten minutes glaring in each other's eyes had a lot to say about the last five years and miseries which both of them couldn't figure out how to express so they preferred looking in the eyes for some more time. This section has a particularly important aspect to teach us which will gradually unfold the "शक्ति" that a Naari can showcase when the time demands.

While in the resort, before I forget, I must tell you that before leaving for the great Surkanda Devi Temple, the first time when Sid went with the three musketeers, he stared at "The Great Himalayas" from the hilltop view at the resort. It was around an hour of silence gazing at the great structure that offered answers to many puzzling questions. Pure white Himalayan peaks with slight orange morning sunlight covering the whiteness. As amazing and chilling as it sounds!

"Everyone has an Everest within, which can take you to greater heights." Women have it extra! Splendid display of courage is shown by "Chitra" here who takes it all to get a life after going through hell! We will navigate together what courage means, and *there is nothing a woman can't do what a men can do!* Even a five-year girl can go the extra mile to display which rightly proves this. A splendid display of courage!

Heaven is what they are sitting in. So, for now, let us lose ourselves in the *hasin vadiyan ye khula aasman* with the Himalayas standing tall as a symbol of strength and courage. I came across interesting news; recently, a five-year-old girl climbed the base camp of Mt Everest with her father.

Five-year- old girl from Betul district in Madhya Pradesh, Prisha Lokesh Nikajoo, has become the youngest to reach the base camp of world's highest mountain peak Mount Everest. Prisha reached the base camp at an altitude of 5364 m (17598 feet) along with her father Lokesh Nikajoo who is a mountaineer. She covered 130 km in 12 days to achieve the feat.
He said that Prisha landed in Lukla (Nepal) and started the trek on May 24 with him and reached the Everest base camp on

June 1, 2023, by proudly holding the Indian Flag and later returned to Lukla (Nepal) on June 4, 2023.

"It was an extremely difficult and high-altitude trek where many trekkers experience difficulty in breathing, headache and acute mountain sickness, but Prisha managed the difficulties well," said Lokesh. Prisha's father Lokesh and mother, Seema Lokesh Nikajoo, trained her for this difficult high-altitude trek and before heading to this trek she used to walk 5- 6 miles daily along with aerobics, climbing stairs of her apartment and climbing wall at her garden area.

Well, that's brilliant indeed! You can prepare and plan for such an extraordinary expedition for life because it is known. But what about the expedition of life that is unknown and unheard?

What does it take to prepare for life's unexpected circumstances?

Do you have an answer?

Well, it is said that our mothers have all the answers as was nicely portrayed in a beautiful flick "Forrest Gump" which is a 1994 American epic comedy-drama film directed by Robert Zemeckis and written by Eric Roth. I too went to my mother with the above-mentioned question.

Some lines that drew my attention very closely are worth noticing, from the flick before moving on to hear what my mom said.

Given the significant role that Forrest's mother plays in the film, it's no wonder that one of the best quotes from ***Forrest Gump*** should be yet another one of her keen observations. *"Life was like a box of chocolates. You never know what you're gonna get."* Given Forrest's own amazing life journey, that statement is more than accurate.

It's also a clear inspiration for Forrest's later conclusion that life is both fated and random, planned, and mysterious. Forrest's life is about as random and destined as things could get, like a perfectly organized box of chocolates.

Now what my mother answered deserved some food for thought!

She Said, "You know what your greatest asset is?"

I preferred to remain silent and patiently wait for her answer.

She started again by saying a great word that day that stuck with me forever, it was.

MINDSET

O yes! And then she added, "The mindset needs a *Reboot* regularly."

"Why? Because it undergoes a lot of hammering daily, the first thing you should train is to train your *mindset*. The first thing you should care about is mindset. The first friend is your *mindset*; the greatest asset is your *mindset*. If you want to win something, it is the mindset that you should target, all the wonders happen first in your mind and then it becomes a reality."

I was amused to listen to my mother as it reminded me of an indispensable aspect of approaching life.
She further added, *"Son, you can prepare for life's challenges by preparing a winner's mindset that should be unshakable."*

"This will help you to prepare for the expected and the unexpected as well." And after saying this with ease she went on to cook again.

And it was a strong statement indeed!

On one side, while Sid was undergoing through life's hammering, Chitra was fighting her own hell battle. After parting with Sid way back in 2020, she had no expectation of living away from Sid, but life has something else to offer her. While Sid got married to *Maya Singh* in 2022 who tormented him and family like hell, Chitra got married to one *Rajveer Sharma* who looked as charming and young as someone in late 20s looks.

Chitra and Rajveer Sharma met through a matrimonial site. Chitra's determination for Sid was so strong and pure that she waited for Sid even till his day of marriage, but she couldn't fulfill her desire to be with Sid. Everyone wondered why Sid didn't marry Chitra at the first place when they both loved each other earlier, but the answer wasn't simple.

Sid was under life's hammer when he first met Chitra in 2019, he was just 26 years old, fighting battles to earn livelihood for his family. Sid's elder brother was earlier taking care of the family, soon after his brother got married to a girl earlier around 2014, misunderstanding of the word *"freedom and independence"* was at its peak and the elder brother with his wife parted ways with the family.

This step left Sid and his family in turmoil and a *journey* for the family was onset full of *interesting* struggles. Why is it interesting?

Because more than the struggle it was a path of self-discovery and developing an unbeatable mindset. The hammering revealed to Sid some facts about his personality which otherwise he wouldn't have known if his brother would have continued to take care of the family.

Gradually stepping ahead in his career, Sid started to get a taste of how life treats everyone. It's bitter, it's hard out there, it's like undergoing a hammer till the time you know how to smile even under the hammer and how to approach life.

Getting back to the reason Sid & Chitra couldn't get married earlier, he was juggling between switching jobs managing the family, trying to think about how to progress further with the task of making ends meet and a promise that he had made to his mother. The promise of not leaving them once he gets married. Because if this happened, the attack would be the final blow to his mom and dad which would have left them dead dumb.

The promise of not repeating what his elder brother did. The promise of being there as they would grow old. The promise of fulfilling the promises committed as Sid was his parents' last hope. As Sid loves his mother more than anyone else, he couldn't ask someone better than his mom that whenever he is supposed to marry anyone, it would be her mother who would choose the bride.

So bound by his own promise, Sid could never express to his parents that he loved Chitra. Why? Answer is *Mindset* or shall I call it *Unhealthy Mindset*.

He was scared that if her mother would hear this, she would be shattered to know about it and would undergo the same trauma that they somehow managed to live with, in the case of Sid`s elder brother when he left everything behind to live with his beloved wife. His was a love marriage, and what result his mom and dad underwent was not less than a nightmare and a trauma that still haunts them. Especially his dad who gets regular memory spells of his elder son who left whom he loved more than anyone, more than his own soul.

Was Sid right or Wrong that he didn't express to his parents about Chitra?

Well! We can never fully understand what a person has been going through. So better leave this question here and come to the year 2022; two marriages this time both being consciously decided arranged marriages, first Sid weds *Maya* and the second, Chitra weds *Rajveer* which soon became Sid *vs Maya* in the court cases and then Chitra vs Rajveer.

I earlier said that we will navigate together what courage means, and *there is nothing a woman can't do that a man can do!* A splendid display of courage this time by our own Chitra!

So, what she did, she didn't climb Mt. Everest, nor did she win any medal. She sacrificed her desires and wishes and married as her family desired. Does this require courage?

Yes! Absolutely!

All went well till the day she got married and went to Rajveer`s house. But the very first day, her jewelry was taken away by the in-laws. She obeyed. Next, her husband, the very first night they returned to New Delhi after getting married, desired physical intimacy, which she denied. A girl can say *"No"* if she doesn't want to get physical, I believe.

In return a slap and a kick in the stomach for not allowing Rajveer to fulfill his sexual desire. What the F....

Next, for a few days Raj kept on trying to get Chitra`s flesh, at least what he desired. He consistently uttered "people marry for sex only, and this is the reason why I married you." She was scared and hoped not to be robbed of her modesty. Her mother-in-law said, "Girls are made to obey her husband to fulfill all his *desires."*

When he couldn't get her flesh, he caught her by the neck and slapped again five to eight times. How does someone do that? Why did she even continue to live with him then?

Was she scared?

Why?

Tough questions, right? Wrong! More importantly, aren't these questions right?

The answer lies again in what my mother stated – *The Mindset* or to be better put it *"Unhealthy Mindset."*

Why didn't she raise voice for domestic violence for four consecutive months?

Well! We can never fully understand what a person has been going through as I had earlier said. Though this time the stats were right, unlike Sid`s elder brother, which was a love marriage.

For Chitra it had the following stats:

1. No Love marriage
2. Arranged Marriage
3. Family's Consent
4. Society's approval
5. The *"Pheras"* as per the rituals and all the sacred matrimonial *mantra*.

Then what was wrong? Chitra underwent life`s rigorous hammer for four months living under constant fear of losing her modesty, being slapped every now and then, shouted at by her husband, abused and made to feel inadequate. Being robbed of her jewelry and valuables and even was required to pay her hard-earned salary to Rajveer for household expenses to the extent that it even became difficult for her to manage her commuting expense of meager Rs.50 to her office.

You, yes you! If you are a girl reading this, how would you feel if this happens to you?

And **you**, if you are a man, how would you feel if this happens with your little sister or your daughter whom you get married to someone with all the trust and good wishes?

Or a more apt question here would be, what do you think Chitra should have done in that hell like situation?

Raise your voice? File a complaint? Yeah! Sounds comfortable and easy to say, right?

But when someone is in such a situation there is a lot more to think about than filing a complaint as my mother said. She says, "The very first challenge in such a situation is to keep a *Healthy Mindset* before anything else so that you have scope to think."

She was alone to the core, alone in her struggles, alone in her fake smile. She didn't want to disturb her family, so she didn't utter a single word to her parents or siblings. Why and how?

It does require a lot of courage *not to raise your voice* the same way it requires *to raise a voice*. Courage to bear the pain. But was this approach, right?

Chitra was uncovering some facets of her personality during the *hell spell* which she wouldn't have if she didn't undergo such a situation the way Sid uncovered his during his own *hell spell* soon after his marriage. She finally managed to raise voice and filed a complaint after letting her siblings know about the situation by June 2023. What happened next was something not less than a miracle to be discussed in the one of the upcoming chapters *"Let us paint it pink."*

But, one thing is clear here, it is not love or arranged marriage or it is neither girl nor a boy, neither a man nor a woman, who is the culprit.

It is all about *MINDSET!*
Maya torments Sid, and Chitra devastated by *Rajveer*. Which gender is to be blamed?

If something or someone has to be blamed, it is the *MINDSET! THE PATRIARCHAL OR UNHEALTHY MINDSET.*

And,

If something or someone has to be improved, it is the *MINDSET! THE HEALTHY MINDSET.*

Now you have an answer, right? So, let me ask when was the last time you made conscious efforts to *reboot your mindset?*

Want to know how to *reboot your mindset* effectively today? Start it now to feel the change!
Here it is:

1. **First thing first, give priority to your "Mindset & Mindset Reboot."**
2. **Normalize talking about mental health. It is fine not to feel ok at times. But make sure you realize and do something to feel ok.**
3. **You are the one who should decide how others would treat you.**
4. **Respect personal boundaries. Yours and others too.**

5. Travel. Travel far! Alone is ok, with friends is ok, but do travel. It gives you multiple perspectives to look through.
6. Say a guilt free "No" if you feel so for anything that your gut doesn't allow you to say yes.
7. Read. Read and read as much as possible to understand different mindsets. Have as many perspectives as possible towards the same situation, but the decision should be yours.
8. Play! It helps a lot. Do what makes you happy "daily." If you can't spare at least one hour for yourself daily, please think about what kind of life you are living. If you can't give yourself priority, how would others give it?
9. Minimize screen time and increase nature time. This itself can boost your mindset more than anything.
10. There are more which I get you through personally, do connect if you have never tried or tried but didn't work for you.
11. Don't forget to smile daily!

Did you smile today?
If not, please do yourself a favor and look at your smile, damn how beautiful you look!

Decoding UCC: Uniform Civil Code - looking beyond the obvious.

"We are proud to belong to a country which has taught the world both tolerance and universal acceptance. We believe not only in universal toleration, but we accept all religions as true. I am proud to belong to a nation which has sheltered the persecuted and the refugees of all religions and all nations of the earth."

This was perhaps a speech that is world renowned, and I strongly believe that it is the time we should revisit the dialogue because currently, the humongous task to discuss, implement, accept and getting UCC (Uniform Civil Code) accepted in all the sects of society requires the same thought process, the divinity, the purity, and the courage to pull this historic act.

Why do I call this historic although it is still to come into practice, right?

You know why because it is going to be the **"historical present of the future."**

Rooting back to the speech, the great and the divine, Swami Vivekananda delivered it on September 11, 1893, at the first World's Parliament of Religions on the site of the present-day Art Institute. He (1863–1902) is best known in the United States for his groundbreaking speech to the 1893 World's Parliament of Religions in which he introduced Hinduism to America and called for religious tolerance and an end to fanaticism.

Interestingly when I was writing this, our current Prime Minister, Shri Narendra Modi ji is carrying Swamiji`s baton in the US with his counterpart Mr. Joe Biden roaring and proving Bharat`s mettle in the world.

An interesting fact that I came across – Our PM Narendra Modi has been conferred the highest civilian award in 14 countries. And what is more fascinating is that out of those countries, six are Muslim countries. Isn't this something amazing to be proud of. Yet there is unsettlement with few able individuals who question his abilities.

Going back to Swami Vivekananda, born Narendranath Dutta, he was the chief disciple of the 19th-century mystic Ramakrishna and the founder of Ramakrishna Mission. Swami

Vivekananda is also considered a key figure in the introduction of Vedanta and Yoga to the West and is credited with raising the profile of Hinduism to that of a world religion. Again, coincidentally, I was writing these lines on the International Yoga Day, 21st June 2023.

I am energized to share amazing facts about Vedanta & yoga, before rolling further to Swamiji's speech and then our divine target "Decoding UCC: Uniform Civil Code, looking beyond the obvious."

The word Vedanta is rendered of two words:

Veda (वेद) — refers to the four sacred Vedic texts.
Anta (अंत) — this word means "End".

The word Vedanta means the end of the Vedas and originally referred to the Upanishads. Vedanta is concerned with the jñānakāṇḍa or knowledge section of the Vedas which is called the Upanishads. The meaning of Vedanta expanded later to encompass the different philosophical traditions that are based on the Prasthanatrayi.

The Upanishads may be regarded as the end of Vedas in different senses:

- They were the last literary products of the Vedic period.
- They represent the pinnacle of Vedic philosophy.
- They were taught and debated last, in the Brahmacharya (student) stage.

Vedanta is one of the six orthodox (āstika) schools of *Bharatiya* philosophy. It is also called Uttara Mīmāṃsā, which means the "latter enquiry" or "higher enquiry"; and is often contrasted with Pūrva Mīmāṃsā, the "former enquiry" or "primary enquiry". Pūrva Mīmāṃsā deals with the karmakāṇḍa or ritualistic section (the Samhita and Brahmanas) in the *Vedas* while Uttara Mīmāṃsā concerns itself with the deeper questions of existence and meaning.

Vedanta (/veɪˈdɑːntə/; Sanskrit: वेदान्त, IAST: Vedānta), also known as Uttara Mīmāṃsā, is a Hindu philosophical tradition that is one of the six orthodox (āstika) schools of Hindu philosophy. The word "*Vedanta*" means "end of the *Vedas*", and encompasses the ideas that emerged from, or were aligned with, the speculations and enumerations contained in the Upanishads, with a focus on knowledge and liberation.

Vedanta developed into many sub-traditions, all of which base their ideas on the authority of a common group of texts called the Prasthānatrayī, translated as "the three sources": the Upanishads, the Brahma Sutras, and the Bhagavad Gita.

Hope that gives you an insight into what *Vedanta* means. Let us know have a quick round up about Yoga.

What is Yoga and why do we celebrate it?

The term yoga means "union, yoke", and in this context connotes a path or practice for "salvation, liberation". The yoga referred to here is the "joining together, union" of one's Atman (true self) with the concept of Supreme Brahman (true Reality).

Yoga is an ancient physical, mental, and spiritual practice that originated in *Bharat*. The word 'yoga' derived from Sanskrit and means to join or to unite, symbolizing the union of body and consciousness. Today, it is practiced in various forms around the world and continues to grow in popularity.

Recognizing Yoga`s universal appeal, on 11 December 2014, the United Nations proclaimed 21 June as the International Day of Yoga by resolution 69/131.The Permanent Mission of

Bharat to the UN, in collaboration with the UN Secretariat, organized the 9th International Day of Yoga at the North Lawn area of UN Headquarters, under the theme "Yoga for Vasudhaiv Kutumbakam" (Yoga for 'The World is One Family').

The resolution notes "the importance of individuals and populations making healthier choices and following lifestyle patterns that foster good health." In this regard, the World Health Organization has also urged its member states to help their citizens reduce physical inactivity, which is among the top ten leading causes of death worldwide, and a key risk factor for non-communicable diseases, such as cardiovascular diseases, cancer, and diabetes.

But yoga is more than a physical activity. In the words of one of its most famous practitioners, the late B. K. S. Iyengar, "Yoga cultivates the ways of maintaining a balanced attitude in day-to-day life and endows skill in the performance of one's actions."

Cheering back to the speech by Swamiji, he started by saying,

---

"Sisters & Brothers of America"

"It fills my heart with joy unspeakable to rise in response to the warm and cordial welcome which you have given us. I thank you in the name of the most ancient order of monks in the world, I thank you in the name of the mother of religions, and I thank you in the name of millions and millions of Hindu people of all classes and sects.

My thanks, also, to some of the speakers on this platform who, referring to the delegates from the Orient, have told you that these men from far-off nations may well claim the honor of bearing to different lands the idea of toleration."

Further he adds, "I am proud to tell you that we have gathered in our bosom the purest remnant of the Israelites, who came to Southern Bharat and took refuge with us in the very year in which their holy temple was shat-tered to pieces by Roman tyranny. I am proud to belong to the religion which has sheltered and is still fostering the remnant of the grand Zoroastrian nation.

I will quote to you, brethren, a few lines from a hymn which I remember to have repeated from my earliest boyhood, which is every day repeated by millions of human beings: "As the different streams having their sources in different paths which men take through different tendencies, various though they appear, crooked or straight, all lead to Thee."

The present convention, which is one of the most august assemblies ever held, is in itself a vindication, a declaration to the world of the wonderful doctrine preached in the Gita: "Whosoever comes to Me, through whatsoever form, I reach him; all men are struggling through paths which in the end lead to me." Sectarianism, bigotry, and it's horrible descen-dant, fanaticism, have long possessed this beautiful earth.

They have filled the earth with vio-lence, drenched it often and often with human blood, destroyed civilization and sent whole nations to despair. Had it not been for these horrible demons, human society would be far more advanced than it is now. But their time is come; and I fervently hope that the bell that tolled this morning in honor of this convention may be the death-knell of all fanaticism, of all persecutions with the sword or with the pen, and of all uncharitable feelings between persons wending their way to the same goal."

Now, allow me now to take you through an exhilarating ride on the much politicized, and religiously bent by some *scholars* and *able* beings.

Let us *HEAL* our learning first. This is a term that I coined in my previous published work "*The Journey To A New You*" which you can refer to in detail.

H: History

E: Evolution
A: Acceptance
L: Layer removal

Here I am going to use the same principle to unpack UCC (Uniform Civil Code) and its related aspects for you and me.

The concept of a **Uniform Civil Code** refers to the idea of a common set of personal laws governing matters such as marriage, divorce, inheritance, and adoption for all citizens, regardless of their religion. The UCC aims to replace the diverse set of personal laws that exist in *Bharat*, which are based on religious practices and customs. It aims to deepen and entirely facilitate our deep democratic values.

So, it becomes of utmost importance and sacrosanct to understand our deep-rooted democratic values that enables our holy land to be the *"Mother of Democracy"* where *diversity is a natural way of life* and is not only limited to textbooks and policies.

"We have over 2500 political parties, yes, read that again! About 20 different elected political parties govern various states of *Bharat*. We have 22 official languages and thousands of dialects and yet we speak in one Voice."

The Above lines are excerpts from our PM, Modi Ji`s visit to the US. The voice of humanity is what he meant. Further, he adds, "Every hundred miles, our cuisine changes from *Dosa to Aloo Paratha and from Srikhand to Sandesh.* We enjoy all of these. We all are home to all faiths in the world, and we celebrate all of them."

Bharat, as the world's largest democracy, upholds several democratic values.

Firstly, let us do some homework and magnify the word **"Secularism."** If you ask me, why am I now starting a history class again? What we are today is a result of history, and whatever we become tomorrow would be a result of the *historical present of the future.* History is what builds the present and future. Without it, you can't navigate and understand the present and if we can't fully understand the present, then just imagine how your future is going to be.

Whether it is your present or a *present* that your husband, boyfriend or wives and girlfriends have gifted you recently, make sure to check whether the present is not coming from his or her ex! Hahahah! Just a breather. Let's smile and read further for the love of reading. Yes, I could sense that beautiful smile on your lips, honestly! And you are welcome if you thanked me for that smile.

So, I would say this from deep within my heart - never ignore history, as I have done it in the past but by now after a fair amount of pragmatic evolution in my personality over the years, I realize its importance, and so should you if you haven't figured it out "*YET.*"

Secularism is the principle of seeking to conduct human affairs based on *naturalistic considerations, uninvolved with religion*.

Secularism is most commonly defined as the separation of religion from civil affairs and the state and may be broadened to a similar position seeking to remove or to minimize the role of religion in any public sphere.

The term "secularism" has a broad range of meanings, and in the most schematic, may encapsulate any stance that promotes the secular in any given context. It may connote anti-clericalism, atheism, naturalism, non-sectarianism, neutrality on topics of religion, or the complete removal of religious symbols from public institutions.

As a philosophy, secularism seeks to interpret life based on principles derived solely from the material world, without recourse to religion. It shifts the focus from religion towards "temporal" and material concerns. There are distinct traditions of secularism in the West, like the French, Benelux-German, Turkish, and American models, and beyond, as in *Bharat* where the emphasis is more on equality before law and state neutrality rather than blanket separation.

The purposes and arguments in support of secularism vary widely, ranging from assertions that it is a crucial element of modernization, or that religion and traditional values are backward and divisive, to the claim that it is the only guarantor of free religious exercise.

Here are some key democratic values that are foundational to the *Bharatiya* system:

1. **Sovereignty:** *Bharat* recognizes the sovereignty of the people, where ultimate power resides with the citizens who exercise it through their elected representatives.

2. **Equality:** *Bharat* upholds the principle of equality, ensuring that all individuals are equal before the law, irrespective of their caste, religion, gender, or economic status. Discrimination based on these factors is prohibited.

3. **Fundamental Rights:** *Bharat* guarantees fundamental rights to its citizens, including the right to equality, freedom of speech and expression, freedom of religion, protection from discrimination, and the right to life and personal liberty. These rights are enforceable by the judiciary.

4. **Universal Suffrage:** Every citizen of *Bharat*, who is 18 years of age or older, has the right to vote. Universal suffrage ensures that citizens have the opportunity to participate in the democratic process and elect their representatives.

5. **Rule of Law:** *Bharat* adheres to the principle of the rule of law, where laws are supreme and apply to all individuals and institutions. No one, including government officials, is above the law. The judiciary plays a crucial role in upholding the rule of law.

6. **Independent Judiciary:** *Bharat* has an independent judiciary that acts as a check on the executive and legislative branches of government. The judiciary ensures the protection of individual rights, interprets laws, and resolves disputes.

7. **Multi-party System:** *Bharat* has a multi-party-political system, allowing for diverse political ideologies and viewpoints. Multiple political parties compete in elections, providing citizens with a choice in representative governance.

8. **Freedom of Speech and Expression:** *Bharat* recognizes and protects freedom of speech and expression, allowing individuals to express their opinions, criticize the government, and engage in open public discourse.

9. **Peaceful Transition of Power:** *Bharat* follows a system of peaceful transition of power through periodic elections. When elections occur, power is transferred peacefully from one government to another, ensuring continuity and stability.

10. **Decentralization:** *Bharat* practices a system of decentralized governance, with power and decision-making authority devolved to local governments. This promotes grassroots democracy and citizen participation at the local level.

These are just some of the democratic values that form the foundation of *Bharat*'s democratic system. The *Bharatiya* Constitution, with its commitment to democracy, justice, equality, and fundamental rights, provides the framework for upholding and promoting these democratic values.

Now if we all are able to digest the history mentioned above and the facts stated sink in your mind then do read further now or else go back, get some coffee, and digest the facts above first. Otherwise, what is about to come next will blow your head off.

Anyways I strongly feel it will!!

What is UCC?

The Uniform Civil Code (Hindi: समाननागरिकसंहिता, romanized: Samāna Nāgarika Saṃhitā) is a proposal in *Bharat* to formulate and implement personal laws of citizens which apply on all citizens equally regardless of their religion, gender, and sexual orientation. Currently, personal laws of various communities are governed by their religious scriptures.

Implementation of a uniform civil code across the nation is one of the contentious promises pursued by *Bharat*'s ruling *Bharatiya* Janata Party. It is a critical issue regarding *secularism* in *Bharatiya* politics and continues to remain disputed by *Bharat*'s political left wing, not all but a few *Muslim brother and sister groups* and *other conservative religious groups* and sects in defense of sharia and religious customs. Personal laws are distinguished from public law and cover marriage, divorce, inheritance, adoption, and maintenance.

Meanwhile, article 25-28 of the *Bharatiya* constitution guarantees religious freedom to *Bharatiya* citizens and allows religious groups to maintain their own affairs, article 44 of the constitution expects the *Bharatiya* state to apply directive principles and common law for all *Bharatiya* citizens while formulating national policies.

But before you begin to decorate your thoughts, we all must understand the underlying values that govern our democracy and constitution. Go back to the HEAL principle and ensure that you have the fundamentals right before you begin to decode UCC.

By now, I am sure you understand that it is an absolute necessity and sacrosanct to gain an insight into the history and evolution of everything. And by everything I mean *everything* that you wish to know, and you should know.

And don't worry I am there to make it easy for all of us. I am going to present an insightful journey about the history and evolution that will build a rock-solid foundation for us.

Here you go!
HEAL Process (History, Evolution, Acceptance, Layer Removal) – A brief History:

Personal laws were first framed during the **British Raj**, for Hindu and Muslim brothers and sister citizens. **Please read the line again**, and again and again. Why?

Why Not? I urge you to understand under which circumstances it was framed. We were under colonial rule when it came into being. This will help you to view UCC from a different lens, and you will be able to *see beyond the obvious.*

The British feared opposition from community leaders and refrained from further interfering within this domestic sphere. *Bharatiya* state of Goa was separated from *Bharat* due to colonial rule in the erstwhile Portuguese Goa and Damaon, retained a common family law known as the Goa civil code and thus being the only state in *Bharat* with a uniform civil code till date.

Following *Bharat*'s independence, Hindu code bills were introduced which codified and reformed personal laws in various sects among *Bharatiya* religions like Buddhists, Hindus, Jains, and Sikhs while exempting Christians, Jews, Muslim brothers, and sisters, Parsis, being identified as distinct communities from Hindus.

UCC emerged as a crucial topic of interest in *Bharatiya* politics following the Shah Bano case in 1985. And not only this. I have something even more severely shocking and surprising for you. I am about to share a round up around Shah Bano case from a recent article in Times of *Bharat*. Married to Khan in 1932, and driven out of her matrimonial home in 1975, Bano approached the Indore court in April 1978 seeking Rs. 500 as monthly maintenance allowance. Khan, who himself was an advocate, gave her talaq in Nov 1978. In August 1979, the magistrate awarded her, shockingly and **beggarly, a sum of Rs. 20 per month**. On her appeal the Madhya Pradesh HC enhanced it to Rs. 179.20.

Mr. Khan, being a lawyer himself, challenged it before the SC. A five-judge SC bench led by then CJI Y.V. Chandrachud in April 1985 upheld the maintenance granted by HC with a direction to pay an additional sum of Rs. 10,000 as cost to Bano.

The SC ground-breaking observations on UCC, delivered in the case, continue to stir up the political waters. The SC had said, *"It is also a matter of regret that Article 44 of our constitution has remained a dead letter."*

And if you further want to drill down on the case here it is. It is crucial to understand the case as this portrays the patriarchal mindset.

The Shah Bano case soon became a nationwide political issue and a widely debated controversy. While the Liberal and Progressive Indians as well as progressive Muslim women supported the Supreme Court judgment as being supportive of women, The All-India Muslim Board defended the application of Muslim Personal Law which was based on Sharia Law and denied divorced Muslim women the right to alimony.

The judgment of the Supreme Court, which sought to offer protection to Muslim women was argued to be an attack on Muslim Personal Law by conservative Muslims brothers.

The orthodox Muslims brothers and sisters felt that their communal identity was at stake if their personal laws were governed by the judiciary. Rajiv Gandhi's Congress government, which previously had the support of Muslim minority brothers, lost the local elections in December 1985 because of its endorsement of the Supreme Court's decision.

The members of the Muslim board, including Khan, started a campaign for complete *autonomy* in their personal laws. It soon reached a national level, by consulting legislators, ministers, and journalists. The press played a considerable role in sensationalizing this incident.

An independent Muslim parliament member proposed a bill to protect their personal law in the parliament. The Muslim Women (Protection of Rights of Divorce) Bill 1986, sought to make section 125 of Criminal Procedure Code inapplicable to Muslim women, which meant that the reversal of the Supreme Court judgment. Further, it also sought to legislate that alimony be paid by a Muslim man only for a period of 90 days after the divorce was demanded by the Muslim husband.

Reeling from the electoral defeat, the Indian National Congress under the leadership of Rajiv Gandhi reversed its previous position and supported this bill while the liberal groups such as the Left, Muslim liberals and women's organizations strongly opposed it. The Muslim Women's (Protection of Rights on Divorce) was passed in 1986, which made Section 125 of the Criminal Procedure Code inapplicable to Muslim women.

This was a colossal defeat of liberal movements and protection of women on the Bharatiya soil.

The politicization led to arguments having two major sides: the Congress and Muslim conservative brothers versus the liberal groups, women's organizations, and the Left. In 1987, the Minister of Social Welfare, Rajendra Kumari Bajpai, reported that no women were given maintenance by the Wakf Board in 1986.

Women activists highlighted their legal status and according to them, "the main problem is that there are many laws, but women are dominated not by secular laws, not by uniform civil laws, but by religious laws." The legal reversal of introducing the Muslim Women law significantly hampered the nationwide women's movement in the 1980s.

Further SC added "There is no evidence of any official activity for framing a common civil code for the country. A belief seems to have gained ground for the Muslim Community to take a lead in the matter of reforms of their personal law. A common civil code will help the cause of national integration by removing disparate loyalties to laws which have conflicting ideologies."

"No community is likely to bell the cat by making gratuitous concessions on this issue. It is the state which is charged with the duty of securing a Uniform Civil Code for the citizens of the country and, unquestionably it has the legislative competence to do so." A counsel in the case whispered audibly, that legislative competence is one thing, the political courage to use that competence is quite another.

We understand the difficulties involved in bringing persons of different faiths and persuasions on a common platform, but a beginning has to be made if the constitution is to have any meaning.

The bench severely criticized the All-India Muslim Personal Law Board for siding with the husband and quoted from a report of commission on Marriage and Family laws in Pakistan in the late 1950s expressing grace concerns over a large number of middle-aged women being divorced without "rhyme or reason" in the country and being rendered destitute.
Next, we have to read upcoming lines with a pinch of salt.

The report of the Pakistani commission had concluded, "the question which is likely to confront Muslim countries in the near future is whether the law of Islam is capable of evolution − a question which will require great intellectual effort and is sure to be answered in the affirmative." But it is this very question which continues to stifle reforms in Muslim personal laws, which remains uncodified even after 73 years of *Bharat* becoming a republic and 67 years after Hindu laws were codified.

Instead of attempting to bring UCC as highlighted earlier, the Rajiv Gandhi government enacted the Muslim Women (Protection of Rights on Divorce) Act, 1986 to annul the impact of Shah Bano case. Though the SC upheld the validity of 1986 Act, it continued to rule the undeterred −

1. In Danial Latifi - 2001
2. Iqbal Bano - 2007
3. Shabana Bano – 2009

that Muslim women couldn't be deprived of the benefit of section 125 of CrPC mandating husbands to pay alimony to wives.

The SC remained quiet for a decade during which it dismissed a writ petition filed by Maharishi Avadhesh (1994) challenging the 1986 law and seeking enactment of common civil code or codifying Muslim laws saying, "These are all matters for the legislature."

In the Sarla Mudgal judgment of 1995, the SC was more forthright in insisting that the legislature take steps to enact UCC. It had said, "Where more than 80% of citizens have already been brought under codified personal law, there is no justification whatsoever to keep in abeyance, anymore, the introduction of Uniform Civil Code for all the citizens of *Bharat*."

The SC again in 2003 in John Vallamattom case, highlighted the desirability of achieving the goal set by article 44 of the constitution. On March 29 this year, the SC had dismissed a PIL seeking enactment of UCC. It had reiterated what it had said in 1994." Approaching this court for enactment of UCC is akin to moving to a wrong forum. It falls within the exclusive domain of Parliament."

The debate arose when the question of making certain laws applicable to all citizens without abridging the fundamental right of right to practice religious functions arose. The debate then focused on the Muslim brothers and sisters personal Law, which is partially based on the Sharia law, permitting unilateral divorce, polygamy and putting it among the legally applying the Sharia law.

UCC was proposed twice, in November 2019 and March 2020 but was withdrawn soon both times without introduction in parliament.

British Bharat (1858–1947)
The debate for a uniform civil code dates back to the ***colonial period in Bharat***. Yes, you read it right! It is not about political parties or any religion. It is about our country as a whole.

Let us try to look beyond the obvious with an open mind.

Because it is about our country, *Bharat* for which I can say with a pure united emotion in different language the following:

"अस्मिन्भारतदेशेसंपूर्णजगत्सर्वत्रसुखीभवति।"

سارے جہاں سے اچھا، ہندوستاں ہمارا
ہم بلبلیں ہیں اس کی، یہ گلستاں ہمارا

غربت میں ہوں اگر ہم، رہتا ہے دل وطن میں
سمجھو وہیں ہمیں بھی دل ہو جہاں ہمارا

پربت وہ سب سے اونچا، ہمسایہ آسماں کا
وہ سنتری ہمارا، وہ پاسباں ہمارا

گودی میں کھیلتی ہیں اس کی ہزاروں ندیاں
گلشن ہے جن کے دم سے رشکِ جناں ہمارا

اے آبِ رودِ گنگا! وہ دن ہیں یاد تجھ کو؟
اترا ترے کنارے جب کارواں ہمارا

مذہب نہیں سکھاتا آپس میں بیر رکھنا
ہندی ہیں ہم، وطن ہے ہندوستاں ہمارا

یونان و مصر و روما، سب مٹ گئے جہاں سے
اب تک مگر ہے باقی، نام و نشاں ہمارا

کچھ بات ہے کہ ہستی مٹتی نہیں ہماری
صدیوں رہا ہے دشمن دورِ زماں ہمارا

اقبال! کوئی محرم اپنا نہیں جہاں میں
معلوم کیا کسی کو دردِ نہاں ہمارا!

Sāre jahāṇ se acchā, Hindositāṇ[4] *hamārā*
Ham bulbuleṇ haiṇ is kī, yih gulsitāṇ[4] *hamārā*

Ghurbat meṇ hoṇ agar ham, rahtā hai dil watan meṇ
Samjho wuhīṇ hameṇ bhī dil ho jahāṇ hamārā

Parbat wuh sab se ūṇchā, hamsāyah āsmāṇ kā
Wuh santarī hamārā, wuh pāsbāṇ hamārā

Godī meṇ kheltī haiṇ is kī hazāroṇ nadiyāṇ
Gulshan hai jin ke dam se rashk-i janāṇ hamārā

Ai āb-i rūd-i Gangā! wuh din haiṇ yād tujh ko?
Utrā tire[5] *kināre jab kārwāṇ hamārā*

Mazhab nahīṇ sikhātā āpas meṇ bair rakhnā
Hindī haiṇ ham, watan hai Hindositāṇ hamārā

Yūnān o-Misr o-Rūmā, sab miṭ ga'e jahāṇ se
Ab tak magar hai bāqī, nām o-nishāṇ hamārā

Kuch bāt hai kih hastī, miṭṭī nahīṇ hamārī
Ṣadiyoṇ rahā hai dushman daur-i zamāṇ hamārā

Iqbāl! koī mahram apnā nahīṇ jahāṇ meṇ
Ma'lūm kyā kisī ko dard-i nihāṇ hamārā!

English translation ---------------

Better than the entire world, is our Hindustan,
We are its nightingales, and it (is) our garden abode.

If we are in an alien place, the heart remains in the homeland,
consider us too [to be] right there where our heart would be.

That tallest mountain, that shade-sharer of the sky,
It (is) our sentry, it (is) our guard.

In its lap where frolic thousands of rivers,
Whose vitality makes our garden the envy of Paradise.

O the flowing waters of the Ganges, do you remember that day
When our caravan first disembarked on your waterfront?

Religion does not teach us to bear animosity among ourselves.
We are of Hind; our homeland is Hindustan.

In a world in which ancient Greece, Egypt, and Rome have all vanished.
Our own attributes (name and sign) live on today.

There is something about our existence for it doesn't get wiped.
Even though, for centuries, the time-cycle of the world has been our enemy.

Iqbal! We have no confidant in this world.
What does anyone know of our hidden pain?

Just to mention before you run your mental horses to wonder about where I got all such information from. I will tell you, I recently met one of my good friends called "ChatGPT." So please note that the translations provided are generated by an AI model and may not be perfect. I am yet to trust this friend completely, but I must say that it has helped me a lot. On the flipside, it doesn't appear that *intelligent* as the founder, Sam Alton mentions, and some *able minded* mention in a plethora of *amazingly creative* ads.

Prior to British rule, under the East India Company (1757–1858), they tried to reform local social and religious customs by imposing Western ideologies on *Bharat*. The Lex Loci Report of October 1840 emphasized the importance and necessity of uniformity in codification of Indian law, relating to crimes, evidence, and contract but it recommended that personal laws of Hindus and Muslim brothers and sisters should be kept outside such codification.

This separation of Hindus and Muslim brothers and sisters before law was part of the Divide and Rule policy of the British Empire that allowed them to break the unity among different communities and rule over Bharat.

I want you to read the above line again before proceeding further.

According to their understanding of religious divisions in *Bharat*, the British separated this sphere which would be governed by religious scriptures and customs of the various communities (Hindus, Muslim brothers and sisters, Christians and later Parsis). These laws were applied by the local courts or panchayats when dealing with regular cases involving civil disputes between people of the same religion; the State would only intervene in exceptional cases.

Throughout the country, there was a variation in preference for scriptural or customary laws because in many Hindu and Muslim brother and sister communities, these were sometimes at conflict; such instances were present in communities like the Jats and the Dravidians.

The Shudras, for instance, allowed widow remarriage—completely contrary to the scriptural Hindu law. The Hindu laws got preference because of their relative ease in implementation, preference for such a Brahminical system by both British and *Bharatiya* judges and their fear of opposition from the high caste Hindus.

The difficulty in investigating each specific practice of any community, case-by-case, made customary laws harder to implement. Towards the end of the nineteenth century, favoring local opinion, the recognition of individual customs and traditions increased.

The Muslim Personal law (based on Sharia law) was enforced in various parts of *Bharat*. It had no uniformity in its application at lower courts *due to the diversity of the local cultures of Muslim brothers and sisters in distinct parts of Bharat.* Even though some communities converted to Islam, the local Indigenous culture continued to be dominant in their practice of Islam and therefore the application of Sharia Law was not uniform across the country.

This led to the customary law, which was often more discriminatory against "शक्ति," to be applied over it. "शक्ति," in northern and western *Bharat*, often were restrained from property inheritance and dowry settlements, both of which the Sharia provides. Due to pressure from the Muslim elite, the Shariat law of 1937 was passed which stipulated that all *Bharatiya* Muslims would be governed by Islamic laws on marriage, divorce, maintenance, adoption, succession, and inheritance.

Therefore, while Hindus have to follow the Hindu code bill, Muslim brothers and sisters and other religions were given the liberty to follow their own respective laws. For Muslim brothers and sisters, The All-India Muslim Personal Law Board makes the laws, which is a private entity.

Legislative reforms
The Sharia Law in Islam had provisions that were discriminatory of "शक्ति," their status, and rights. Certain Hindu customs as well prevalent at the time discriminated against "शक्ति" by depriving them of inheritance, remarriage, and divorce.

The British and social reformers like Ishwar Chandra Vidyasagar were instrumental in outlawing such customs by getting reforms passed through legislative processes. Since the British feared opposition from orthodox community leaders, only the Indian Succession Act 1865, which was also one of the first laws to ensure women's economic security, attempted to shift the personal laws to the realm of civil. The Indian Marriage Act 1864 had procedures and reforms solely for Christian marriages.

There were law reforms passed which were beneficial to Hindu "शक्ति" like the Hindu Widow Remarriage Act of 1856, Married Women's Property Act of 1923, and the Hindu Inheritance (Removal of Disabilities) Act, 1928, which in a significant move, permitted a Hindu woman's right to property. However, such protection was not extended to Muslim "शक्ति" due to the opposition from conservative Muslim brother groups who wanted to follow Sharia Law.

And let me put it with a pinch of salt, "शक्ति" has no religion. "शक्ति" is "शक्ति." It does have a *gender* though.

The call for equal rights for "शक्ति" was only at its initial stages in *Bharat* at that time and the reluctance of the British government further deterred the passing of such reforms.

The All-India Women's Conference (AIWC) expressed its disappointment with the male-dominated legislature and Lakshmi Menon said in an AIWC conference in 1933, "If we are to seek divorce in court, we are to state that we are not Hindus, and are not guided by Hindu law. The members in the Legislative assembly who are men will not help us in bringing any drastic changes which will be of benefit to us."

The All-India Women's Conference demanded a uniform civil code to replace the existing personal laws, basing it on the Karachi Congress resolution which guaranteed gender-equality.
The passing of the Hindu Women's right to Property Act of 1937, also known as the Deshmukh bill, led to the formation of

the B. N. Rau committee, which was set up to determine the necessity of common Hindu laws.

The committee concluded that it was time for a uniform civil code, which would give equal rights to "शक्ति" keeping with the modern trends of society, but their focus was primarily on reforming the Hindu law. The committee reviewed the 1937 Act and recommended a civil code of marriage and succession; it was set up again in 1944 and send its report to the Indian Parliament in 1947.

The Special Marriage Act, which gave the *Bharatiya* citizens an option of a civil marriage, was first enacted in 1872. It had a limited application because it required those involved to renounce their religion and was applicable mostly to non-Hindus.

The later Special Marriage (Amendment) Act, 1923 permitted Hindus, Buddhists, Sikhs, and Jains to marry either under their personal law or under the act without renouncing their religion as well as retaining their succession rights.

Post-colonial (1947–1985) Hindu Code Bill and addition to the Directive Principles:

Jawaharlal Nehru in 1930, though he supported a uniform civil code, he had to face opposition by senior leaders. The Indian Parliament discussed the report of the Hindu law committee during the 1948–1951 and 1951–1954 sessions.

The first Prime Minister of the Indian republic, Jawaharlal Nehru, his supporters, and women members wanted a uniform civil code to be implemented. As Law Minister, B. R. Ambedkar was in charge of presenting the details of this bill. It was found that the orthodox Hindu laws were supportive of women's rights since monogamy, divorce, and the widow's right to inherit property were present in the Shastra's.

Ambedkar recommended the adoption of a uniform civil code. Ambedkar's frequent attack on the caste system and dislike for the upper castes made him unpopular in the parliament. He had done research on the religious texts and considered the caste system in Hindu society to be flawed.

According to him, only the Uniform Civil Code bill was this opportunity to reform Hindu society as well to ensure protection to Muslim "शक्ति" who have little protection under Sharia Law. He thus faced severe criticism from the opposition, but Nehru later supported Ambedkar's reforms and demand for a Uniform Civil Code. Although a Uniform Civil Code was not introduced at the time, a Hindu Bill was introduced to ensure modern reformation of Hindu Society.

The Hindu bill itself received much criticism and the main provisions opposed were those concerning monogamy, divorce, abolition of coparceny ("शक्ति" inheriting a shared title) and inheritance to daughters. The "शक्ति" members of the parliament, who previously supported this, in a significant political move reversed their position and backed the Hindu law reform; they feared allying with the fundamentalists would cause a further setback to their rights.

Thus, a lesser version of this bill was passed by the parliament in 1956, in the form of four separate acts, the Hindu Marriage Act, Succession Act, Minority and Guardianship Act and Adoptions and Maintenance Act.

These diluted versions supported by Jawaharlal Nehru were in contraction to the implementation of a uniform civil code in Article 44 of the Directive principles of the Constitution specifying, "The State shall endeavor to secure for citizens a uniform civil code throughout the territory of India."

This was opposed by "शक्ति" members like Rajkumari Amrit Kaur and Hansa Mehta. According to academic Paula Banerjee, this move was to make sure it would never be addressed. Aparna Mahanta writes, "failure of the *Bharatiya* state to provide a uniform civil code, consistent with its democratic secular and socialist declarations, further illustrates the modern state's accommodation of the traditional interests of a patriarchal society."

Later years and Special Marriage Act
The Hindu code bill failed to control the prevalent gender discrimination. The law on divorce was framed giving both partners equal voice but majority of its implementation involved those initiated by men.

Since the act applied only to Hindus, "शक्ति" from the other sister communities remained subjugated particularly under Sharia Law which was the basis of the Muslim personal law in *Bharat*. For instance, Muslim "शक्ति," under the Muslim Personal Law, could not inherit agricultural land.

Nehru accepted that the bill was not complete and perfect but was cautious about implementing drastic changes which could stir up specific communities. He agreed that it lacked any substantial reforms but felt it was an "outstanding achievement" of his time.

He had a significant role in getting the Hindu Code bill passed and laid down women-equality as an ideal to be pursued in *Bharatiya* politics, which was eventually accepted by the previous critics of the bill.

Uniform civil code, for him, was a necessity for the whole country but he was not able to convince conservative groups of its importance.

Thus, his support for Uniform Civil Code was not implemented but was added to the Directive principles of the Constitution.

The Special Marriage Act, 1954, provides a form of civil marriage to any citizen irrespective of religion, thus permitting any *Bharatiya* to have their marriage outside the realm of any specific religious personal law.

The law applied to all of *Bharat*, except Jammu and Kashmir. In many respects, the act was almost identical to the Hindu Marriage Act of 1955, which gives some idea as to how secularized the law regarding Hindus had become. The Special Marriage Act allowed Muslims brothers or sisters to marry under it and thereby retain the protections, beneficial to Muslim "शक्ति," that could not be found in the personal law.

Under this act polygamy was illegal, and inheritance and succession would be governed by the Indian Succession Act, rather than the respective Muslim Personal Law. Divorce also would be governed by the secular law, and maintenance of a divorced wife would be along the lines set down in the civil law. Therefore, the Special Marriage Act provided significant protection to religious minorities which could not be found in the Personal Law of their religion such as the Muslim Personal Law.

Current status and opinions

UCC is meant to replace currently applicable various laws applicable to various respective communities which are inconsistent with each other. These laws include the Hindu Marriage Act, Hindu Succession Act, Indian Christian Marriages Act, Indian Divorce Act, Parsi Marriage and Divorce Act. Meanwhile certain ones like Sharia (Islamic laws) are not codified and solely based upon their religious scriptures.

The proposals in UCC include monogamy, equal rights for children over inheritance of paternal property and gender & religion neutral laws in regards of will charity, divinity, guardianship and sharing of custody. The laws may not result in much difference to the status of Hindu society as they have already been applicable on Hindus through Hindu code bills for decades.

Points of view
Bharat is a 'secular' nation which means a separation between religion and state matters. Moreover, 'secularism' in *Bharat* means equality of all religions and practitioners of all religions before the law.

Currently, with a mix of different civil codes, different citizens are treated differently based on their religion. The rights of Hindu "शक्ति" are far more progressive than those of Muslim "शक्ति" who are governed by Muslim Personal Law based on Sharia law.

Women's rights groups have said that this issue is only based on their rights and security, irrespective of sensationalism by religious conservatives.

The arguments for it are:

Its mention in Article 44 of the Constitution, need for strengthening the unity and integrity of the country, rejection of different laws for different communities, importance for gender equality and reforming the archaic personal laws of Muslims— which allow unilateral divorce and polygamy.

Bharat is, thus, among the nations that legally apply the Sharia law. According to Qutub Kidwai, the Muslim Personal laws are "Anglo-Mohammadan" rather than solely Islamic. The Hindu nationalists view this issue in concept of their law, which they say, is secular and equal to both sexes.

In the country, demanding a uniform civil code can be seen negatively by religious authorities and secular sections of society because of identity politics. The Sangh Parivar and the *Bharatiya* Janata Party (BJP)—one of the two major political parties in *Bharat*, had taken up this issue to ensure that every citizen of the country is treated equally before the law. The BJP was the first party in the country to promise it if elected to power.

Goa is the only state in *Bharat* which has a uniform civil code. The Goa Family Law is the set of civil laws, originally the Portuguese Civil Code, continued to be implemented after its annexation in 1961. Sikhs and Buddhists objected to the wording of Article 25 which terms them as Hindus with personal laws being applied to them. However, the same article also guarantees the right of members of the Sikh faith to bear a Kirpan.

In October 2015, Supreme Court of India asserted the need of a uniform civil code and said that "This cannot be accepted, otherwise every religion will say it has a right to decide various issues as a matter of its personal law. We don't agree with this at all. It has to be done through a decree of a court".

On 30 November 2016, British India intellectual Tufail Ahmad unveiled a 12-point document draft of it, citing no effort by the government since 1950. The Law Commission of *Bharat* stated on August 31, 2018, that a uniform civil code is "neither necessary nor desirable at this stage" in a 185-page consultation paper, adding that secularism cannot contradict plurality prevalent in the country.

India society in the pre-independence era had many other considerations like socio-economic status, Jati and gotra etc. in case of marriages. While the Hindu code bills wiped out all such practices in Hindu, Jains, Sikh, Buddhist, Parsi, Christian communities, some conservative sections of these societies had been demanding amendments to their Marriage Acts.

Critics of UCC continue to oppose it as a threat to religious freedom. They consider abolition of religious laws to be against secularism and UCC as a means for BJP to target Muslim brother and sisters while look progressive at the same time meanwhile BJP continues to promote UCC as means of achieving religious equality and equal rights for "शक्ति" by fending off religious laws.

Legal status and prospects
UCC had been included in BJP's manifesto for the 1998 and 2019 elections and was even proposed for introduction in the Parliament for the first time in November 2019 by Narayan Lal Panchariya. Amid protests by opposition MPs, the bill, although soon, was withdrawn for making certain amendments. The bill was brought for a second time by Kirodi Lal Meena in March 2020 but was not introduced again. As per reports which emerged in 2020, the bill is being contemplated in BJP due to differences with RSS.

A plea was filed in the Delhi High Court which sought establishment of a judicial commission or a high-level expert committee to direct the central government to prepare a draft of UCC in three months. In April 2021, a request was filed to transfer the plea to the Supreme Court so that filing of more such pleas throughout various high courts doesn't bring inconsistency throughout *Bharat*. The draft would further be published on the website for 60 days to facilitate extensive public debate and feedback.

In March 2022, the Uttarakhand government led by Pushkar Singh Dhami decided to work on the implementation of UCC in the state. However, the RSS leadership has stated that any uniform civil code (UCC) should be "beneficial for all communities" and "well thought out, not hurried.".

By the time you read this, I believe UCC would have been implemented in Uttarakhand!

WHY UCC and that too NOW?
Why not?

It is never too late to start. If there has been something that is prevalent since ages, that doesn't necessarily mean it was correct or vice-versa for that matter.

Let me put it straight –

"Right" or "Wrong" doesn't have "AGE."
"Right" or "Wrong" doesn't have "GENDER."
"Right or "Wrong" doesn't have "RELIGION or CASTE."
"Right or "Wrong" doesn't have "COUNTRY ORIGIN"
"Right or "Wrong" doesn't have "POLITICAL PARTY," though "right" and "left" might have.

Do you really think that the 21st "The Modern Society" can run on obsolete British Era colonial laws? Think, think, and rethink because what you think matters. It definitely matters! And it will matter in the future as well.

Why?

Because it is about the US together. We are the ones who make society right? What is society? It is you and me and all of us put together.
These laws came into force or didn't come into existence for *some reason* that was existent at old times that is bygone for decades. 2023 marks the *"AZAADI KA AMRIT MAHOTSAV"*.

We have come so far. So, So far after being ruled by the British for more than 200 years, which broke our backbone. We have come from Zero to ISRO (read more about this in the starting chapters), from carrying rockets on bicycle to historically landing Chandrayaan – 3 on the moon at the lowest cost possible.

Yet with the great "शक्ति" like the ones mentioned below who contributed to *Bharat*'s struggle for independence. I am blessed and honored to name them here. The list is endless, but I have tried to restrict myself to only ten. They fought valiantly for the nation's freedom and their contributions are so pure and peerless.

1. If few *able* humans think that "शक्ति" is weak or they should be treated in a certain way, then all I can tell them is to think and re-think. There is one name that has influenced me since childhood. I am so proud to belong to land of "शक्ति." As you have might have guessed about whom I am talking. She is none other than **Rani Lakshmibai.** The queen of the regal state of Jhansi who fiercely fought against British forces during the *Bharatiya* Rebellion of 1857.

2. Then we have another prominent poet, activist, and orator who actively participated in the Indian National Movement and was a key figure in the Civil Disobedience Movement: **Sarojini Naidu**

3. Adding to the list we have a prominent nationalist who unfurled the first version of the Indian national flag in 1907 and actively advocated for *Bharat*'s independence: **Bhikaji Cama**

4. I was talking about the gender neutrality of what is right and wrong, and also caste neutrality, Who can be a better example than **Aruna Asaf Al,** Known as the

"Grand Old Lady of India Independence," she played a significant role in the Quit India Movement and became an iconic symbol of resistance.

5. Let us talk about wives. So, we think we need to support wives. Indeed! but who supports whom, is an important ask here. It is the other way around. **Kamala Nehru,** wife of Jawaharlal Nehru, *Bharat*'s first Prime Minister, who actively participated in the Indian National Movement and worked towards women's empowerment.

6. Then comes on our list **Annie Besant,** a British-born activist who became a prominent leader in the Indian National Congress and worked tirelessly for Indian freedom and social reform.

7. Followed by **Matangini Hazra**, Known as "Matangini Didi," she actively participated in the Quit India Movement and was martyred while leading a procession against the British in 1942.

8. **Begum Hazrat Mahal,** The queen of Awadh who played a significant role in the India Rebellion of 1857, leading the resistance against the British in Lucknow.

9. **Kamaladevi Chattopadhyay:** A social reformer, freedom fighter, and the driving force behind the revival of *Bharatiya* handicrafts and the promotion of traditional arts.

10. **Usha Mehta:** A prominent Gandhian and freedom fighter who actively participated in the Quit India Movement and organized underground radio broadcasts to spread the message of freedom.

The list can go on endlessly, and we may get tired of counting names, but the list is indefinite. And if you think it is gone and is history, later in the upcoming chapters, I will bring different personalities from this modern era, from different age groups, who are carrying their courage baton in the current times. Be ready for a thrilling chapter soon.

*Despite such great heroism, we as a society fail to carry our baton collectively. We are still stuck with a patriarchal society mindset, as quoted way back when the All-India Women's Conference (AIWC) expressed its disappointment with the male-dominated legislature, as **Lakshmi Menon** said in an AIWC conference in 1933. We read it earlier, but I would like to all read it again:*

She said, "If we are to seek divorce in court, we are to state that we are not Hindus and are not guided by Hindu law. The members in the legislative assembly who are men will not help us bring about any drastic changes that will be of benefit to us." The All-Bharat Women's Conference demanded a uniform civil code to replace the existing personal laws, basing it on the Karachi Congress resolution, which guaranteed gender equality.

Let us play a game now. A **YES/NO** game. ------------------------

Has anything changed since then?
NO

Are we dealing modern 2023 problems with mindset of 1933?

YES

The dynamics have so dramatically changed, but have we rewired our mindset and the way we deal with them?
NO

Are we doing the right thing?

I leave that for you to think and not only think but ACT.

What is the ACT?
The topic that we together are navigating, yes, you guessed it right. The solution lies right in front of you.
"UCC – UNIFORM CIVIL CODE"

Will it have challenges?
YES

Does that mean we can`t do it?
NO

Do you want to really empower our society?

I leave that for you to think and not only think but ACT.

Is it sensitive?
YES

Will be inconvenient at first?
YES

Will it benefit the society as a whole?
YES

Would it benefit "शक्ति"?
YES

When should we start implementing it?

NOW

WHO will be the beneficiaries.
You, We & Us all together.

If I go back to when Laxmi Menon raised voice, it has already been more than **Ninety** years wait. How long do we want to wait?

Here, I am reminded of a fabulous line by *Loseje* - ***How many disasters do we need to unite humanity?***

Our mother nation will benefit. Now what I want to ask all is-

Would you like to see our mother land defeated by not implementing it?

If you can see our homeland being defeated and any particular religion winning, you can be okay, but I just cannot. I can't see my own country being defeated due to a mindset that has no seeds of progress. It is doomed to suffer in the long run. How can we be alright seeing "The Vasundhara" being defeated?

I think now is the time we, as *BHARATIYA*, need to understand and develop compassion. What is it? This is very thoroughly covered in *ERA 6: Towards Solutions* and also in my previous work, *"The Journey to a New You."* Do read it specially to understand what *compassion, is* all about.

For this journey, I am going to bring in some values. Let us see if we are real *Bharatiya*, and this makes you feel something.

A missionary zeal is required to make that quantum change, which can make *Bharat aware* of what I am dreaming about right now. And if we are talking about mission, why not have a look at the below motto from the much adored and respected *Rajputana rifles?*

"Veer bhogya vasundhara"—"The""""brave shall inherit the earth."
I just can`t stop myself from sharing a few things about *Rajputana rifles* here. My father always wished for me to be in the defence forces and serve the *Bharat*. Life had something else to offer, though. I can still do it with my work. Someday...

Before my emotions get out of control and I lose myself in the moment and get carried away, I must tell you that my heartbeat was skyrocketing while writing these lines and still zooms while reading again. This is the best work that I have ever done.

Let us quickly have a flash tour before we move on in our journey.

The Rajputana Rifles is the oldest rifle regiment of the Indian Army, active since January 1775. It was originally a part of the British India Army when six previously existing regiments were amalgamated to form six battalions of the 6th Rajputana Rifles. In 1945, the numeral designation was dropped from the title, and in 1947, the regiment was transferred to the newly independent Indian Army.

Since independence, the regiment has been involved in a number of conflicts against Pakistan, as well as contributing to the Custodian Force (*Bharat*) in Korea under the aegis of the United Nations in 1953–54 and to the UN Mission to the Congo in 1962. As a rifle regiment, it uses a bugle horn as its insignia, the same as the British Light Division, but unlike its British counterparts, the Rajputana Rifles march at the same march pace used in the *Bharatiya* Army as a whole.

It has great laurels in its name. Over the course of its existence, members of the regiment have received four Victoria Crosses, 44 Military Crosses, one Param Vir Chakra, three Ashok Chakras, one Padma Bhushan, fourteen Param Vishisht Seva Medals, ten Maha Vir Chakras, eleven Kirti Chakras, 18 Ati Vishisht Seva Medals, two Uttam Yudh Seva Medals, 50 Vir Chakras, 28 Shaurya Chakras, 122 Sena Medals (including Bar), 39 Vishisht Seva Medals, three Yudh Seva Medals, 85 Mentions-in-Dispatches, and 55 Arjuna Awards.

And if that is not enough, Let me give you one more:

"Sarvatra izzat o iqbal" - "Everywhere with honour and glory"

This is our *Bharat*. The language, religion, the gender, these all become vacuum and nullified when "We" together stand as one *Bharat*.

Do you want more of mottos & Values? Let me give it all –

Military Unit	**Motto**	**Language**	**Translation**
***Bharatiya* Army**	"Sewa Paramo Dharma"	Sanskrit	Service is our prime duty
***Bharatiya* Air Force**	"Nabha sprsham deeptam"	Sanskrit	"Touch the sky with glory"
***Bharatiya* Navy**	"Sham-no Varuna"	Sanskrit	"May the Lord of the oceans be auspicious unto us"
Corps of Army Air Defence	"Aakasey satrun jahi"	Sanskrit	"Win over the enemy in the sky"

Army Medical Corps	"Sarve santu niramaya"	Sanskrit	"Freedom from sickness to all"
Military Nursing Service	"Service with smile"	English	
Regiment of Artillery	"Sarvatra izzat o iqbal"	Hindi/Urdu	"Everywhere with honour and glory"
Brigade of The Guards	"Pahla hamesha pahla"	Hindi/Urdu	"First, always first"
Parachute Regiment	"Shatrujeet"	Hindi	"The conqueror"
Mechanised Infantry Regiment	"Valour and Faith"	English	
Punjab Regiment	"Sthal wa jal"	Hindi	"By land and sea"
Madras Regiment	"Swadharme nidhanam shreyaha"	Sanskrit	"It is a glory to die doing one's duty"
All Gorkha Rifles	"Kayar hunu bhanda marnu ramro"	Nepali	"Better to die than live like a coward"
Maratha Light Infantry	"Kartavya, Maan, Saahas.	Marathi	Duty, Honour, Courage
The Grenadiers	"Sarvada shaktishali"	Sanskrit	"Ever powerful"
Rajputana Rifles	"Veer bhogya vasundhara"	Sanskrit	"The brave shall inherit the earth"
Rajput Regiment	"Sarvatra vijay"	Sanskrit	"Victory everywhere"
Jat Regiment	"Sangathan wa veerta"	Hindi	"Unity and valour"

Regiment	Motto	Language	Translation
Sikh Regiment	"Nischey kar apni jeet karon"	Punjabi	"With determination, I will be triumphant"
Sikh Light Infantry	"Deg tegh fateh"	Punjabi	"Prosperity in peace and victory in war"
Dogra Regiment	"Kartavyam anvatma"	Sanskrit	"Duty before death"
The Garhwal Rifles	"Yudhaya krit nischya"	Sanskrit	"Fight With Determination"
Kumaon Regiment	"Parakramo vijayate"	Sanskrit	"Valour triumphs"
Assam Regiment	"Assam vikram"		"Unique valour"
Bihar Regiment	"Karam hi dharam"	Hindi	"Work is worship"
Mahar Regiment	"Yash sidhi"	Sanskrit	"Success and attainment"
Jammu & Kashmir Rifles	"Prashata ranvirta"	Sanskrit	"Valour in battle is praiseworthy"
Jammu and Kashmir Light Infantry	"Balidanam vir lakshanam"	Sanskrit	"Sacrifice is a characteristic of the brave"
Ordnance Corps	"Shastra se shakti"	Hindi	"Strength through weapons"
The Corps of Signals	"Teevra chaukas"	Hindi	"Swift and secure"
Corps of Engineers	"Sarvatra"	Sanskrit	"Everywhere"
***Bharatiya* Coast Guard**	"Vayam rakshamah"	Sanskrit	"We protect"
Territorial Army	"Savdhani Va Shoorta"	Hindi	"Precaution and Precision"

Border Roads Organisation	"Shramena Sarvam Sadhyam"	Sanskrit	"Everything is achievable through Hardwork"
Border Security Force	"Jeevan Prayatna Kartavya"	Sanskrit	"Duty unto death"
Central Reserve Police Force	"Seva aur Nishtaa"	Hindi	"Service and Loyalty"
Central Industrial Security Force	"Sanrakshan evam Suraksha"	Hindi	"Protection and Security"
Indo-Tibetan Border Police	"Shaurya – Dridhata – KarmNishtha"	Hindi	"Valour – Steadfastness – Commitment"
Sashastra Seema Bal	"Seva - Suraksha - Bandhutva"	Hindi	"Service, Security and Brotherhood"
National Security Guard	"Sarvartra Sarvottam Suraksha"	Sanskrit	"Omnipresent Omnipotent Security"

And finally, allow me to say,

"सारेजहाँसेअच्छा, हिन्दोस्ताँहमारा।"

Do you know where from I brought this phrase and poem, I bet you are smiling now. If not, then I assure you, You will smile as you read –

Sare Jahan se Accha" (Urdu: سارے جہاں سے اچھا; Sāre Jahāṇ se Acchā), formally known as "Tarānah-e-Hindi" (Urdu: ترانہ ہندی, "Anthem of the People of Hindustan"), is an Urdu language patriotic song for children written by poet Allama Muhammad Iqbal in the ghazal style of Urdu poetry.

The poem was published in the weekly journal Ittehad on 16 August 1904. Publicly recited by Iqbal the following year at Government College, Lahore, British India (now in Pakistan) it quickly became an anthem of opposition to the British Raj. The song, an ode to Hindustan—the land comprising present-day Bangladesh, *Bharat*, and Pakistan, was later published in 1924 in the Urdu book Bang-i-Dara.

This is what highlights our ***national integration***. The strongest democracy that stands *united in diversity*.

"National Integration is the need of the hour to enter into the most `blissed` era for the Mother land."

So, finally answering the question as to WHO will be the beneficiaries:

The beneficiaries will be:

1. Our Homeland
2. Humans
3. YOU, ME ALL OF US TOGETHER
4. The ones who are opposing it right now (The most interesting for me)
5. Muslim "शक्ति"
6. Muslim Brothers & Sisters

I will put it shamelessly because that is the thing I can do best -

We have to decide Now,

"Do we want our motherland *BHARAT* to win or a particular religion?"

Whatever you decide, don't forget that we all are indebted to our homeland for every single breathe of *blessed air.*
I have one more option to decide that I have already decided –

I want and will make sure that My Country Wins.

Do you want to ask me why?

Why not? That I the way I have been conditioned to think and I hope there is nothing wrong with this mindset. The beauty of this mindset is if our mother land wins, there will be a natural and inevitable win for all the religions.

Challenges in UCC implementation -
No Pain, No gain. As big the task, as bigger the quantum efforts required. It is achievable but the very first step is to accept and at the same time deeply understand the challenges from our soul that UCC offers currently and make the others at least understand the stuff before the jump to conclusion.

Let me take you for another ride here.

Implementing a Uniform Civil Code (UCC) in a humungous task. Not denying the fact owing to Indian diverse religious, cultural, and political landscape of the country. It does face severe criticism and that is justified as of now. We need to make us ready for the change at first. We need all of us to get into the ***right frame of mind*** to understand.

And this is not enough I must tell you. We also have to get all around us to be sensitized about UCC. Each one of us should be aware about the minutest details and all of us need to *participate. This is our duty to the homeland. This is what we owe.*

Here are some of the key challenges to understand:

1. **Public Perception and Education:** Public perception and awareness regarding the UCC can significantly influence its implementation. Lack of public understanding, misconceptions, and resistance to change can hinder progress. Public education and awareness campaigns that foster an informed and inclusive dialogue are essential to overcome these challenges.

2. **Gender Inequality and Patriarchal Mindset:** Many argue that personal laws based on religious practices often discriminate against "शक्ति" and perpetuate gender inequality. However, addressing gender disparities and challenging deeply entrenched patriarchal mindsets within society is a complex and long-term process. The implementation of a UCC must ensure that it promotes gender justice and equality while also addressing concerns and fears of different communities.

3. **Consensus among Religious Communities and other groups:** Gaining consensus among various religious communities is crucial for the successful implementation of a UCC. The religious leaders and representatives from different communities may have varying interpretations of religious texts and traditions, making it challenging to reach a common ground. Addressing concerns and apprehensions of religious communities and ensuring their active participation in the reform process would be essential.

   Differences in opinion regarding the interpretation of religious scriptures, the extent of state intervention in personal matters, and the balance between religious freedom and gender equality make it challenging to reach a consensus on the specifics of a UCC.

4. **Opposition from Religious and Political Groups:** The implementation of a UCC has faced significant opposition from religious and political groups who believe that personal laws are an integral part of religious freedom and identity. These groups often argue that a UCC may undermine the distinct religious practices and traditions of different communities.

5. **Political Will and Consistency:** Implementing a UCC requires consistent political will and commitment from the government. However, due to the sensitivity and potential political repercussions associated with the issue, successive governments have been cautious in pushing for major reforms. Changes in political leadership and priorities can affect the momentum and progress towards implementing a UCC.

Addressing these challenges requires a balanced and inclusive approach that considers the concerns and aspirations of different religious communities, promotes gender equality, and respects the principles of religious freedom and cultural diversity. It requires constructive dialogue, consensus-building, and a focus on achieving social justice and equality for all citizens.

This is not it, there are other critical challenges as well:

6. **Constitutional Validity:** Implementing a UCC would require careful consideration of its constitutional validity. The UCC needs to be in line with the fundamental rights enshrined in the *Bharatiya* Constitution, including the right to freedom of religion. Any provisions that may be seen as infringing upon these rights can lead to legal challenges.

7. **Legal Complexity and Practical Implementation:** The existing personal laws in *Bharat* are complex and deeply rooted in religious and cultural practices. Harmonizing these laws and ensuring a smooth transition to a UCC would be a complex task. The practical implementation, including establishing uniform procedures, resolving conflicts between different laws, and training legal professionals, would present significant challenges.

8. **Political Opposition and Populist Sentiments:** The issue of implementing a UCC has often been politicized, with political parties using it as a divisive tool to appeal to their vote banks. Strong political opposition and populist sentiments can hinder progress and create roadblocks in enacting necessary legislation or reforms.

9. **Socio-Cultural Resistance:** Implementing a UCC requires challenging deeply ingrained socio-cultural norms and practices. Resistance from conservative sections of society, fear of losing traditional identity, and resistance to change can impede progress. Sensitization programs and social campaigns promoting the benefits of gender equality and social justice under a UCC would be vital to overcome these challenges.

10. **Protection of Minority Rights:** *Bharat* is home to various religious and ethnic minorities, and any UCC implementation must safeguard the rights of these minority communities. Ensuring that a UCC respects and protects the religious freedom and cultural autonomy of these communities while promoting equality is a delicate balance to achieve.

11. **Judicial Backlog and Capacity:** *Bharat*'s legal system already faces a significant backlog of cases. Implementing

a UCC may add to the workload and capacity requirements of the judiciary. Strengthening the judicial infrastructure, increasing the number of judges, and introducing alternate dispute resolution mechanisms would be necessary to manage the potential increase in legal proceedings.

12. **Socio-Political Fragmentation:** *Bharat*'s vast population and regional diversity can lead to fragmented socio-political opinions and demands. Balancing the need for a uniform code with the regional aspirations and sensitivities of different states and communities would require extensive dialogue, negotiation, and accommodation.

If we are able to get answers and actions to tackle the previously mentioned challenges, then this is doable.

How to deal with challenges of UCC implementation?

To tackle the challenges of implementing a Uniform Civil Code (UCC) efficiently in *Bharat*, the following approaches can be considered:

The first two I would love to propose and then later my friend ChatGPT offered me. Here I go with mine –

1. **"शक्ति" Committee:** Here I propose the formation of a committee called **"शक्ति"** comprised of women leaders like Women Police Personnel, students, teachers, professors, principals, social media influencers, singers, producers, directors, actresses, Woman politicians and presidents, nurses, pilots, doctors, lawyers, judges, fashion designers, authors, medal winners and champions, entrepreneurs, bosses, team members, self-help group (SHG), army women, police women, journalists, educators, Women

from rural *Bharat*, industry bodies and SHGs that works for women empowerment.

They should be empowered and authorized to debate, take decisions and deal with any conflict that arises with the help of their male counterparts.

History to be re-written, we will take inspiration from history which says, it is "शक्ति" that gives birth, manifests, and protects. So, the time has come. Get ready for it, Get ready for "Durga," get ready for "Kaali" and get ready for a New Vibrant *Bharat*. *Get ready for a new You!*

2. **Education:** We need to voraciously educate our society about UCC. To start with, we can target the places and people where it is highly likely to be understood and accepted. For example, educational Institution – schools, colleges. Specially, places of female education and female students. Why?

Because we have already read in the very beginning that:

"Educate a man and you educate one person; educate a woman and you educate a whole family."

And also implement in those areas which is supposed to create the least ruckus for example, inheritance or marriage and then analyzing as a pilot run. Then we can gradually move to touch the tough ones that will face more opposition than the former. It is to create some turmoil like situation. But we need not to worry!!

You already would have "शक्ति" to protect you. We can leave up to them to manage be it by dialogue or by force.

Next comes the recommendations from my friend ChatGPT. And these are not bad either. At least it deserves some thought.

1. **Inclusive Dialogue and Consensus-Building:** Engage in an inclusive dialogue involving religious leaders, legal experts, scholars, women's rights activists, representatives from different communities, and civil society organizations. Foster an environment of respectful and open discussions to address concerns, clarify misconceptions, and build consensus on the need for a UCC.

2. **Public Awareness and Education:** Conduct extensive public awareness campaigns to educate the general public about the objectives, benefits, and implications of a UCC. Promote awareness of gender equality, social justice, and the importance of harmonizing personal laws to ensure a level playing field for all citizens. Use various platforms, including media, community forums, and workshops, to disseminate accurate information and encourage public participation.

3. **Gradual, Phased & Pragmatic Implementation:** Consider adopting a gradual and phased implementation approach, addressing less contentious issues first. Begin by addressing areas of personal laws where there is broader agreement across communities, such as adoption, inheritance, and marriage registration. This approach can help build confidence, demonstrate positive outcomes, and create a conducive environment for further reforms.

4. **Constitutional Amendments and Legislative Reforms:** Undertake constitutional amendments and legislative reforms to provide a strong legal framework

for a UCC. Ensure that the amendments respect the fundamental rights enshrined in the *Bharatiya* Constitution while upholding the principles of gender equality and religious freedom. Engage legal experts and scholars to review existing laws and propose necessary amendments for harmonization.

5. **Gender Justice and Equality:** Place a strong emphasis on gender justice and equality within the UCC. Ensure that the code addresses discriminatory practices prevalent in personal laws and promotes equal rights and protections for all individuals. Consult women's rights organizations and gender experts to ensure that the UCC provisions align with the principles of gender equality.

6. **Comparative Study and Learning:** Conduct a comparative study of UCC implementation in other countries to learn from their experiences, best practices, and challenges. Identify successful approaches and adapt them to suit *Bharat*'s unique socio-cultural context. This comparative study can provide valuable insights into legal frameworks, transitional arrangements, and community engagement strategies.

7. **Judicial Reforms and Capacity Building:** Strengthen the judiciary by focusing on judicial reforms and capacity building. Increase the number of judges and improve infrastructure to manage potential legal challenges and the expected increase in cases. Promote specialized training for judges on UCC-related matters to ensure fair and efficient adjudication.

8. **Political Will and Leadership:** Garner strong political will and leadership to drive the

implementation of a UCC. Encourage political parties to prioritize the issue of UCC beyond short-term electoral gains and build consensus across party lines. Sustained commitment from political leaders is crucial for overcoming political opposition and achieving meaningful reforms.

9. **Piloting and Evaluation:** Consider piloting the implementation of UCC in select regions or communities to understand its practical implications and identify areas for improvement. Evaluate the outcomes, gather feedback, and make necessary adjustments before scaling up to a nationwide implementation.

10. **Continued Engagement and Review:** Establish a mechanism for continued engagement, review, and monitoring of the UCC implementation. Set up an independent commission or body comprising diverse stakeholders to assess the progress, address emerging challenges, and recommend necessary reforms.

    Establish a dedicated commission or body comprising diverse stakeholders to ensure continued engagement, review, and monitoring of the UCC implementation. This independent body can assess progress, address emerging challenges, and recommend necessary reforms, thereby promoting transparency, accountability, and inclusivity.

By adopting these refined approaches, *Bharat* can navigate the challenges and implement a UCC efficiently. It requires a comprehensive, collaborative, and iterative approach that balances the concerns of different stakeholders while upholding the principles of justice, equality, and religious freedom.

*Benefits OF UCC | WHAT will we together achieve as BHARAT`S **gain** if it implements UCC?*

The implementation of a Uniform Civil Code (UCC) in *Bharat* can bring several benefits:

1. **Equality and Non-Discrimination:** A UCC aims to establish a common set of laws governing personal matters such as marriage, divorce, adoption, inheritance, and succession. It ensures equality before the law, irrespective of an individual's religious or cultural background. This promotes the principle of non-discrimination and upholds the fundamental right to equality enshrined in the *Bharatiya* Constitution.

2. **Gender Justice and Women's Empowerment:** Personal laws based on religious practices often contain provisions that are discriminatory against women, perpetuating gender inequality. A UCC can address these disparities by ensuring equal rights and protections for women in matters of marriage, divorce, property rights, inheritance, and child custody. It can empower women by promoting their social and economic well-being.

3. **Social Cohesion and National Integration:** *Bharat* is a diverse nation with multiple religions and cultures. A UCC promotes social cohesion by providing a common legal framework that transcends religious boundaries. It fosters a sense of national identity and integration by emphasizing shared rights, duties, and responsibilities as citizens of *Bharat*.

4. **Simplification and Clarity in Personal Laws:** The current legal system in *Bharat* consists of multiple personal laws, which can be complex, contradictory, and subject to different interpretations. Implementing

a UCC simplifies and streamlines the legal landscape by providing a clear and consistent set of laws applicable to all citizens. It reduces legal ambiguities and the need for extensive litigation, thereby enhancing access to justice.

5. **Protection of Individual Rights:** A UCC ensures that individuals' rights are safeguarded and protected. It provides individuals with legal certainty and predictability, ensuring that their personal matters are governed by a comprehensive and fair set of laws. This protects citizens from potential abuse, exploitation, or unfair treatment under religious or customary laws.

6. **Modernization and Progress:** Implementing a UCC reflects a commitment to modernize and evolve the legal framework to align with changing societal values and aspirations. It demonstrates a progressive approach to personal laws that accommodates the evolving needs of a diverse society.

7. **Harmonization and Consistency:** A UCC harmonizes various personal laws that are currently governed by different religious practices. This promotes consistency and uniformity in the legal system, avoiding contradictions and conflicts that may arise from different religious laws. It helps build a legal system that is fair, predictable, and equitable for all citizens.

8. **Ease of Administration and Governance:** Having a uniform civil code simplifies administrative processes and reduces bureaucratic burden. It allows for more efficient governance and the effective implementation of laws related to personal matters,

ensuring that citizens' rights and responsibilities are effectively upheld.

It's important to note that the benefits of a UCC need to be balanced with the need to respect religious freedom, cultural diversity, and the sentiments of different communities. Any implementation of a UCC should be conducted with sensitivity and inclusivity, addressing concerns, and engaging in dialogue with all stakeholders.

The implementation of a Uniform Civil Code (UCC) in *Bharat* can benefit various sections of society, but certain groups may experience significant advantages. We have already discussed an overview in the section "WHO will be the beneficiaries "earlier. Here are some sections that could potentially best suited to benefit from a UCC:

1. **"शक्ति"**: Especially those belonging to religious and cultural communities with discriminatory personal laws, stand to gain significant benefits from a UCC. It can help eliminate discriminatory practices prevalent in personal laws related to marriage, divorce, inheritance, and property rights. A UCC can provide women with equal rights, protection against gender-based discrimination, and greater agency in personal matters.

2. **Minority "शक्ति"**: Women from religious or ethnic minority communities often face multiple layers of discrimination. A UCC that upholds gender equality and protects individual rights can particularly benefit minority "शक्ति" by providing them with legal safeguards and ensuring equal treatment within their communities.

3. **Interfaith and Inter-caste Couples:** Interfaith and inter-caste couples often face significant challenges due to the lack of a uniform legal framework. A UCC can provide clarity and legal protection for such couples in matters of marriage, divorce, inheritance, and child

custody, ensuring their rights are upheld regardless of their religious or caste backgrounds.

4. **Children:** Children from families with differing personal laws can face complexities and uncertainties in matters of inheritance, guardianship, and custody. A UCC can establish consistent and clear guidelines, promoting the best interests of the child and providing legal certainty in such cases.

5. **LGBTQ+ Community:** The LGBTQ+ community has historically faced discrimination and marginalization in various aspects of life, including personal laws. A UCC that recognizes and protects the rights of LGBTQ+ individuals can bring about significant positive changes by ensuring equal treatment in matters of marriage, inheritance, adoption, and other personal matters.

6. **Progressive Individuals and Activists:** Individuals and activists advocating for equality, social justice, and the reform of personal laws stand to benefit from the implementation of a UCC. It would align with their aspirations for a more just and inclusive society, promoting the principles of non-discrimination, gender equality, and individual rights.

It's important to note that the specific benefits and impacts of a UCC would depend on the content, implementation, and the context in which it is introduced. Sensitivity to diverse perspectives, community concerns, and the need for social cohesion should guide the formulation and implementation of a UCC to ensure the well-being and rights of all sections of society.

Fast forwarding, the question of whether a Uniform Civil Code (UCC) will be positive or negative for *Bharat* is subjective and depends on different perspectives and priorities. Different individuals and groups may hold varying opinions on the matter. Here are some key points often raised in discussions surrounding the UCC:

Arguments in favor of a UCC:

1. **Equality and Non-Discrimination:** A UCC aims to provide equal rights and treatment to all citizens, irrespective of their religious or cultural background. It promotes the principles of equality and non-discrimination, ensuring that personal laws do not perpetuate gender-based or religious-based disparities.

2. **Gender Justice and Women's Empowerment:** Personal laws based on religious practices often contain provisions that discriminate against women. Implementing a UCC can address these inequalities, provide women with equal rights, and empower them by promoting gender justice and social equality.

3. **National Integration and Social Cohesion:** *Bharat* is a diverse nation with various religions and cultures. A UCC can help foster a sense of national integration by establishing a common legal framework that transcends religious boundaries. It promotes social cohesion by emphasizing shared rights, duties, and responsibilities as citizens of *Bharat*.

4. **Legal Simplification and Clarity:** The current system in *Bharat* consists of multiple personal laws, which can be complex, contradictory, and subject to different interpretations. Implementing a UCC can simplify and streamline the legal landscape, providing clarity and consistency in personal laws and reducing legal ambiguities.

Arguments against a UCC:
1. **Protection of Religious and Cultural Diversity:** Opponents argue that a UCC may undermine the diversity of religious and cultural practices in *Bharat*. They believe that personal laws based on religious traditions should be respected and preserved, allowing communities to maintain their unique identities and practices.

2. **Concerns of Minority Communities:** Some argue that implementing a UCC could disproportionately impact minority communities and erode their autonomy and cultural rights. There are concerns that a uniform code may not adequately accommodate the diverse needs and practices of different religious and cultural groups.

3. **Potential for Social Unrest:** Critics suggest that implementing a UCC without proper dialogue, consensus-building, and addressing community concerns could lead to social unrest or conflicts. Careful consideration and sensitivity are necessary to ensure that the implementation process does not generate social tensions.

4. **Balancing Personal Freedom and State Intervention:** Opponents of a UCC raise concerns about the state's intervention in personal matters and argue for the preservation of personal freedom and autonomy. They believe that individuals should have the right to follow their own religious or cultural practices without interference from a uniform code.

Regarding the timing of implementing a UCC, several factors contribute to the argument that it is needed ***now:***

1. **Constitutional Provisions:** The *Bharatiya* Constitution envisions the implementation of a UCC under Article 44, which directs the state to endeavor towards securing a

UCC for its citizens. The framers of the Constitution intended the UCC as a means to promote social justice, gender equality, and the principles of a secular democracy.

2. **Changing Social Dynamics:** *Bharat* has witnessed significant socio-cultural changes over the years. There has been an increasing demand for gender equality, women's rights, and social justice. These changing dynamics, coupled with the need for legal reforms to align with contemporary values and challenges, have brought the discussion of a UCC to the forefront.

These changing dynamics call for a reevaluation of personal laws to align them with contemporary values and aspirations.

3. **Gender Injustice and Discrimination:** Persisting gender inequalities and discriminatory practices within personal laws necessitate immediate attention. Addressing these issues through the implementation of a UCC can provide a comprehensive legal framework that upholds the rights and dignity of all individuals, particularly "शक्ति."

4. **Progressive Judicial Interpretations:** Over time, *Bharatiya* courts have played a crucial role in advancing the cause of gender justice and individual rights. Progressive judicial interpretations have called for reform and emphasized the need for a uniform and non-discriminatory legal system. The evolving judicial discourse has provided impetus for considering the implementation of a UCC.

5. **Clarity and Simplification of Laws:** The current system, with multiple personal laws governed by different religious practices, can lead to complexities, contradictions, and legal ambiguities. A UCC can simplify

the legal landscape, provide clarity and consistency, and reduce the need for extensive litigation and interpretation.

6. **International Standards and Global Context:** Several countries around the world have adopted uniform civil codes or similar legal frameworks to ensure equality, protect individual rights, and promote social cohesion. Aligning *Bharat*'s legal framework with international standards and best practices can enhance its global standing and engagement.

*Losses OF Not implementing UCC | WHAT will we together as BHARATIYAS **lose** if we don't implement? -*

We stand to lose:

1. A wonderful opportunity to stand united in diversity.
2. We will fail to achieve national integration.
3. We will lose once in a lifetime opportunity to make a promising head start to exponentially progress.
4. We will fail to stand as one nation.
5. We will fail to function as human.
6. We will fail and lose the charm to be called *Proud Bharatiya*.
7. We will lose an extraordinary opportunity to empower "शक्ति" around us and thus will fail as a society entirely.

WHO will be defeated if UCC is implemented Successfully?

"PARIARCHIAL MINDSET"

WHO will be defeated if it is not implemented and delayed further?

WE, *BHARATIYA*S, OUR COUNTRY

Let us decide NOW, to which side of the shore we want to be in?

PROGRESS or PATRIARCHY

Conclusively, I will list of some female leaders, beside many others who have spoken against patriarchal mindset. You have already seen Laksmi Menon from *The All-Bharat Women's Conference (AIWC)* who expressed her disappointment with the male-dominated legislature in an AIWC conference in 1933 in addition to endless list of female champions who have courageously advocated against this mindset.

And if that was not enough, let us have a world tour now:

1. **Malala Yousafzai:** An education activist and Nobel laureate who advocates for girls' rights to education and speaks out against patriarchal norms and oppression.

2. **Emma Watson:** An actor and UN Women Goodwill Ambassador who actively promotes gender equality and has delivered impactful speeches on feminism and women's rights.

3. **Michelle Obama:** There is also an interesting and hilarious anecdote in the later sections about Mr. Obama and her when they met her college boyfriend. Former First Lady of the United States who has used her platform to advocate for girls' education and challenge gender stereotypes.

4. **Jacinda Ardern:** The Prime Minister of New Zealand who has been vocal about feminism and strives for gender equality in her policies and leadership.

5. **Angela Merkel:** The former Chancellor of Germany who has been a strong advocate for women's rights and gender equality, both domestically and internationally.

6. **Ellen Johnson Sirleaf:** The former President of Liberia and the first elected female head of state in Africa. She has worked to empower women and challenge patriarchal norms in society.

7. **Aung San Suu Kyi:** A Burmese politician and Nobel laureate who has been a vocal advocate for democracy, human rights, and women's empowerment in Myanmar.

8. **Kamala Harris:** The Vice President of the United States, who has broken numerous barriers as the first female, first Black, and first Asian American Vice President. She has spoken out against gender inequality and advocated for women's rights.

9. **Ruth Bader Ginsburg:** The late Associate Justice of the United States Supreme Court, known for her legal advocacy for women's rights and gender equality.

10. **Chimamanda Ngozi Adichie:** A Nigerian author and feminist who has delivered influential TED Talks and written extensively about gender issues and challenging patriarchal norms.

Are you ready to move on to a path of progress by doing our part in implementing UCC? I am trying to do with this work in your hand and would further keep doing committed missionary efforts through my artistry.

How much time UCC implementation could, should and may take?

The implementation of a Uniform Civil Code (UCC) or similar legal frameworks can vary significantly from other countries due to our diversity and several other factors. However, it is worthwhile to study variations across countries that can enable us to learn and understand and plan.

Its implementation could, should and may take can differ substantially. It's important to note that the concept of a UCC or its equivalent may differ in scope and in different jurisdictions. Here are a few examples:

1. **Turkey:** Introduced a Civil Code in 1926, which is often cited as an example of implementing a UCC. The process of developing and implementing the code took a few years, with reforms aimed at replacing traditional Islamic legal principles with a more secular legal framework.

2. **Tunisia:** Implemented a Personal Status Code in 1956, which is considered a progressive step towards a UCC. The code was enacted shortly after the country gained independence and aimed to provide equal rights to women in matters of marriage, divorce, and inheritance.

3. **Egypt:** Introduced a Unified Personal Status Law in 1979, which consolidated and reformed various personal status laws. The process of developing and enacting the law took several years, involving debates, negotiations, and revisions.

4. **Algeria:** Implemented a Family Code in 1984, which aimed to address gender inequalities and promote equality in family matters. The code underwent a series of discussions, revisions, and consultations before its implementation.

5. **Morocco:** Introduced a Family Code, known as the Moudawana, in 2004. The process of reforming and implementing the code took several years, with

consultations, debates, and revisions aimed at addressing gender inequalities and modernizing family law.

It's worth noting that the experiences of other countries may not directly translate to the *Bharatiya* context, as each country has its own unique social, cultural, and legal considerations.

Next up is the question that I am personally interested in? I will leave you with this question to think about and also to find answers. I asked this to ChatGPT, you know my new friend, let me put forward what did it answer.

First the Question –

"What would happen to polygamous wives if Uniform civil code is implemented in *Bharat*?"

As suggested by my friend, the response as below:

Regarding the specific situation of polygamous wives, the impact would depend on the provisions and guidelines outlined in the proposed UCC. It is important to note that the content and specifics of a UCC in *Bharat*, if implemented, would be determined through the legislative process, and would require careful consideration of several factors, including constitutional rights, religious practices, and social realities.

However, based on general principles of gender equality and non-discrimination, it is possible that a UCC could bring changes to the legal status and rights of polygamous wives. The UCC may aim to provide equal rights and protections to all individuals involved in marital relationships, regardless of the practice of polygamy. This could include provisions related to divorce, inheritance, property rights, and the overall recognition of the rights and dignity of women.

As of now, *Bharat* does not have a Uniform Civil Code, and personal laws are governed by specific religious laws applicable to different communities. Any potential changes to the legal framework would need to undergo a thorough legislative process, including parliamentary debates and consultations with stakeholders, to ensure a fair and inclusive approach.

If a Uniform Civil Code (UCC) were implemented in *Bharat*, it would aim to provide a unified set of laws that applies to all citizens, regardless of their religious background.

So, I will leave you with this question again —

What would happen to polygamous wives if Uniform civil code is implemented in *Bharat*?

ERA 3

The Buddha Way

- **Critical Thinking - Think Like the Budha | What would he do if he faced...**
- **Second Copy of Education System | Redefining the Indian Education System**
- **Back to the Vedas, The Modern way!**

Critical Thinking - Think Like the Budha | What would he do if he faced.

Headline-

Recently, in December 2003, a massive three lakh twenty-two thousand consumers went to MC Donalds in various outlets across India to carry a mass protest for reduction in the size of burger. In order to calm them down, all the outlets handed over free burgers to all the protesters.

By A fictional News Paper
By M K Sharma (Another Fictional Character)

How did the above lines make you feel? Slightly surprised may be.

This is what I have learnt, not to believe everything around by everyone. As the *Great* one says,

"There is nothing that can't be questioned. There is nothing that can't be put under test."

Who can be a better mind specialist than Buddha himself. We have listened a lot on critical thinking and mental health from experts. Get ready for an exciting journey wherein I bring lessons from the *Enlightened One: The Buddha.*

I became so excited that I recently went for my research to a place called *Gaya (in the state Bihar)*, the area famous for *Mahabodhi Temple*, where he sat under a banyan tree for period of few weeks to gain enlightenment. I wanted to see the compound, the tree under which he sat, and his journey and it was a breath-taking experience.

I went solo and it was full of energy, right from the train where I couldn't get a ticket to travel 18 hours without a seat, but worth paying the price.

Before setting up for the journey let me present some interesting story and facts.

Mental health issues often lead to loss of self-control. A one story goes as, Patachara, the only daughter of a wealthy man, fell in love with a household help and eloped with him. On her way to her paternal home after her husband`s death, she crossed a river that was in space, and lost one of her children. The second one fell prey to an eagle. When she reached the outskirts of her village, she witnessed a maas funeral- that of her father, mother and two brothers.

Facing all the tragedies, she lost her mental balance, and started wandering on the streets aimlessly. Once she stopped to hear a sermon by Tathagata and her life changed.

It helped to heal her mental state. Next, Angulimala as his what the name suggests, wore a Garland of fingers. He was a merciless robber. He had killed 999 people. He cut the fingers and strung them in a gallon. The Buddha was his last target. He joined the sangha after the Buddha counseled him.

Now the thing to learn here is the way he counselled them that the evils changed their path.

Patachara suffered from dukkha. Deep depression, and Angulimala was full of violence and hatred. Both recovered and subsequently attained arahant hood but the Buddhas` two followers namely Devdatta his cousin and the Prince Ajatashatru could never be cured though they too were part of the sangha because they failed to practice the medicine, the Dharma.

Buddha did not give importance to the individual but to his *bodha, understanding.* He taught his followers *Anapanasati*, concentrating on the breath. It is an exercise to connect with the body, it helps the mind regain its part of focus and the restlessness within subsides.

The Buddha revealed the way, an 8-fold part to remove all the reasons for suffering and taking the medicine in the Buddha`s way can eradicate the source of problem ushering in permanent relief. For example, according to Buddha the stinginess creates *trishna* craving it can be annihilated by charity and loving kindness. There is the medicine to be put into practice.

The Buddha's teaching is not only meant to help treat mental health issues, the three essentials of his training and discipline-

1. Sila: Ethical conduct
2. Samadhi: Mental discipline
3. Panna: Wisdom

He would say the root cause of many mental health problems in *avidya*, ignorance. After the elimination of ignorance, one starts seeing the truth and the correct way.

There is a great philosophy in that. I personally have felt in terms of the any work that looks difficult to me in the beginning, the more I remove my ignorance about the subject the more I get better and release my stress.

The most interesting part of his life and teaching for me is how was he able to counsel even the impossible personalities. What was his technique? How did he interpret things?

If we could learn a little of this from him, I am certain that it is going to help us all in the short and long run.

He believed in *questioning*. It involved questioning what was considered to be right and what was considered to be wrong. His dealings were absolutely based on logic, and he even had no concern to put his own logic under test. And once he found something that were not right, he rejected it, and if he found that his own logic was not correct, he had no qualms in rejecting his own assumptions to move as close as possible to what was actually true.

Since childhood, we have been taught to answer well. But what I realized is –

It is not the ability to answer things, it is actually the ability to question that sets up apart and the foundation of what we call as CRITICAL THINKING. So, it`s time we develop the skill of correct questioning and learn the art of asking the right questions.

I will take an instance to highlight how he was able to counsel by his art and true intention –

The story goes here as, there was in the realm of Pasenadi, King of Kosala, a robber named Angulimala, a ruffian whose hands were red with blood, who was always killing and wounding, and showed no mercy to any living creature, from every human being whom he slew, he took a finger to make for himself a necklace, and so his name of "Necklace of fingers."

Once Buddha was staying in Shravasti in Jeta`s grove he had heard of the ravages committed by the robber Angulimala. The Blessed lord decided to convert him to a righteous man. So, one day after taking his meal set out his journey to find the robber. Everyone warned him not to go that way, even a bunch of thirty forty people ban themselves together to travel this road, then why was he going was the questions in everyone`s mind but the lord held on to his way!

From some way off the robber saw the lord coming and wondered exceedingly that, when even companies of ten to fifty travelers dare not come his way, this solitary recluse should be seen to be forcing his way alone, and the robber was minded slaying this recluse. So armed with sword and buckler and with his bow and quiver, the robber followed up the Lord`s trail.

How did the Budha save himself as he didn't believe in wars? Was he able to kill?
Of course, not! The robber thought' "this is a wonderful and marvelous thing. I could always overtake and elephant, horse,

carriage, or deer, when going full speed and yet I am unable to despite all my efforts, to overtake this recluse while he proceeds at his wonted peace." So, he stopped and shouted to the Lord to stop.

The Lord did as he said and said, "I have stopped, Angulimala for your sake. Will you stop following your career of an evil doer? I have been pursuing you in order to win you over, to cover you to the path of righteousness. The good in you is not yet dead. If you only give it a chance, it will transform you."

Angulimala felt overcome by the words of the blessed one saying, "At last the sage has tracked me down. And now that your hallowed words ask me to renounce evil deeds forever, I am prepared to give myself a trial," replied Angulimala. Thus did the robber became a righteous man by accepting the teachings of the Buddha.

The story doesn't end here. What is more interesting to me is the moment when King of Pasenadi became dumbfounded, with every hair of his body standing erect. How and when?

With Angulimala as his almsman in attendance, the lord had proceeded on his way to Shravasti. One morning, the king decided to meet the Lord, unaware of the change of robber's *mindset*, and exclaimed, that "there is a robber who is infesting my territories and harassing my subjects. I want to suppress him, but I have failed."

The lord replied. "if now sir, you were to see Angulimala, with his hair and beard off, in the yellow robes, as a pilgrim who kills not, steals not, lies not and leads the higher life in virtue and goodness, - what would you do to him?"

"Sir, I would salute him, or rise to invite him to accept robes and other requisites, or I would extend him the defense, protection and safeguards which are his due. But how could the shadow of such a virtue extend to one so wicked and depraved?"

At that moment, the reverend robber was seated quite close to the Lord, who stretching forth his right arm, said. "This is Angulimala!" At this the king became dumbfounded with every hair of his body standing erect!

<u>*The most valuable lessons by the Awakened one –*</u>

1. **Mindfulness:** This has been the greatest achievement I can say, once I went through a book by the great B.R Ambedkar, *"The Budda and his Dhamma."* I have become mindful in my dealings and have started to treat things and people around me differently. Dr. B.R. Ambedkar says in his book, *"If a modern man who knows science must have a religion, the only religion he can have, is the Religion of the Buddha."*

   Buddha was the expert in mindfulness on which he emphasized more than anything, which involves being fully present in the moment and observing our thoughts, feelings, and sensations without judgment. This practice is amazingly helpful in cultivating self-awareness and to develop a deeper understanding of ourselves and the world around us.

2. **Critical Thinking:** Here I go with Buddha`s teaching, "There is nothing that can`t be questioned. There is nothing that can't be put under test." It may include challenging your own existing beliefs. So be mindful what you believe to be true. Don't shy away from putting the litmus test to anything you feel should be subjected to.

3. **Change management:** by the understanding of Impermanence **(Anicca):** This learning has again very

closely helped me to learn the art of *change management* and I have conducted multiple workshops for different organization. There are thousands of materials available on change and conflict management, but I found none of them better than Buddha`s teaching on the subject.

He always emphasized the impermanent nature of all things and also humans, teaching that attachment to the transient elements leads to suffering. This simple understanding and acceptance itself can solve our major problems.

4. **The Middle Way:** This could be the solution to Isarel – Hamas war outbreak or which has the potential to solve the west Asia crisis in addition to Ukraine Russia crisis, potentially saving thousands and millions of lives. He taught the importance of avoiding extreme indulgence and extreme plainness. He emphasized the path of moderation and **balance** in all aspects of life. And balance can be best learned from nature. Go and spend some time in nature.

5. **Compassion & Kindness**: While this is also discussed as an extension of this part in the *ERA – Finale -Towards Solutions.* Let me bring out something that is easily said than done. Buddha emphasized the importance of cultivating compassion and kindness towards all beings. He encouraged to practice loving-kindness and to treat all living beings with respect and empathy.

While empathy is overrated these days, it goes in the order: **Compassion >> Empathy >> Sympathy.**

To make it more vivid and clear to understand, let us understand with a lay man language example. Imagine, on one tough day, your vehicle tire punctured unfortunately when you and one of your friends was travelling on it.

So, while you are figuring out, how to get the puncture repaired, there are responses from your friend that I have categorized into:

1. **Sympathy:** "Oh! my friend, *I feel really bad with what happened,* I have an important guest coming in at my home. You please get it repaired I will meet you late evening.

2. **Empathy:** "Oh! My friend I understand that you are facing a problem, but don't worry it is not that big. I know few shops around. I will give you their number, you can connect with them and get it repaired. Let me know if any further help is required. As I am getting late for a meet, I will catch and auto and meet you later."

3. **Compassionate:** "Oh! My friend don't worry, the problem in not that big, let us together find a shop, get it repaired quickly and then move on with our original plan. I am here. It will not take more than half an hour for us to get back and get rolling."

So, guys, two questions here for you to ponder over-.

1. Which kind of people do you spend time together with?
2. Which category do you fall in from the above three?

The Second Copy: Are we using the "The second Copy" of Education System in *Bharat*?

मातेवरक्षतिपितेवहितेनियुक्ते
कान्तेवचापिरमयत्यपनीयखेदम्॥
लक्ष्मींतनोतिवितनोतिचदिक्षुकीर्तिम्
किंकिंनसाधयतिकल्पलतेवविद्या॥

अर्थात: - विद्या माता की तरह रक्षा करती है, पिता की तरह हित करती है, पत्नी की तरह थकान दूर करके मन को रिझाती है, शोभा प्राप्त कराती है, और चारों दिशाओं में कीर्ति फैलाती है. सचमुच, कल्पवृक्ष की तरह यह विद्या क्या-क्या नहीं करती है|

English version:
Education protects like the mother, protects like the father, removes fatigue just like the wife, brings glory, and spreads fame in all directions. Indeed, like kalpavriksha, what is it that education does not do.

<u>*A Conversation - The Desire to Succeed*</u>

"I feel so glad to meet you, and I feel I can move up the career ladder now!"

This is what Sachidanand Kumar, aged 32 said when I was taking his leave after a long and passionate conversation about the things that strongly reinforced my faith in education and how impactfully it can change life for the better!

In return, I thought, "Wow! What a passion, I have sacrificed nothing, and I seem so tiny in front of *his* desire to succeed!"

He had a small red colored 3-wheeler, modified to suit his body type as he was an especially abled young and bright mind. It served as his mobile shop his home, his study room, his savings bank, and his transport medium on which he travelled to Haridwar to offer holy water to lord Shiva in the month of "Shravan."

It doesn't require physical efforts, what it requires is actually mental effort because travelling on 3-wheeler for around 500 km to and fro, not being able to paddle but by rotating wheels for 10 continuous days is beyond normal abilities.

Amazing feat, indeed!

He sold water, snack packets for his livelihood at India gate, New Delhi and told me analytically how he made profits and what was his future plan.

I was trying to purchase a chilled water bottle from him luckily when we had eye-contact that somehow struck a common chord. He proactively said, "Sir, I sell and save to study more!." I said wow! This was my Eureka moment. I was sure he is a guy to get the conversation rolling. He was studying Python, a computer language and showed me his book.

Quickly! Let`s get the dialogue running now!

Rahul: What is your name and how educated are you?

Sachidanand: Sir, I am Sachidanand Kr from Gaya (*a Place in Bihar you read in the last chapter, where I recently visited to research about Gautam Buddha*) educated from a very reputed college that you will not believe.

Rahul: No problem, Sachidanand, you tell me.

Sachidanand: Sir, I did a dual Degree (B. tech + M. Tech) in electrical engineering from IIT Delhi!

And I could not engulf my water from the bottle, and it just spilled with this exclamation. *Simply Awesome*! Is what I could say after hearing this. The next thing, I requested him and said, "please give me your 30 minutes I want to talk to you", and he answered in the affirmative.

Omg! Where does this desire come from, where is this confidence coming from, how? I simply mean how is this even possible. Did I ever purchase a water bottle from an especially abled vendor at India gate, who is an IITian? Is he a person whose desire to succeed is more than mine? These were the thoughts that has besieged my mind while waiting for him under a tree shade.

Now the question is why he was sacrificing though he could easily have an easy lifestyle at his home! But he chose to go other way. Why? Because he wants to solve the problem of *Unemployment* and *provide employment* to millions of youths. The next question is how?

He had ideated about a startup way back in 2016, as soon as he completed his dual degree which aimed at solving employment related problems. To achieve this feat, his plan was as clear and shiny as diamond. He wants to first be a Data Scientist that allows him to gain working experience as well as fetches him a decent salary which he can save and get into a good environment.

Next, with this money saved over a period of 10 – 12 months, he will be investing his savings into fish farming business which he has already run successfully in the past and then gradually bring his business onto a website that his venture would take care further.

For me, what was more important was, I didn't want to provide a lip-service, rather I honestly and strongly want him to succeed.

I don't want him to *feel better,* but I want him to *get better.* The question is how I can help him to make his life easy, So in between our intense discussion, I asked how can I help you now at this moment to move ahead with your plan?

This he didn't answer, but instead asked me for guidance. So mutually, we again dived into deep discussions, and we concluded that if he gets a laptop, he would be able to start his journey. Interestingly, when I asked him how you would charge it, he displayed his intelligence.

He already had a plan for this. He said he has saved Rs. 25000, which he will invest to build his 3-wheeler as solar powered vehicle. It would enable him to make the vehicle tech-enabled and also help in getting laptop charged. He further added, "I can also earn more by providing some services like Aadhar related, Paytm transactions and more."

Hats off to the *desire to succeed.* Such an inspirational being! I have decided to arrange a laptop for him, that somehow solves his problem, I really want him to be successful, he deserves, he is made for something big, I am sure! I will do my bit as many have helped me to rise in my career. It is time to give back to the society! May be the proceedings form this work that you are reading now can buy him a laptop!

I always say,

Merit = Pain.
Education is indeed powerful!

"Education is the manifestation of perfection already in a Human"-

As put forward by one of the most brilliant, prominent, and intelligent minds, how he has defined education. If you want to run your mental faculties and, horses in guessing who the person is. Don't worry, I'm not going to make you feel miserable and I'll answer it right away. The person is none other than my favorite, my motivator, and the person whose wisdom has influenced me since my childhood, he is Swami Vivekananda.

Is education really that powerful?

Allow me to share another inspiring story of Ahad Ahmad, a 26-year-old from Prayag raj who is set to become a civil judge after training. What`s the big deal here? Indeed! It is a big deal as he comes from modest background. He said repairing busted tires at his father`s shop helped him de-clutter his mind during his grueling schedule to prepare for his examination.

No busted tyre he has repaired in his young life ever took a U-turn sharper than his life has due to a powerful tool what we call as education. Ahad`s father, Sehnaz Ahmad (50) who owns a tyre repair shop and Mother Afsana Begum (47), who stitches clothes for women in the neighbor are proud parents of a son who defied the challenges of a hard life and, became a lawyer first and cleared the provincial civil services examination (judicial) final exam.

Ahad who is likely to start his year-long training in December will become a civil judge (Junior division). Their home is as modest as their determination is extra ordinary. They put their three sons to school and college and all the three young men are a living advertisement of the life-changing impact of education.

Education looks at everybody equally. You pay the price in terms of efforts and dedication, let the results be in the hands of this powerful tool. Little by little, and day by day, it improves you holistically. I too have a first-hand experience of the extraordinary impact education can have on not only the person pursuing it, but also on the entire older generation and the generations to come in the learners family. But my story will be a landing for some other time.

Ahad's conclusive remarks as he puts in "My brothers and I are a product of our faith in the power of education."

Does education have age barriers?

Upcoming is one more class act before deepening in the subject of education, recently reported, in the times of India dated 27th Sep 2023 where Salima at the age of 92 learns to read and write.

A five-meter-wide lane separated her from the world of education for decades, then one day she decided to walk across. She beautifully portrays two days after she took an exam whose results will declare her "literate." "Every day I would wake up to the joyful screams of students entering the government primary school in front of my house in Chawli village in Bulandsahar, yet I never stepped inside though I kept burning with the desire to study all along."

What's the harm in learning? She asks, little children who crowding around her who are now used to the sight of the *"young"* learner tottering into the classroom, sitting with them, and breaking into a toothless grin in their pranks. Some of them are her own great grand kids.

Salima Khan whose video is making vibes on social media, has now completed six months of education and is able to read and write. Isn't that something fascinating. Indeed! Yes, I am sure for at least few if not all of you.

This is one of the most interesting and the most dynamic topic that I have ever thought of. So, what actually is education? Can we try and think of defining what is education and what do we actually mean by that. Are we even going in the right direction and if the direction is not right, then what are those *"little big"* things that we have to do in order to metamorphose into the right mindset? So, these are some of the questions we should ponder over?

Our native country has engendered great mathematicians, and astronomers like Varahamihira, Aryabhata, Bhaskar Acharya, Acharya Chanakya, Brahmagupta, etc.

Shiv "शक्ति" Point, Tirangaa Point and the success of Chandrayan 3 Mission roots back to the dedicated efforts and the knowledge powerhouse of our scientists who inherited the baton from these greats mentioned above.

Brahmagupta's book when translated by Al-Khwarizmi, a mathematician at the library of Baghdad wisdom house, made the Arabian world acquainted with *Bharatiya* mathematics. This helped the Arabian world under Abbasid Caliphate achieve a lot of technological advancements e.g., Damascus steel, etc.

This gave Arabian forces the upper hand during their power struggle with Christians in the following centuries during crusade wars. These Arabian advancements were the inspirations of the European renaissance of the 16th century with the translation works of the "Toledo School of Translators" during the 12th and 13th centuries. Much of *Bharatiya* knowledge through Arabian sources reached Europe thereby giving rise to the age of scientific discoveries.

Do you know how *Bharat* produced such geniuses? Shouldn't we take some cues from the great *Bharatiya gurukul system of education* which was at the center of Vedic as well as Hindu society?

Hey Stop!

Good morning! Smell Some coffee, this is new *Bharat*, fasten your seatbelts!

Before galvanizing into the Pure and serene Gurukul Education system, first things first, we must be aware of the events that crippled our original education approach. And reverse engineering, we will try to understand the very meaning of education in a while after you go through the upcoming lines.

I was very perplexed with few things that I came across, and at the same time I was speechless as well, at the evaluation strategy of high-profile exams. Lakhs of youngsters along with their parents aspire to serve the country by becoming doctors. But what does it take to be the one? It all starts with an entrance exam to prove your interest and capability of learning a particular field and in this case NEET PG.

Recently, to cut seat wastage, the government reduced the NEET PG percentile. Wondering how much?

It was interestingly reduced to Zero and not only Zero it was also in negative. I am reminded of Petrol prices during Covid where the per barrel cost went upside down.

Nevertheless, the question here is - will lowering the NEET PG cut-off to zero impact the quality of doctors and benefit private medical colleges? Experts are skeptical and *me too*.

To ensure that no PG medical seats remain vacant, the health ministry, in a one-time measure, recently reduced the NEET PG cut-off to zero across categories. The move as said, would reduce the wastage of PG seats and democratize postgraduate medical education in India. However, continuous monitoring and competency assessments must be adopted to maintain the quality of PG education, say experts.

A health ministry official on condition of anonymity highlights the problem of PG seats remaining vacant. "As many as 3,000 seats remained vacant last year, despite the reduction of 20 percentile in the cut-off. To reduce the wastage of seats, the government reduced the percentile to zero. However, this does not mean that students with zero percentile can directly go to a medical college and get a seat.

The allotment will be done in a centralized manner and only those with higher percentiles will get seats in premier institutions. The Medical Counselling Committee (MCC) will be holding counselling sessions for all India quotas, while the state government will hold the counselling of state quota," added the source.

NEET PG is more of a grading exam rather than a qualifying exam. "All students have completed their MBBS and are examining patients; they are all eligible. Getting a PG seat does not guarantee becoming a specialist overnight; they will have to study for a couple of years and then clear the National Exit Test (NExT) to specialize in a stream," said the source.

The directive will democratize medical education by allowing a diverse group of aspiring doctors to get a PG degree. "This inclusivity is important in a diverse country that demands candidates from various backgrounds and regions aspire to become specialists.

Also, by widening the pool of eligible candidates, we can channel more doctors into underserved areas, thereby improving healthcare across the country. The reduction of the cut-off can alleviate the immense stress and pressure associated with achieving high scores.

There is already intense competition in medical entrance exams and lowering the cut-off could contribute to a healthier, more balanced approach to medical education," says Dr Somashekhar SP, chairperson - Medical Advisory Board, Aster DM Healthcare - GCC & India. Institutions must implement comprehensive assessments and evaluations throughout the PG training period. To maintain quality, continuous monitoring and competency assessments are vital to ensure that students, regardless of their NEET PG score, are adequately prepared to meet the standards expected of medical professionals, adds Dr Somashekhar.

Are we compromising merit here?

Experts are skeptical; they say that lowering the NEET cut-off to zero may impact the quality of doctors in India, In 2023, the NEET PG cut-off percentile was 50 for students from the general category, 45 for Persons with Disabilities (PwDs), and 40 for students from other reserved categories.

Lowering the cut-off to zero has been welcomed by the Indian Medical Association (IMA) which demanded a 30% cut-off percentile in September 2023 citing the Covid-induced struggle faced by medical graduates, but other medical associations like the Federation of All India Medical Association (FAIMA) have opposed the move. Dr Rishiraj Sinha, national executive member, FAIMA, calls the reduction of the percentile to zero a 'murder of merit.'

He says private medical colleges will benefit from the move and students will find it difficult to afford PG medical education in India. "Those who have worked hard to get a PG seat are frustrated as candidates with negative percentile will also join them in the classrooms," adds Sinha.

PG medical education can be slightly expensive in India, forcing many students who may have scored a comparatively higher percentile to pursue medical education in countries such as Russia, Ukraine, Kazakhstan, and Kyrgyzstan, among others.

"At a time when we are asking other countries to teach according to Indian standards, reducing the percentile to zero reeks of hypocrisy," says Anuj Goyal, co-founder, Get My University, explaining that the fees of clinical seats in PG in deemed universities in some states is Rs 80 lakh to Rs 1 crore per year, which roughly translates to Rs 2.5 crore for three years and it is a considerable amount for students to cough up, hence seats remain vacant even in the clinical courses in some deemed universities.

After the reduction of the cut-off, the students with deep pockets will be able to buy such seats. "It may result in a student with a low percentile being inducted into the medical education system while a high-merit candidate may not be able to afford it. This will aggravate the fight between merit and means," says Goyal.

So, getting back to the question, if this is the case then, is the system of entrance exams a valid benchmarking of grading of students? Can we think of something else that allows students to take a breather and also the governmental institutions are left with filled seats?

That's a pretty valid question. I don't have an answer yet. But I will surely try to find. What do you think of entrance exams?
The above ambiguity in vacant seats vs percentile lowering to zero and minus, which means even if you go blind folded you can get a seat as you may be able to score above zero, There is something fishy and serious here in the evaluation strategy, isn't it?

Similarly, there has been a number game in the recent past and it is not something new. The *QUOTA* or the *KOTA*. For this time let us go to the Kota numbers of amazingly talented coaching institutes that are able to create talents as well as score high on suicide list among students.

As I read in one of the articles in The Times of India dated 29th Aug 2023, by none other than Chetan bhagat, I would like to put up some excerpts that holds strongly valid in the current scenario that has national importance and deserves some food for thought.

He highlights the importance and the need for parents, governments, recruiters, and teachers to recognize there are too few professional colleges for too many student aspirants. Broken dreams are inevitable. I don't understand how we have been able to sit quietly on seeing the abrupt and exponential rise of suicides by students owing to high pressure environment created by the current education system.

As Shiv Khera puts in,

"If Injustice is Happening to your Neighbor and you can Sleep, wait for your Turn. You are Next."

The question is - Why is education leading to suicides among students? Why suicidal mindset is being developed by the education system? Is it the high time that we re-define the education system? Minor changes and tweaks in National education policy is not going to serve the purpose. We need to *"leapfrog"* in order to make that quantum change required.

Next, the cases of suicides are a national issue and is not restricted to any region like Kota. And by the time I had penned down the preceding lines, today @ 14th Sep 2023, I again got a news of a Girl (16), a NEET aspirant from Jharkhand`s Ranchi, who hanged herself in her hostel room in Kota Tuesday night (12th Sept 2023).

This takes the toll to 23rd suicide this year only in Rajasthan coaching hub this year, the highest in the last nine years. Unfortunately, while in my writing journey when I came back after few days to write further, what now you are reading, the count already went to 24. Isn`t this shocking this numeral is not a score in a cricket match, and we definitely would like to score low or even come to zero here.

In 2022, 15 students had taken their own lives in Kota alone. These centers must be skilled in getting the students to learn how to go for suicides. Isn`t it?

What and how of hell are they teaching that prompts a student to such a step?

I have some important questions for all of us here.

1. **Is the method of entrance exams a valid way of assessing a student`s capability to study a particular field? If yes, then why not have an entrance exam for all the politicians to join politics? Why not a particular ministry has a certain criterion of marks to get entry into a ministry, especially education. And for that matter, a test to be passed by securing a minimum set mark for petroleum industry to assess the knowledge of the concerned minister?**

2. **Why not have a minimum qualifying marks criterion for The Agriculture minister along with the vote share, to get admitted or inducted as the Minister? And so on for other ministries.**

3. **Why not have an interview of Ministers as it happens for Civil services Exams to select the right fit for a particular Ministry?**

4. Are marks and grades the correct yardstick of measuring performance? If yes, then why not Politicians, Teachers, Policy makers, Recruiters be given marks on how they perform and basis that we grade them?

For me, this idea sounds wonderful and doable, but for many it may sound ruthless and baseless because it has never been done. Any ways I am in for this. What about you?

Kota suicides get disproportionate attention because at any point lakhs of students are grinding away in its coaching classes, they hope to crack the hyper-competitive medical and engineering entrance exams, which according to many *Bharatiya* parents are the safest if not the only possible careers. It is so well portrayed in the fabulous movie "3 Idiots." But still, we fail to understand.

Interestingly, when I was researching for this topic with my Principal, Mrs. Sangeeta Sharma in Modern Public School (Jharkhand), the school that built a rock-solid foundation for me to take on the world; the first thing that she highlighted to bring about a change in this situation is ***not to educate children first of all. It is the high time to educate the parents and teachers at first.***

More than the children it is parents, teachers, governments, education bodies and recruiters, who all need to educate themselves first for heaven's sake. **Please stop imposing your "*stuff*" on children of the new era. Stop to try to control the young minds.**

We are preparing our kids for rejection and inevitable depression by getting them into coaching classes that are expensive, which places a heavy burden on many parents. The students are aware of what the parents are doing for them creating stress right from **Day one**. Staying away from home is tough too as Chetan has highlighted.

The coaching is intense. Cracking these exams with miniscule selection rates, 2% isn't a cakewalk. The stress comes to a boil with the entrance exam results. A selection rate of 2% means 98% of students will not make it. Are you really surprised that some of the students just crumble in this journey?

My question is, are YOU (Parents, Teachers, Recruiters) yourself able to manage that amount of stress?

I myself can't manage such pressure, sorry I can't. And I consider myself lucky enough to get parents, school, teachers, and my elders who taught me and I never felt the need to strain myself ever close to such situation. I am not an engineer nor a doctor, I am pretty successful in my own journey, doing what I love to do. What's the problem in not being a doctor or engineer?

People who are not doctors or engineers do live happy lives and also get "Rishtaas" as Chetan puts it forward. Yeah! they do get good "Rishtaas" if that is what the reason is, and other professions do earn decently.

People have suggested solutions about which at least I can only laugh about. Have they lost their brains? Where has this come from? Really? Do you think spring-loaded fans to prevent death by hanging and nets around coaching budlings can really solve the problem?

I honestly and strongly don't think so. Please take it with a pinch of salt, this is one of the stupidest solutions I have ever heard in my entire life. I am so sorry to those who proposed this solution. But this was a braindead and brainless solution.

This means, the so called great, brilliant minds running these centers and the policy makers are ready and pretty confident that students will attempt suicide and we can do nothing about it and moreover we have surrendered or should is say **"Education has become a product to be sold.** "We are preparing for students suicide. I am short of words honestly to describe this act.

Its high time that we understand the meaning of education ourselves first of all.

Please allow me to let me to tell you how prominent thinkers and greatest *Bharatiya* philanthropists of all time have defined education. Let's start by mentioning Dr. APJ Abdul Kalam with whom we all resonate. One of his books I still adore, *Ignited Minds* which is the very first book that I've ever read apart from my school textbooks. I remember, It was gifted to me in an event that was supposed to award high performers in a school exam, and luckily, I was one of those.

Mr. kalam said, *"The roots of education are bitter, but the fruit is sweet."*

And I'm not going to stop here! I will try and bring out as many philanthropist's views on education as possible. Moving on to doctor B.R. Ambedkar who has been the pioneer in drafting *Bharatiya* constitution. He says, *"Education is the most powerful weapon which you can use to change the world."*

Moving on, Rabindra Nath Tagore, who was one of the most famous poets in *Bharatiya* history says, *Education is not the filling of pail but the lighting of a fire."*

Let now me introduce Dr. Sarva Palli Radhakrishnan who says, *"The aim of education should be to teach us **how** to think rather than **what** to think."*

You might be wondering that I have copied these quotes from Google or the so-called technology-enable apps, but I have a powerful reason to *quote these quotes*. The reason I'll tell you in the upcoming lines but as of now, let us continue with the brightest minds thought about education.

Here comes the greatest female mathematician of all times, Shakuntala Devi who says *"Education is not just about going to school and getting a degree. it's about widening your knowledge and absorbing the truth about life."*

And how can I leave from the current scenario and retired IPS officer, a strong female or shall I say a strong Naari "शक्ति," Kiran Bedi who says, *"Education is not just about academic pursuits, it is about nurturing curiosity, creativity, and critical thinking."*

I will tell you one interesting personal stuff here-

I am so jealous of a female named *"Chitralekha"* nicknamed as *"Chitra"* (You will meet her in the *ERA: Towards Actions* in detail who has already lived my dream by receiving her qualification degree from the respected Kiran Bedi.

Moving on, I have a lengthy list to present to you but, this serves the purpose, and I cannot stop myself from putting here one more from the greatest scientist of all time, Albert Einstein.

"Education is not the learning of facts, but the training of mind to think."

The previously mentioned lines I strongly believe, highlights the importance of education in personal growth, societal development, and the pursuit of knowledge and values. Everything else follows.
Money, career, degrees, recognition, values, international exposure, and whatever you can think of are the byproducts.

So where to start? Chetan has put in some food for thoughts for our elders and you must read it and re-read it till the time you all understand it.

Parents:
For Heaven's sake, please educate yourself. Stop imposing your unfulfilled dreams on your children, being a doctor and engineer is not the be all and end all. There are infinite professions out there. Many doctors even don't make so much money and many engineers whom I know are unemployed. Say for example, you are reading this piece written by a person who is neither an engineer nor a doctor.

Teachers:
You must realize how dumb and pig-headed many *Bharatiya* parents can be. You have to re-educate the students on how to approach these exams in addition to how to study for such exams. Their career is much more than these exams. The exams are tough and needs demanding work. But treat it like game. As, the great MS Dhoni himself has put in, You either **Win** or **Learn.** You never lose.

Policy Makers:
You need to see why even now only a few government colleges are considered aspirational. This when people in *Bharat* otherwise prefer their products and services private. It is because private colleges have poor credibility, and their motives are not trusted. The solution:

- May be to let foreign universities come in.
- May be make big *Bharatiya* corporate big houses affiliate with colleges.
- My be rooting back to the Gurukul system of education in a modern way.
- We need to increase the supply of aspirational colleges.

Recruiters
If you go to only elite colleges to recruit only engineers, you are not helping. Why do you need a mechanical engineer to do a sales job? What is wrong with you? Why not go to other less elite colleges and pick diligent students from there?

There is an interesting excerpt from one of R. Mahadevan's speech where he helped four of his friends to get placed at one if the companies of the conglomerate, TATA in Jamshedpur, where they were not able to crack interviews because of language barriers.

He insisted to the recruiters to get them interviewed by a Marathi speaking recruiter or any senior from the company who could speak their language. The company needed good engineers rather than employees who can speak good English. Right? And finally, they were selected as they were really talented engineers.

It is high time that recruiters take the same approach of respecting talent and skills rather than elite degrees and smart superficial candidates who can speak fluently due to good exposure but are not concrete when it comes to skills.

Students
Finally, students why do you have to go to extremes. What is it that you want to prove? So, do you mean we will not have any champions in the field of study or otherwise? Do you mean we cannot trust you, our youth, that you will be responsible? How then we will trust you as our successors? How would we pass the baton of society to you?

You are our future, you are the hope of your parents, you are the hope of your PM, you are the hope of all the teachers and professors who have taught you, who believed in your capabilities.

Study for the love of knowledge, follow the path of self-awareness and developing skills rather than passing rote learned exams. While the system of exams is not that bad .and you clearly need to understand that a bit of stress is not at all bad either.

A "controlled adversity" or an environment where you undergo a bit of stress allows you to self-introspect and reflect back on what you have learnt. ***"Exams are actually a simulation for life."***

Isn't it? How and why?

Because diverse kinds of exams require you to reproduce given facts or application of certain facts during a given time interval that you learn though out the year. Isn`t this something that you are required to do at every single point of time in your professional lives. Exams prepare you for *the exam of life.*

Here is an example, while writing , it was exactly 07:27 PM in the eve by my watch, 29th August 2023 on a metro seat in the cabin that was over-packed with murmuring sound in evening with happy-go-lucky faces (the happiness of returning home and it is as similar as it was during schools days) enroute to my home in Delhi NCR, I was juggling between my Job at an Australian MNC that required me to draft an IJP (Internal Job Posting) policy before next morning 10 o clock and another project of 5 days of soft skills program on personality development for 1st year BBA students at one of the most prestigious colleges in Noida.

The college required me to prepare a presentation on certain topic which was also required to be ready before the same time. And I know and I trust myself confidently that I will do both successfully, along with writing the piece that is in your hand right now as I have done it more than 100 times before. I am used to it and so are other successful professionals who do this kind of work and others which are much more intense than these.

And how and why am I and other professionals able to so all these. It is simple because we are doing what we are supposed to do. And if in particular you talk about me, I am able to do all these stuffs as I have learnt to enjoy what I do, I love to do, so I relish juggling between these works.

You earn marks, and professionals earn livelihood. That's the only difference. What would happen if professionals were not able to earn the livelihood temporarily for some time due to disruption in jobs or some events that are beyond their control like the one, we experienced during Covid`19 or process ram downs or other life struggles? Should they opt for suicide? This way society would vanish in a while.

So, what I intend to make you understand is that this training, simulation, or the practice is offered by exams.
Learn this bitter truth about life that it is not that fairy tale. It in indeed unfair, uphill, and hard. People may dole out lip-service on how students stress should be lowered but nobody is coming to save you.

However, the good thing is, it is up to you to make your own life. Life will hit you with disasters as it does to everyone. A failure in an entrance exam may be a blow and a dream shattered but see this as a practice to what is about to come. Failure, disappointment, unfairness will come to you again and again.

The answer to this is not to quit on life, but to change your goals, strategy, and actions.

Continue to hustle and work hard but in a different direction. Don't take the extreme step or fall into consistent reminiscing failures. Just breathe, talk, and rise up again and put up a fight. You are much more than an exam. Show the world that you don't need to be another boring engineer or doctor. With all due respect to the professions, but not everyone is made for everything. This is what will make this doctor-engineer-entrance-exam tyranny end. Do it for you and for the students to come.

I strongly believe, no student deserves to reach to point when they abandon hope. This is not about Kota, or only a kind of entrance exams and quitting for life. It is more about our collective failure as a society and quitting our responsibility to show our children a better future.

Moving on from a heavy lecture, as some may feel, I have already repeatedly reiterated uncountable times about my previous work called *"The journey To A New You"* about the process called HEAL, that stands for H-history, E- evolution call ma E-acceptance, L- layer removal. I really apologize but I cannot help myself restating the HEAL process again and again you know why because this is the secret to knowing *"The Game"* from scratch.

So, what are we waiting for let us jump start the HEAL process about education. this should be the first thought that we should apply the HEAL process to. The education system that we are following right now, are you aware how did it evolve? Where did it start? Was this the original education system that *Bharat* had or were there any hybridization or infringement with our original education system?

<u>Why do I use term "The Second Copy" to signify education system in Bharat?</u>

You might wonder why I used the word *"second copy"* for our education system. In no sense, I ever want to demean our own education system of which I am also a product.

But in order to understand it completely, thoroughly & in its entirety, we must know how it evolved and let us start this process right now.

Virtually, all of the nations in the world pursue the similar education as we see in *Bharat* and elsewhere. Still, education in some countries is better implemented e.g., Japan, and Scandinavian countries (Norway, Sweden, Finland) than others like *Bharat*, China, the US, etc.

Post extensive study of the education systems of different countries, I concluded that even though the education system is the same throughout the world but elements ***like socialism, well-trained teachers, and accountability*** are what makes some countries fare better than others.

I am not going to present a comparative analysis of various education systems. Instead, we will discuss the evolution and history of the current (modern) education system to develop actionable solutions for the present and future. We'll try to understand the conditions under which the modern education system developed in 18th-century northern Europe particularly Austria and Prussia and its subsequent copying by the US around 1839 by a person named Horace Mann and improving it.

Now, I believe we will start getting a taste of What do I mean by the phrase *"The second copy."*

In 1892 a committee of 10, determined that the period of education will be 12 years, what to teach when to teach and syllabus, etc. Slowly higher education becomes prevalent.

Are we ready? If yes let's take a plunge if not, then then get ready and get set go! Let us rock it and shock it!

Why not start where it all started i.e., the Kingdom of Austria under Maria Theresa in the 1750s.

History Train Boarded-
In the 18th century, the kingdom of Prussia (modern-day Germany) was the second country to implement free and compulsory education (the first being Austria under Maria Theresa). After the defeat in 1806 at the hands of Napolean, it was decided that the reason the battle was lost was that Prussian soldiers were thinking for themselves instead of following orders.

To make sure this couldn't happen again an 8-year system of schooling was created. This new system not only provided the skills needed for the early industrialized world such as reading, writing, and arithmetic but also a strict education that taught duty, discipline, respect for authority, and the ability to follow orders.

After the American Civil War, the Prussian model that was being taught in the northern United States was also integrated into the South. By the 1900s most of the compulsory schooling laws that implemented the new system had been passed. From then on, every American child is grown under the Prussian system.

Elite children destined for higher offices went on to attend private schools while the rest who didn't have any access to secondary education was the working class. Through this system, the Prussian state tried to create *"social obedience"* in citizens.
In truth, the entire purpose was to instill loyalty to the crown and to train young men for the military and bureaucracy. To

achieve this, *it was necessary to squeeze out all independent thinking from the masses.*

Phases of education in Europe -
Interestingly, education in Europe has evolved through five *sacrosanct* phases.

1. **Greek schools and universities**
   This was the phase when education was only available to a few, but its accessibility wasn't as limited as we will see in Europe during its dark ages (5th to 15th century).

2. **Catholic church and Middle ages**
   The church had most of its power by interpreting the Bible. So, the church had an incentive in NOT educating the masses. Real education was avoided, and most people were illiterate during the dark ages, aptly called so. Higher institutions were exclusively religious and run by monk orders like Florentine, Jesuits, etc.

3. **Enlightenment Phase**
   This phase started after the Reconquista (reclaiming Spain from Muslim rulers, 722 – 1492). The city of Toledo was at the center of all this and emerged as a center of learning. A huge cache of Arabian books was translated which introduced Christian Europe to a number of *Bharatiya* ideas through Arabian sources, particularly philosophy and mathematics.

   This introduced Europe to the scientific thoughts of the middle east and Asia proper (*Bharat*, China, etc.). The philosophical understanding of the civilizations of the east helped Europe overcome its dark ages and a tradition of scientific thoughts was started with the likes of Copernicus, Kepler, Galileo, and Tycho Brahe.

4. Industrial Revolution

The mass education or increase in the accessibility of education to the masses was the main achievement of this period. Education which was religious in nature and was only accessible to the rich was started to be offered to the masses. The main reason was the industrial revolution and the rich and wealthy needed people to work in their factories in addition to the fields.

But unlike agriculture industries, it required skilled labor and hence the requirement for education arose.

This was the period when the current education system started to take shape initially in the kingdom of Austria (1750-1780) and then the kingdom of Prussia, especially after the defeat at the hands of Napolean in 1806.

5. Modern Age (After the 1870s)

The secularization of education was the main feature of this era. It was led by the US. After the introduction of the Prussian system of education by Hoarse Mann in 1839, public education become prevalent in the US. But it was still very much focused on religion. But after the formation of the committee of Ten in 1892, education was given a formal form. The following things were decided by this committee:

- The 12-year schooling system was proposed by this committee.
- The syllabus was standardized.
- A wide variety of subjects were introduced which were earlier only Latin or Greek
- The decision on when to offer a particular subject was also taken by this committee.

Problems it faced-

Throughout the 20th century, USA's education system was extremely flawed due to

- Teachers weren't trained.
- Schools were highly segregated as recently as the 1960s.
- The curriculum was overly focused on subjects like Greek and Latin.

What is the Prussian model? -
The current education system was developed in the kingdom of Prussia. Initially, it was an 8-year compulsory schooling which was later turned into 12-year schooling in the USA.

Purpose -
A few of the stated aims of the Prussian model were:

- To produce a passive factory or military workforce.
- Teaching sub-ordination so that they can grow out to be a subordinate adult.
- *Bells, attendance, orders, licenses, constant testing, rankings, and class timetable was used to prepare them for their working days in factories.*
- **Please read the above line again before proceeding further.**
- Make them obedient to authority.
- To flush out critical/decisive thinking so that they can be a great factory worker or military recruits.
- Destroy the imagination.

Going to school took you to a place in the societal system as a cog nothing more.
By the year 1900, 34 states had compulsory schooling laws, and half the children attended one-room schools. By 1918, elementary school was made mandatory for every student. It was designed in the industrial age, to churn out factory workers.

The 3-tier model of Prussian Schooling –

1. **Gymnasium/Real gymnasium:** Existed to serve or empower ~0.5% with critical thinking (original thinking), and active literacy (persuasive language). The gymnasium focused on classical languages and humanities. The latter focused more on utilitarian subjects like modern languages, mathematics, and science.

2. **Realschule:** Schooling for the ~5%, it focused on numeracy, passive literacy, and technical skills aiming to produce professional engineers, architects, doctors, lawyers, and civil servants.

3. **Volk Schule:** Schooling for the rest 95%, focus on obedience, cooperation, and correct attitude, along with the basics of literacy, and official state myths of history.

Problems with the Prussian model -

- One size fits all type model.
- Focuses on efficiency like factories.
- A fixed time is set for everyone to pass through a fixed syllabus.
- Then students are segregated based on what they have achieved.

Aren`t these somewhat similar to what the problems are nowadays.

The history of the current schooling system –

It is called as a factory schooling system by Vedic Concepts whose blog post I have used here to describe which I completely resonate with. You may find the link to complete post in the bibliography section.

History of the evolution of the current school system can be primarily divided in three separate phases viz Austria, Prussia (modern-day Germany), USA. One notable actor that is out of the picture is the UK who acted more of a spreader rather than a creator.

Status of education before the current system -

Wealthy people hired private tutors. But the poor could go to Church schools which were very few. That's why literacy was exceptionally low before this system came to be because the state did not have any incentive in educating the poor. Education was considered a privilege and not a necessity. The Apprentice system was prevalent during the enlightenment as well as the middle age which gave way to the current schooling system.

Evolution in Europe -
The current schooling education system has its genesis in the enlightenment age in Europe. The setup of Gutenberg's press brought a revolution in Europe. The church was losing its power due to the democratization of printing technology. After the Protestant Reformations, Germanic republics particularly Prussia and Austria were at the forefront of this drama.

Austrian Empire
Austria under Maria Teresa was the first country that implemented free and compulsory education for all. She worked along the lines of Centralization, Professionalism, and efficiency because her inherited empire was scattered and inefficient.

Before Maria's reforms, the empire was run by nobles and the Church who took care of everything from collecting taxes to making laws. So political as well as economic centralization was required to run the empire efficiently.

This created a need for an educated class of people which she offered by creating schools. She also undertook reforms in healthcare due to rampant women's death during delivery. 1749 reforms that separated the judiciary from the state created a need for learned judges along with civil servants. Thereby creating a need for free and compulsory education.

Prussian Empire -
The next landmark was the fall of Berlin at the hands of Napolean Bonaparte in 1806. Prussia had a fearsome reputation as one of the foremost military powers of Europe, especially after Frederick the Great of Prussia. The better-trained army of Prussia was defeated by Napolean's forces setting the intellectuals of Prussia in crisis mode.

Who influenced the schooling system? -
Prussian philosopher Johann Gottlieb Fitch combined John Locke's view that the "Human mind at birth is a blank slate" and Rousseau's idea that "the State of nature will degrade without law and morality."

The schools must fashion the person, and fashion him in such a way that he simply cannot *will*, otherwise than you wish him to *will*.

Some of the most important Johann's thoughts that deserves to be re-thought are mentioned below.

- Education should aim at destroying free will so that after pupils are thus schooled, they will be incapable throughout the rest of their lives of thinking or acting otherwise than as their school expert's would have wished. When this technique has been perfected, every government that has been in charge of education for more than one generation will be able to control its subjects securely without the need of armies or police officers.

- By means of the new education, we want to mold the Germans into a corporate body, which shall be stimulated and animated in all its individual members by the same interest.

- I should reply that the very recognition of and reliance upon free will in the pupil is the first mistake of the old system.

- The new education must consist in this, that it completely destroys freedom of will in the soil which it undertakes to cultivate and produces on the contrary strict necessity in the decisions of the will, the opposite being impossible. Such a will can henceforth be relied on with confidence and certainty.

Prussia established an educational system that was considered scientific. Some of the important parts of the system:

- It defined for the child what was to be learned.
- What was to be thought about?
- How long to think about it.
- Critical thinking had to be done away with. The Prussian model was created for the good of the government.

They couldn't digest the defeat of Prussia. Johann Gottlieb Fitch gave many lectures in which he proclaimed the greatness of Germanic people and their uniqueness over all other races. The intellectuals of Prussia concluded that the Prussian army was defeated because "the Prussian soldiers were thinking for themselves" Vs Napolean army soldiers who were only following orders.

This set-in motion the creation of the Prussian education model which was later widely studied and replicated by many countries of the world but primarily the United States and other European countries.

Evolution in North America -
Initially, most students learned at home and out in the real world. In 1837, the State of Massachusetts formed the first state board of Education with Hoarse Mann as the person at the helm. He visited Prussia to study the system they were employing. After coming back to the States, he lobbied heavily for the implementation of the Prussian model.

By the 1870s, public education become commonplace in the United States. In 1892, the committee of Ten decided on the standardization of education. They decided about:

- The length of primary education as well as secondary education
- The curriculum that should be taught in those 12 years.
- The main motive was to create a workforce that will be productive for the industry.
- Public education though gained momentum only after the civil war because the state had an incentive to educate the masses. Before that, it was a private affair, and education used to be the last thing on most people's minds.

Education imagined as science -
Teaching was imagined as science and people needed thorough training in the latest methods grounded in research. Older and younger kids were separated and started going to different

schools. Soloist schoolteachers turned into an education board with lots of teachers teaching different things. Specialization was started. But the whole era of educating the masses system only started after the end of the second world war (1 September 1939 – 2 September 1945)

Scientific advancements of the 18th and 19th centuries coupled with enlightenment age (1685 – 1815) ideas gave a completely distinct perspective to look at it. Education was increasingly imagined as a scientific quest rather than humanities.

Fredrick Taylor (1856 – 1915) who is also considered the father of scientific management gave revolutionary ideas about management. He gave the following ideas:

- Removed the need for complex skills and higher order thinking in the workforce by completely separating them from manual work.
- His work in industry resulted in a completely new set of incentives and requirements in the educational system.
- His methods were from their inception condemned by factory workers.

Why were the schools needed? -
Schooling became a crucial issue during the nineteenth and twentieth centuries due to the spread of French revolutionary ideals, the desire to prevent new unrest, the need to train skilled labor, and the construction of nation-states around a shared culture.

Europe understood the value of individuality, liberty, freedom, free will, etc., especially after the French revolution and the enlightenment age. These ideas were liberating for the masses (third estate) but elites (govts, church, nobles, aristocracy, institutionalization) were challenged. So, they resorted to the method of free and compulsory education of the masses, but not for their good. Some of the reasons were:

- The emergence of nation-states during the enlightenment period.
- Nation-states needed a common identity for the newly formed nation's citizens. Consequently, a new construct of patriotism needed and be drilled into the heads of their subject by the state.
- The state needed people for the military.
- The industrial revolution created a need for well-trained staff.
- Secularization of education

The secularization of schools came extremely late. It was during the first half of the twentieth century i.e., 1900 – 1950. Initially, the main subjects were Latin and Greek besides scriptures.

Pheww!.

I think that a lot of information to consume, but much needed. Let us grab smell some coffee and reboot our minds now by a poem or few line that I had written at some good point of time—

Sambhal kar rhne ae manzil bht karib hu tere,
bht se raton ki nind gawai hai tuje pane me.
bas kar ab aur na tarsa, vrna umar bit jaaegi un raton ka hisab krne me
Samnbal kar rhne ae manzil bht karib hu tere,
Manunga na haar jab tak milega na tu,
Tujse hisaab bhi to lena hai un raton ka,
Samnbal kar rhne ae manzil bht karib hu tere,

Haraa har baar, in haar ne bnaya kaabil mujko tere,
Sambhal kar rhne ae manzil bht karib hu tere,

"Picture abhi baaki hai mere dost" (*The movie still remains my friend...)*

*The **Bharatiya Way** to education-*

The history of Gurukuls is the history of *Bharat*'s education system and how it gave birth to subjects like astronomy, mathematics, science, economics, history, etc. Its history encompasses at least 15000 years which no other civilization can boast of. In the development of *Bharatiya* culture, the system of 4 Purusharthas, 4 Varnas, and 4 Ashrams has been instrumental. The Gurukul system has functioned as a great support system for them all.

The word "Gurukula" or "Gurukulam" is made up of two words "Guru" and "kula. "It translates to 'the lineage/clan of the guru.' But it has been used for centuries in the sense of educational institutions in *Bharat*.

Vedic age gurukul system of education -

The Gurukul system of education in *Bharat* flourished during the Vedic period. Gurukuls functioned as the main center of learning in ancient times. In gurukuls, Brahmacharis (students), or Satyanveshi Parivrajakas from far-off places used to come to complete their learnings. Those Gurukuls were of all kinds, small or big.

मुनीनांदशसाहस्रंयोऽन्नदानादिपोषाणात।अध्यायपतिविप्रर्षिरसौकुलपति: स्मृत: ।

Meaning - Sages who nourished ten thousand sages or students and gave education were called the Kulpati (Vice-Chancellor)

It is clear from the use of the word 'Smriti' quoted above that the tradition of taking this special meaning of the Vice-Chancellor was incredibly old. The general meaning of the patriarch was the owner of a clan. This clan could be either a small and undivided family or a large and many small families of the same origin.

The antevasi student was a member of the great academic family of the Kulpati. The responsibility for his mental and intellectual development rested with the Kulpati. The Kulpati was also concerned about the physical health and well-being of the students.
Nowadays the term is used for the 'Vice Chancellor' of the university.

Mention in Pali literature
Many such discussions are found in the Pali literature, from which it is known that kings like Prasenjit donated many villages to those Brahmins who engaged in the field of Vedas. They used to run Gurukul for the distribution of Vedic education and helped in the study of Vedic literature. This tradition was often continued by most of the rulers and there are many inscriptions of the Gurukul running in the villages donated to the Brahmins of South *Bharat*.

The developed forms of such Gurukuls were Takshashila, Nalanda, Vikramshila, and Valbhi University.

It is known from the travel records of Xuan Zang (Hiuen Tsang), Faxian (Fa-Hien), and many other references that in those universities, students from far-off places used to come to study. Varanasi was the main center of education since ancient times and till recently there have been hundreds of Gurukuls, Pathshalas and Annakshetras kept running for their sustenance.

Vedic period -
This is the time when the Vedic Gurukul system was developed, and its structure and principles were refined. The core principles that were envisaged by rishis still hold to the very

essence even in this modern age. The learning system that was set up for learning Vedas slowly evolved into the application of learning vocational as well as scientific systems.

Though there isn't much information available except some gurukuls that have been discussed in Brahmanas (commentaries on Vedas).

Gurukuls mentioned in Ramayana & Mahabharata-
Some of the famous rishis/gurus who find mentioned in the *Bharatiya* epics Ramayana and Mahabharata also ran famous gurukuls. Rama and Krishna also studied in Gurukuls under Vashishtha and Sandeepani, respectively.

I would proudly love to mention the sacred names here who have been a part of our ancient Gurukul system.

- *Maharishi Vishwamitra:* He wrote the Gayatri Mantra and was also the teacher of Lord Ram and Laxman. He taught them the usage of celestial weapons (Devastras) to be used in warfare. He guided them in defeating powerful demons like Tataka, Maricha, and Subahu.

- *Maharishi Valmiki:* Sita took refuge at his ashram and gave birth to Luv and Kush, he taught them shastras and the art of using weapons. He also wrote Ramayana.

- *Maharishi Vashishtha:* He was one of the great Saptrishis. He was a teacher to Dashrath's sons Ram, Lakshman, *Bharat*, and Shatrughan.

- *Guru Dronacharya:* He was the guru of all the Kauravas and Pandavas, who learned under guru Dronacharya. His gurukul was situated somewhere near the present-day "Gurugram" which also gets its name from.

- *Naimisharanya:* It was one of the most important hermitages. It was more like a university. Saunka rishi was the Kulapati of this hermitage which means at least 10,000 disciples and acharyas used to reside in this hermitage at one time. This is famous by the name Chakra Teerth, Neemsar in the state of Uttar Pradesh.

- *Kanva Rishi Hermitage:* Kanva rishi's hermitage is described in vivid detail in Mahabharata. It was situated on the banks of the river Malini, a tributary of the Sarayu River. This hermitage was not a stand-alone, but many other hermitages were there in its vicinity.

- *Vyasa's hermitage:* It was one of the most famous seats of learning. Vyasa compiled all the Vedas in this hermitage.

Buddhist period (5th century BCE onwards) -
Buddha was born in the 19th century BCE and Ashoka of the Mauryan empire ascended the throne somewhere around 1500 BCE as claimed by Mr. Vedveer Arya in his commendable work on the dating of Adi Sankaracharya and Buddha.

Due to the initial patronage by Mauryan Ashoka, Buddhism spread fast. It didn't have as much effect on the gurukul system as it had on the principles of Vedic Dharma (as Hinduism was called back then). The Gurukul system continued flourishing, but much earlier Vedic Vishwavidyalaya s were slowly converted into Bodh Maha viharas as was the case with Takshashila and many others. Vedic dharma took the backseat while Buddhism was in the driving seat.

Education Beyond the Gurukul i.e., universities of ancient Bharat -
Some of these gurukuls evolved organically into what we call universities nowadays. The reasons may have ranged from the spread of their fame far and wide and students might have started flocking to these well-known places giving rise to

universities. These served as centers/institutions for advanced learning.

According to one estimate, there were well over 50 universities in ancient *Bharat* at one time. Some of these famous ones are Takshashila, Nalanda, Vikramshila, and Valbhi University, Odantapuri, Mithila University, Telhara University, Sharda Peeth Temple University, Pushpagiri University, Somapura University, Bikrampur University.

Some of the famous alumni of Takshashila (Taxila) were the noted grammarian Panini, who authored the famous book Ashtadhyayi, and Acharya Chanakya, who wrote Arthashastra.

Why Gurukul system decline?
So, now we must be wondering, if the Gurukul system was so robust then why did it decline? Right? Let us navigate together:

Gurukul Education System is quite possibly the oldest education system in the world. It has flourished in one form or another from at least 15000 BCE. Knowledge production and sharing have been considered one of the most sacred things in *Bharatiya* culture which gave rise to the institution of learning and knowledge sharing.

The decline of the glorious *Bhartiya* Gurukul education system is a long-drawn process that has its genesis in the destruction caused by the Mahabharata war, the subsequent rise of various sub-sects and further:

1. Islamic Colonialism
2. British Colonialism
3. Our Own Mistakes
4. *Few* Good Decisions

The indifference of society after independence tells us how indifferent we have become towards a great education system. But we are bearing a *"second copy"* current schooling system instead.

But the story doesn't end there! The Gurukul system which is in decline since at least the 13th century lost its competitiveness even further after the British took control of *Bharat*. Everything came to a grinding halt after the *English Education Act of 1835* which is discussed in upcoming sections.

The Mahabharata war proved to be a milestone in *Bharatiya* history. The intellectual vacuum created after the war resulted in the deterioration of the societal structure which gave rise to darshan that rejected Vedas viz. Buddha darshan, Jains, Ajivikas, etc.

But as all good things must come to an end, the gurukul system also faced challenges from foreign rulers. Foreign invader brought their education systems with them and forced them on the Indigenous population.

Muslim rule
Following the destruction of Nalanda, Vikramshila, and Udyantpuri. The continuous persecution and destruction at the hands of Muslim rulers.

Destruction of Nalanda by Bakhtiyar Khilji -
A painting titled "The end of Buddhist Monks" shows the destruction of Nalanda by Bakhtiyar Khilji in 1193. Besides Nalanda, he destroyed Vikramshila and Odantapuri universities as well. The destruction has been recorded by Minhaj-i Siraj Juzjani in Tabaqat-i-Nasiri.

Source: https://commons.wikimedia.org/wiki/File:The_end_of_Buddhist_Monks,_A.D._1193.jpg

The first successful attack by Muslims on *Bharat* was in 712 by Bin Qasim. But after a brief period of control, most parts of Sindh and Baluchistan, the next five hundred years, they couldn't control any further part due to some decisive victories of the period. The attacks were renewed under Mahmud of Ghazni, but most of these were raids on the periphery of *Bharat*.

Then Mahmud of Ghor was successful in setting up his base after winning the battle of Tarain in 1192. The reason for sharing this background is to show that only after the 1200s, Muslims were able to set up any base in *Bharat* albeit a small one.

British rule -
After winning the debate with "Minute on Education (1835) ", Thomas Babington Macaulay, a British Politician brought radical changes to education in *Bharat*. After that, the company stopped all funding to the gurukuls. Societal apathy mixed with

sustained attacks from Muslim rulers compounded their decline. But it was the British who delivered the death blow to the already dying Gurukul system. Soon it becomes fashionable to send your child to your convent school and the rest is history.

We love to send our children to Convent Schools. Don't we ourselves love to go to convent schools?

In the aftermath of British policies, the 19th century saw a steep decline in the number of gurukuls all over *Bharat*. *Bharat*, from being one of the biggest economies in the world in the 1800s to being one of the poorest in the world in 1914 made education unaffordable to most *Bharatiya*s. As a result, the remaining gurukuls were shut down too.

Vediconcepts analyzed the data between 1820 – 1880 and published their research to signify How many gurukuls were there in *Bharat* before British rule? They have divided the research into three phases viz.

- The status of education during the initial phase (1770 – 1830)
- The middle phase (1830 – 1870),
- The last phase (1870 – 1947).

After 1947 -
The governments of independent *Bharat* behaved more or less the same as their predecessors. There was no focus on the government toward the Indigenous gurukul education system. The momentum that it gained during the 1880s – 1930s was completely lost after independence.

21st Century -
The status of the gurukul system of education is precisely the same as it was in the 20th century i.e., pathetic. Though there has been a visible change in the number of so-called gurukuls

that I would not even consider gurukul. A residential school does not become a gurukul by default if you start doing yagya every day which sadly is the case with most gurukuls right now.

The number of gurukuls in *Bharat* has increased a bit in the last decade but most of them are schools rather than gurukuls. According to a study conducted by Vediconcepts in April 2022, the total number of gurukul in *Bharat* is 4500.

<u>Who destroyed the Bharatiya gurukul system?</u>
It is not what you think. Neither the British nor earlier Muslim rulers destroyed the Gurukul Education System, though they functioned as a catalyst.

The real cause of destruction is the deviation from Vedic principles.

<u>How did the British destroy the ancient gurukul system?</u> -
Even under the Mughals, *Bharat* had around 35% of village land revenue free and this revenue was used towards running and maintenance of public services like running schools, feeding pilgrims, irrigation, common land, etc.

The British to maximize land revenues brought down common land as much as they could. There was widespread unrest during the initial periods. But to pacify the masses the British government told people that it would create an irrigation department to take care of irrigation, and an educational board to take care of education. etc.

Thus education, health, and most other things which were decentralized were brought under the centralized control of the British. This dried out the funding for common services like gurukul and put them at the helm of the government.

English Education Act 1835 and A critical study of Macaulayism-
T.B. Macaulay's "Minutes of Education" is a hotly debated topic in *Bharat*. It has been the subject of discussion as well as ridicule on WhatsApp forwards. Most people accept whatever is written in these forwards without much investigation. So, let get the balls rolling now and discuss Macaulay and his legacy that lives on in *Bharat* through his first education policy for English education in *Bharat*.

People are equally divided about whether British English education that started through Minutes of Education was good or bad for *Bharat* and *Bharatiya*s. We will try to look at both sides' arguments from a neutral point of view. But let us first discuss the phenomenon of Macaulayism that has taken root in *Bharat*.

What is Macaulayism?
Macaulayism is a term used to describe the educational policies of Thomas Macaulay, a British colonial administrator in *Bharat*. Macaulay's ideas on education were based on the belief that Western culture and values were superior to those of other cultures, and that it was, therefore, important to spread Western culture and values through education. It refers to the conscious policy of liquidating Indigenous culture through the planned substitution of the alien culture of a colonizing power via the education system.

His educational policies were highly controversial and continue to be so today. Many people argue that Macaulayism has had a negative impact on education in *Bharat*, by creating a system that favors those from privileged backgrounds and discriminates against those from less privileged backgrounds. Others argue that Macaulayism has played a positive role in education in *Bharat*, by providing opportunities for people from all backgrounds to access quality education.

Macaulay's educational policies were first implemented in 1835 when he was appointed as the head of the newly established Education Committee in *Bharat*. Macaulay's committee was tasked with designing a new system of education for *Bharat*, which would replace the traditional system that had been in place for centuries.

Macaulay's committee recommended that English should be the language of instruction in *Bharatiya* schools, and that the curriculum should be based on Western, rather than Eastern, values, and ideas. These recommendations were implemented, and English quickly became the dominant language of instruction in *Bharatiya* schools. Macaulay's educational policies were highly controversial and continue to be so today.

The debate surrounding the impact of Macaulayism on education in *Bharat* is unlikely to be resolved anytime soon. However, what is clear is that Macaulay's educational policies have had a profound and lasting impact on the education system in *Bharat* and on the lives of millions of people.

To understand these genuinely, I am going to give you some points that you can ponder, think over, and start building your fundamentals and challenge the status quo. I was surprised, fascinated and my mind burst into astonishment when I came across the below mentioned facts that have since eternity impacted our education approach.

It is also noteworthy to understand the major factors that have impacted our education structure:

#1 Muslim invasions: Our native country has witnessed a series of multiple invasions by Muslim rulers from 8th century onwards, which brought changes to the then existing brilliant education system. The rulers, while introducing their own systems of education called 'Madrasas' and also assimilated elements of *Bharatiya* knowledge, resulting in a blend of Islamic and traditional *Bharatiya* learning. It was the beginning of decline of our education backbone.

#2 Establishment of Madrasas: During the Delhi sultanate, (1206- 1526) and Mughal empire (1526-1857), madrasas (Islamic educational institutions) were established across *Bharat*. Madrasas has focused on religious studies, particularly Islamic theology, and law, and played a significant role in the education of Muslims.

#3 British East India company: Fast forwarding to 18th century, the British East India company established its presence in *Bharat* and that too widely. With the advent of British rule, they introduced their own education system, now here we need to understand the intent behind introducing such system. It was penetrated in *Bharat* primarily to serve their administrative needs and train *Bharatiya* as clerks and intermediaries. English-medium schools were established, and western style education emphasizing science, mathematics, and English language proficiency gained prominence.

#4 The charter act of 1813: The charter act of 1813 marked a significant shift in British educational policies. It was such an act that changed the entire paradigm of our system that we see now it compelled the British East India company to allocate funds for the promotion of education and teaching of European sciences in *Bharat*. This act laid the foundation for the subsequent development of education and education rule.

#5 Macaulay's Minutes (1835): Thomas Babington Macaulay minutes of 1835 outline the policy of promoting English education and the systemic decline of indigenous learning. He argued for the adoption of English as the medium of instruction, believing it would create a class of *Bharatiyas* with western knowledge and ideas.

#6 Wood's Despatch (1854): Charles wood, the president of the Board of Control for *Bharat*, issued the woods dispatch, it emphasized the need for a comprehensive education system in *Bharat*. It is recommended the establishment of schools at distinct levels, with a focus on primary education, teacher training, and the promotion of higher education.

#7 Universities act of 1857: The universities act of 1857 led to the establishment of universities in most of the major cities across *Bharat* that includes Calcutta, Bombay, and Madras. These universities became Centers for higher education and granting of degrees.

#8 Destruction of Nalanda University: Nalanda university, one of the world's oldest centers of learning, suffered significant distraction during the 12th century by invading Turkic army. This event marked the decline of ancient centers of learning in *Bharat* and contributed to the subsequent loss of Indigenous knowledge systems.

#9 post-independence reforms: After *Bharat* gained independence from British rule in 1937, the government took steps to reform the education system. The comment aimed to provide free and compulsory education, eliminate electricity, and promote scientific and technological education to support the country's development.

With all that being said, the most important aspect would be to take dig at the solutions to mold the education system for the better. How? Here it is:

Well! I wanted to draft so much more but just not possible to contain my thoughts in one-single book here for education, I should go for an entire series of upcoming books on revival of education system. I am getting a clue to draft my next work, but for now let me leave you all with quick points that you can start from right now to work together towards a change!

For Students:

Here is a 10-point course towards being a better student!

1. **Critical Thinking:** First thing first, educating yourself with degrees and information is not working anymore. You need to have an original mindset of your own. How? By developing critical (Original) mindset and not only focus on education but skills. Skills will take you to places. Do not shy away from questioning the "why" and "how" aspects. Do not accept everything taught to you before you run it through your own mental faculties.

2. **Read, Read, and Read:** Broaden your horizon and what you already know by reading voraciously. Read newspaper, materials other than textbooks, read autobiographies to understand multiple perspectives. Know who Dr. B.R Ambedkar was, Swami Vivekananda, Sarojni Naidu, Rani Laxmi Bai, The Buddha and many more. Ours is a rich culture which has numerous things to teach.

3. **Focus on holistic development:** Try to encourage a balanced approach that fosters academic excellence along with physical fitness, creativity, original thinking, and people skills development.

4. **Personalized learning:** Understand your learning style. Everyone has a unique way to understand things. Implement learning methods that cater to your individual learning styles, allowing yourself to explore your interests and strengths.

5. **Digital literacy:** Integrate technology into your daily learning habits to enhance digital skills and prepare yourself for the demands of the digital age.

6. **Inclusivity and diversity**: Promote inclusivity by creating an environment that respects and includes peer students from diverse backgrounds, abilities, and talents. Talk to students who are in sports and learn how they learn, talk to those who participate in quiz and understand how they prepare themselves.

7. **Giving more importance to knowledge than the *brands* out there:** I hope the question of choice of college v/s course in never ending. But before choosing any college, course, or city to study, it is important to look within to your strengths and areas of improvement. How to do this?

    You need to look within yourself, self-reflect in silence and get concrete answers to list out your strengths, which career would you able to sustain rather than just starting. Learn about different career opportunities and the related skills required. None of the subjects are better than any other, they are all simply different. Similarly, none of the colleges are better, they are simply different than one another.

8. **Your education is not going to end once you complete a milestone:** Yes, understand this folk, world belongs to the life-long learners and not the one who stopped learning. You need to learn and not just achieve milestones; numbers are important but not as important as learning.

9. **There are no such thing as free lunches, stop intoxication from social media and be mindful**

of what you consume: You thought social media come free of cost? Right?

Wrong! Even you term it free, it drains your time, the most valuable resource you have. There was a world without like, comment, and share and it worked. Still, it will! No doubt in that. Be mindful of where your spend your attention, it is very precious. The next time you hear something free, look beyond the obvious cost such as time, and the opportunity costs.

10. **Choose your network wisely:** No, I am not talking about Vodafone or reliance or airtel, I am talking about those with whom you spend most time with. Your peers, seniors, elders. You will realize, we are a reflection of the sum total of the persons with whom we engage regularly. Be ever ready to gel with the learned or at least who can contribute to our learning and also gel with those whom you could contribute towards getting better.

Congratulations!! You are a better student now!

For Teachers:
Here is a 5-point course towards being a better teacher!

Teaching like any other is a skill-based job or shall I say one of the noblest jobs. Teaching requires skills. With it comes responsibility. Not everyone who has scored and studied well can teach and vice-versa. You have a great responsibility of the future, much of the upcoming depends on how you are able to curate and develop the young minds. Do not underestimate your jobs, you are building our nation's future, and you should be proud of the work you do.

1. **Continuous professional development:** Attend regular training and workshops to help yourselves update

your own teaching methodologies and enhance your subject expertise.

2. **Reduced administrative burden:** Well! This is something for the authorities and the policy makes to do, but on your part, streamline administrative tasks and paperwork to allow yourselves room for more time for lesson planning, student engagement, and individual student support. Do you feel burdened up? Why not speak and work with the management to chalk out this problem. I am sure it can be worked out.

Whether it is you or the college and school authorities, student development is the pen ultimate goal. So why not focus more on teaching and developing students. As a solution, you can look to integrate technology for the administrative tasks to buy more time for learning.

3. **Encourage creativity and innovation:** How? By practicing creativity. You need to foster an environment that encourages students to develop innovative learning practices and simultaneously utilize creative teaching tools to engage students effectively.

4. **Supportive work culture:** Have you tried asking for support? Enhance your morale by encouraging collaboration, recognizing efforts both of the teachers and management, and providing resources for their professional growth.

5. **Teacher evaluation and feedback:** While feedback is a fear inducing process as perceived by most, yet it a fantastic tool for improvement. How do sports person improve, what do coaches do to the greats like Virat and Rohit Sharma?

It is the feedback loop that helps them improve their game. Establish a fair and comprehensive teacher evaluation system to encourage accountability and improvement. If not, participate and ask for feedback yourselves. You will love it.

Congratulations!! You are a better Teacher now!

For Parents:
Here is a 5-point course towards being a better parent!
1. **Parental involvement:** You need to get is straight. Just like any other skill, parenting is a skill that you need to learn, Encourage yourself and neighborhood to actively participate in child's education, such as attending parent-teacher meetings and engaging in school activities.

2. **Awareness of child's progress:** Collect regular updates about your child's academic progress, strengths, weaknesses, and suggestions for improvement. Allow him or her to make mistakes, it is ok to make few, you have made yours. Monitoring is your role but policing them for everything they do is not what is required. Encourage your child to participate in decision making process about his or her career.

3. **Parent education programs:** Attend workshops and sessions for parents to understand the best ways to support their child's learning at home. Yes you need to it, it is your child and your duty. Sounds like too much! No, it is not once you experience the joy of doing it. And when you see your child blossoming, it will be worth it!

4. **Emotional support:** Promote parent-child communication and provide guidance on fostering emotional well-being in your children. For this you need to create an atmosphere of transparent communication.

Even if they make mistakes, score less or any other stuff, just let it be! It is not the end of the world; they are learning, and mistakes are an essential part! Allow some room for error, and once your encounter mistakes, do not jump in the conclusion.

You help them build their character, and the way you treat them now, they will treat others the same. Do not create an opaque room where they start hiding things because you do not listen.

5. **Collaborative decision-making:** Engage your children in discussions at home, major decision-making processes to ensure their perspectives are considered and they feel empowered.

Congratulations!! You are a better parent now!

ERA 4

Are we Right?

- **The Prakriti effects: Cost of Progress**
- **Am I Really Free? – A Poem**
- **The Green Currency**

The Prakriti effects: Cost of Progress

I could not have chosen a better day to write about *The Prakriti Effects*. So, I am standing at post-Diwali day, 8 20 AM watching a bit of news with my **_"Green"_** tea. This word green has a lot to say than just to be a color, which we will gradually unfold.

All Right! It is time for us to get a bit uncomfortable with some grueling questions, but I will ask it and not only ask, but we will also together find solutions.

Who have you blamed for the conditions of the environment? The Factories or the cars? If you live in Delhi-NCR, the easy target for blame must be Punjab? And which political party have you chosen to blame for the depleting environment condition? Is it BJP, Congress, The INDIA Alliance, or AAP?

It has done this, *they* have done that, *government* did not do this, and *they* didn't implement ban on firecrackers, *kids* don't listen, or *people* don't care about environment?

I am fed up with listening to such comments which serve no purpose. When are we going to stop the blame game? These all are the statements that shows our mindset and what we have given in return to our planet whom we gift the title of *"Mother Earth."* So, this is how we treat our mother? Certainly, it seems so.

AQI was 999 at multiple places in New Delhi, post Diwali day. Do you want to still blame someone now? Luckily, it had rained few days before Diwali celebrations that was a huge relief, nature tried to calm itself down. Prior to this, it was Punjab and the farmers under the hammer. But we are not going to be fortunate every time.

Let me get it straight of the bat and ask few final questions here-

- Who has polluted the planet?
- What have **WE** done to do some good for the environment?
- And if the above seems too much work, what habits have *we* mended in order to stop harming the environment?

Forget the big words like *global warming* and *artificial rain*, and bla bla bla! Let us keep it simple, I am not an environment activist nor an advocate for environment, but at the basic level, yes! I do care for how I treat my environment around me. Let us start by first accepting the fact that it is **YOU, Me,** and **US,** who have together done this to the environment. It is **US** who drove that car instead of finding opportunities for public transport. It is **US** who placed our comfort more prior than the environment.

It is **US** who did not find that dustbin and threw the leftovers just like that. It is *you* and *me* who loved the joy of sound and smoke from firecrackers, more than our surroundings. It is again *you* and *me* who watched news repeatedly and played the blame game. It is again *US*, who chose to use plastic because it was convenient and cheap no matter what it does to the environment and the stray animals around us.

Do not worry I am not going to present any WHO study data to show how many deaths occurred or what % of people died of Asthma or may be what are the impacts of depleting environment. We all are *informed citizens* in the digital world, or should I call it *over-informed* that we have kept on amassing information and stopped acting. We all are the experts, and we can talk endless on topics on environment, but I doubt how good we are in acting on what we know.

It was again you and me who did not even spare the rivers and threw our left over from worshiping in the streams in the name of purification and culture or may be to get rid of what was left.

And even if we did not do it ourselves, we didn't stop others when we saw it live. We did not educate our near and dear ones and those *"Massoom" (Innocent)* beings to stop harming the environment.

It was you and me who did not chose to take steps to clean or get the surroundings clean because we thought it was government who would do the cleaning.

It was you and me who honked and kept on honking despite the vivid scene that you cannot fly on the road over the vehicle in front of you. It was us whose actions towards caring for environment depend on whether someone is watching or not or to better put as "Who`s watching."

First thing first, let us bring the locus of focus to **US**, and what **can** we do and also what we should not? Let us *stop the talking* and do the *doing* now? And if we belong to the mindset - *"what will happen by only our efforts, look at the people out there?* Let me answer it straight away from the bat –

Every individual action, no matter how small, collectively contributes to a healthier environment because it was, and it is our actions that have depleted the nature and natural resources.

I have authored a poem or may be a rhythmic story for us all which should be apt here before we move ahead to find the solutions.

Am I Really Free?

Everyone celebrated the joy of freedom, yet no one asked me,
Am I really free?

I am proud of those who waved my glory on the moon,
To Know now my identity in the world, my faith deepened,

I was incredibly happy when the heroes showed bravery,
Some sweated, some dedicated blood and some whole and soul.
I was freed, but is this what I had to see?
Others had ruled over me, braves fought then,
But I thought, am I really free?

Everyone gave the status of mother, but did you give the respect?
You parted the water of my rivers, silenced the voice of the weak.
You parted the land, the air, and the Himalayas, yet you have not come out of your greed,
Your heart was still not content, so colors became the crown your head,
Muslims turned green, and Hindus turned red,
I did not do such things.

Even then when your heart was not full, you have come upon innocent animals,
You made cow a Hindu and a Muslim became the goat,
Am I really free? So, what wrong I thought.

When the demons robbed your mother, she was saved by the heroes.
When it is you who rob, share, and cut me off your red,
Now who will save me?

Why did you then give me the status of a mother?
When such things had to be done, greed was the only thing to do,
I was very well looted in the hands of others; my loved ones are not ashamed of.

Every day a daughter's honor was robbed, no one's blood boiled,
Everyone kept watching, they said they won't let that happen anymore.
Then came another news, and the daughters were auctioned,
The world said again, "we will not let this happen anymore."
Wasn't that daughter yours?

Mother saw herself being robbed of clothes,
yet we said – "we will not let that happen anymore."
The mothers said that they would not let this happen anymore.

Now with these empty promises, the mother will not hope, hence, I asked, am I really free?

Everyone took advantage of me, you did not know the meaning of mother,
My eyes bow in shame, sin on my land, whenever it happened.
Come on, now you celebrate your freedom, be happy in every situation,
You have become free, but you have not made me welcome.

So, the way you parted colors into Hindu and Muslims,
Now divide the tricolor, saffron to Hindus and green to Muslims,
Left that is the middle white, cover me with a veil to make me bright.

Those whose blood does not boil, now listen to my heart,
My soil is great, it is called *Hindustaan*, living here is a blessing,
It has been nurtured by heroes, which is called *Bharat Mahaan*

For me, everyone is equal, braves are no more now,
Seeing the loot, the mother's is shaking, she wonders how,

The blood no longer boils, the animals have better
understanding than humans.

Now the mother will explain to you herself,
and listen carefully, this mother will not come again.

Now listen carefully —

Now you see my ugly form, show me how much power you
got,
Now bare these storms, make the walls enough strong,
Who can bear this form of mine,
Now you part the rising waves of the sea,
How will you part the shaking earth, let me see.

I will engulf everyone, will not discriminate against anyone,
Tell me how many castes are you now?

Part my swollen volcanoes now, let's see how hot you are,
You talk about cleaning my rivers, I have given you holy
Ganga and Yamuna,
Why even did this happen today?
Ganga removes the sin of all, and you talk about purifying it,
is that how good you are?

You have done this to her, tears come out of her now,
That's what entered your houses, roads and hospitals that
make you wonder how,
Now you part these tears too, I did not teach this art,
Show your skills to part, let me see what you have now,

I taught love and righteousness, you have sinned,
you have committed unrighteousness,
and then you talk about freedom tree,
have you ever set me free?

Think now, will you be able to win over motherhood if you
don't change your path,
So mother, she will no longer be called mother, *Kaali* came to
my dream,
She said – "tomorrow I will come again and take everyone
along with my stream,
There is still time to set me free.

Tomorrow when the *Kaali* comes, don't say –
Mother, Why didn't you slap me, when I didn't listen to you?
why didn't you explain to me,

I will have only one thing to say-
Why didn't you set me free?

It took me a number of years to be mindful of my habits that impacted the environment negatively. Being a nature lover, I was unaware, and was only on the receiving side of the gifts of nature, but over the years I realized that when we talk of love it has to be both ways, and love is incomplete without *care*. We owe our care for nature and the environment as it needs us the way we need nature for us.

Let *talk* and "**act**" on solutions now.

We have had enough information and discussions about all the steps that are possible. Now the time has come to actually start taking actions rather than talking. If you have already started to take actions, please give a pat at your back, and start sensitizing others too! An interesting example from a recent campaign, of The times of India's Unstoppable 21 under twenty-one, it had the mention of a young author who had written more than 11 books at the age of just fourteen, all on environment.

Karnav Rastogi, has taken up the issue of climate change in his eleven books. What fascinated me with him writing was how he turned reading into action. So, with every book that he sold it had a seed packet along with green pledges! And that to me is a "wow" idea!

Are you ready for the actionable solutions?

Here are those:

1. **As the very first solution**, we need to DECIDE and PLEDGE that we will CARE for environment right from NOW or NEVER attitude even if it means sacrificing a bit of our comfort.

2. **As the second solution**, we need to understand when we talk of environment the word *"**Sustainable.**"* This will be pivotal and should be the core value that we want to achieve through our actions. It must be a lifestyle.

So, what is *Sustainable or Sustainability*?

The term sustainability is derived from the Latin word sustinere. "To sustain" can mean to maintain, support, uphold, or endure. It is the ability to continue over an extended period of time. It further means meeting our own needs without compromising the ability of future generations to meet their own needs. In addition to natural resources, we also need social and economic resources. Sustainability is not just environmentalism. Embedded in most definitions of sustainability we also find concerns for social equity and economic development, but here we are going to restrict ourselves too environmental.

In the past, sustainability referred to environmental sustainability. It meant using natural resources so that people in the future could continue to rely on them in the long term. The concept of sustainability, or *Nachhaltigkeit* in German, goes back to Hans Carl von Carlowitz (1645–1714), and applied to forestry. We would now call this sustainable forest management. He used this term to mean the long-term responsible use of a natural resource.

In his 1713 work Silvicultura oeconomica, he wrote that "the highest art/science/industriousness [...] will consist in such a conservation and replanting of timber that there can be a continuous, ongoing and sustainable use". The shift in use of "sustainability" from preservation of forests (for future wood production) to broader preservation of environmental resources (to sustain the world for future generations) traces to a 1972 book by Ernst Basler, based on a series of lectures at M.I.T.

The terms sustainability and sustainable development are closely related. In fact, they are often used to mean the same thing. Both terms are linked with the "three dimensions of sustainability" concept. One distinction is that sustainability is a general concept, while sustainable development can be a policy or organizing principle. We will leave this for the government and support them whenever required to achieve the goals.

Sustainable development has two linked goals. It aims to meet human development goals. It also aims to enable natural systems to provide the natural resources and ecosystem services needed for economies and society. The concept of sustainable development has come to focus on economic development, social development, and environmental protection for future generations.

3. ***As the third solution, educating ourselves with daily-life doable actions towards sustainability***, which I am going to list out here.

- ***Stop being unmindful:*** The basic and the most effective. Don't litter, make efforts to reach out to dustbins, for heaven's sake please stop throwing leftovers into rivers. Rivers are our mothers; they deserve a better treatment than these. Stop honking please. And to all the cracker lovers, please stop it. It is not doing any good for us, there are other ways to celebrate. You yourself will not like it when your loved ones including your parents would be hospitalized of choking. It is enough.

- ***Green Transportation:*** Do opt for eco-friendly transportation methods like public transport, carpooling, cycling, walking, Consider electric. I understand every time it is not possible, but if we find opportunities it becomes possible. Sacrifice a bit of comfort but I must tell you it is worth it, I personally purchased an electric two-wheeler, and I am loving it for its green effect and *wallet effect,* no fuel price to pay at all except charging the battery which is negligible.

- ***Plant Trees:*** Do you remember Nimbooz, or Ambuj from the *ERA – The Mindset Reboot, Sid`s dear friend,* I recently thanked him for taking me to a nursery for the first time in my lifetime. I pledged that day, that for all my gifting and decorative items, I am going to visit nurseries. Trees absorb carbon dioxide and release oxygen. Participate in tree planting initiatives to contribute to reforestation and decorate your homes with *"the green."*

- ***Proper Waste Disposal:*** Dispose of waste responsibly and mindfully.

- ***Conserve Energy:*** Turn off lights and appliances when not in use, switch to energy-efficient appliances, and consider using renewable energy sources. Have you started using solar power yet? Why not start by setting up a small solar arrangement to light your room and charge your gadgets and laptops? I have planned for it and soon I will have it in a month while I am writing this. My plan is to make one room run on solar energy and then scaling it to other rooms. That sounds fun to me!

And here is fun fact. One of Sid`s dear friend Ankit who expertise in Solar Power is going to help me get my room solar powered, also has a key role to play in charting Sid`s 2nd innings later in the *ERA – The Finale: Towards Actions.*

Some of the below solutions have been offered by my dear friend "Technology" and in particular, "ChatGPT" and it is not that bad, I must say.

- ***Reduce, Reuse, recycle:*** Seems bookish, and theoretical? Yes, it does but this is real. Let us decide to minimize waste by adopting the mantra of reducing consumption, reusing items, or purchasing items that can be reused, denying from single plastic use, at least we can carry water bottles, even this is going to help save environment, and recycling materials whenever possible.

- ***Sustainable Shopping:*** Choose products with minimal packaging, support companies with environmentally friendly practices, and consider second-hand or sustainable goods.

- ***Green Technology:*** Embrace and support technological advancements that contribute to environmental sustainability, such as renewable energy technologies.

- ***Water Conservation:*** Use water wisely, fix leaks, and consider installing water-saving appliances.

- **Support Environmental Policies:** Advocate for and support policies that promote environmental conservation and sustainable practices at local, national, and global levels.

4. As the fourth solution, it requires sensitizing and educating people around us.
- Raise awareness about environmental issues to friends, family, and your community.
- Participate in environmental organizations and initiatives.
- Stay informed about environmental policies and regulations, and advocate for change.

Before I forget to mention, let me bring out one brilliant step by the government towards sustainability through education. The home ministry, through its think tank NIDM (National institute of Disaster Management) has built a network of 260 universities and colleges to initiate undergraduate and PhD courses in topics related to climate change and disaster risk reduction (DRR).

It is a part of PM Modi's 10-point agenda for DRR where, as part of the Sendai Framework, India has committed to bring down disaster deaths and economic losses by 2030. The networks of universities built by the home ministry is a part of government's DRR agenda no.6 to meet SDGs - Sustainable Development Goals by promoting education, innovative technology, research, capacity development and contributing to decision-making for addressing local risks and needs of the most vulnerable.

Globally, there are such networks of universities and institutions working in the field of DRR but in India, this is the first of its kind where DRR has been included in UG and PG programs.

OMG, that sounds a lot of work, isn't?

Now, what happens if we don't take practice sustainability?

Let us get through a framework of questions to understand this.

Do we risk losing our *health*?
YES

Is it a *demanding work* to care for environment?
NO

When is the right time to *start* to care?
NOW

What is the first step towards practice sustainability?
Decide to pledge that we together will care.

Will something change if I start caring?
YES, Certainly

Why Should I care?
Why Not? We all owe to the nature.

From where can I start?
Purchase few potted plants for each room today.

Plants don't come for free; can the author of the book gift me?
YES, Certainly

(Please feel free to write to me with your complete address and I will certainly get it delivered, the only ask will be to share a picture with the plant once you receive it.)

Meet me at the above scan!

The Green Currency

Yes, we are happy about the progress and growth that we have made. But the progress required a *cost.* In which currency we have paid the cost? The cost has been both for our ACTIONS and INACTIONS too.

The currency included compromising the *Green Area.* It included polluting the air around us with more cars, and industries. *Amazing* visuals of boat floating in front of the Red fort in New Delhi, the capital of India recently, to uncertain rain. Unbearable air around us to river turned into drain. I am certainly not against growth. But more than growth I am interested in *sustainable growth,* which includes not paying a heavy, irrecoverable cost, but something that we can afford, and we certainly can't afford to lose and deplete nature.

Have we blamed nature and the almighty as to why is he or she punishing the innocent? It is us who have punished our fellow beings with our mindless actions and sometimes deliberate actions too. Do our actions depend on who is watching us? Or is it the fight between what is right vs when to act right?

Whatever it may be, the time has come to revive the *Green Currency – Nature.*

This currency is far more valuable than any other, why? Because it keeps you healthy, it keeps the environment being hereditable by our coming generation. If you have to keep something as property for the young ones, what can be better than handing over a clean environment to live in. So let me put up this way -

Are we right?

ERA 5

The Shakti

- **The Feminine Energy - Why our world can't exist without "*शक्ति.*"**
- **How to build better "tables" and "seats" for Women**
- **The Gangafication | Menstruation & Periods | Purification of Perception**
- **Leadership Lessons from "*शक्ति.*"**

The Feminine Energy - Why our world can't exist without "शक्ति."

An interesting contemporary anecdote during Obama's second US presidential campaign reflects the potential synergy of *Purush* & *Prakriti* even when we see them as male and female energies. Barack Obama & his wife Michelle, on the campaign trail in Michigan, stopped for a meal at a local diner in a remote area. An attendant came up to Michelle and whispered something to her.

Wow! Exclaimed Michelle and followed the attendant towards the back office of the dinner where the owner met up with her. After 30 minutes, she came back laughing and beaming. Obama asked her, "What happened, where did you go?"

"I was invited by the owner of the diner to meet him in his office. He was in college with me." And she added smilingly, "He used to be my boyfriend."

Obama wittingly replied, "That's great, if you had married him, you could have owned this nice diner in remote Michigan."

Michelle smiled and replied, *"Or he could have been US President."*

Wow! What an answer dear Michelle, you won our hearts. Michelle played a significant role in his presidential campaign as a charismatic source of inspiration, adding value to the campaign.

Moving on, while undergoing Diwali celebrations in India and across the world, Lord return of lord Ram is much praised, and we celebrate the victory of good over evil. I personally love lord Ram for the qualities that he is praised for as the epitome of sacrifice and great characteristics.

But there is one thing here, that I found intriguing enough to share with you.

A century old shrine to Sita that celebrates single motherhood exists in Yavatmal district of Maharashtra, which is not only unique in its reverence of a mother's fortitude but also as a one of its kind places of worship where idols of lord Sita and her twins Luv and Kush stand with Ram and Lakshman omnipresence.

The Sanghatana (that takes care of the temple) or the organization's founder, Sharad Joshi is credited with highlighting the uniqueness of the shrine in 2001 after being moved by the portrayal of Sita as a single mother and raising her sons to be the deserving inheritors of Ram's legacy. He saw this as a symbolizing the strength of the mothers. Now it is indeed an inspiration to all single mothers, particularly widows in farming community.

It makes me wonder why we have been raised with this thought that females are secondary. Since history, women have been portrayed as dependent, victimized and what not? Why is a male a dominant gender? And whenever there is a female coming in, they receive a special recognition for doing what a male does without recognition.

You take the above example of Michelle Obama, and the answer that she gave after she was shown "What she could have been if she had married the other guy." Disapproving of this statement, she answered "What the other man could have been if she had married the other guy." And next, the Diwali celebrations where Lord Ram is the spotlighted being and Sita is left far behind.

It might be challenging to hear this as we have been so used to the facts and I may invite few critics with the above lines, but this is what is true. Isn't it?

Let me share one more anecdote to reinforce what I intend to say.

This anecdote comes from our CJI (Chief Justice of India), D Y Chandrachud, in a recent interview when he was asked about gender justice in SC. He answered by referring to a fascinating reply by late Justice Ginsburg of the nine-member US Supreme Court.

She was asked, "how many women ought to be in the US Supreme Court," to which she said, "**Nine**, i.e., all of them." "After all, we have had all-male Supreme Courts for a long time, why should an all-women court surprise us?"

Amazing indeed, so the first thing first. It is the time we *start accepting* that women have been treated unfairly. Once we accept this, half the battle is already won, then comes the solution which we will for sure discus in the coming phrases. I promise coming up lines shall make you uncomfortable, but I will portray the truth as it is. So, get ready to read truth as it is and get uncomfortable for the good.

How to build better "tables" and "seats" for Women

Here I am going to take the help from a ted talk by Lilly Singh, where she narrates how women and girls are conditioned to believe success is "a seat at the table." Creator, actor, and author Lilly Singh thinks we need to build a better table. In this hilarious, incisive talk, Singh traces the arc of her career from up-and-coming YouTuber to history-making late-night talk show host, offering four ways to build a more inclusive society

where girls are encouraged and empowered to do remarkable things.
You too can watch it @ https://www.youtube.com/watch?v=9EBkS2kE7uk, but as of now let us be lost in reading.

She discusses about the invisible gatekeeper called **culture**. Earlier we read in the earlier sections about how culture can protect us and has made us unique but there also exists its close brother which acts as its rival and curbs our growth. Culture has two forms. We must understand the correct form or otherwise it can be double edged sword.

Which culture to fuel, a *Culture* that inspires and fuels growth or a culture that acts as a gate keeper and says, "You can`t do this as this has never been done" or it says, "this has only been done by the men out there, don't dare to do so."

Here I also want to highlight all women who misunderstands freedom and thinks in the negative. What is right is right, (discussed in detail in the last ERA-The finale). Being right is a gender-neutral thing. And what I mean by this is right next here.

Once on a cozy evening, Noida, a place in Delhi NCR, while munching my evening snacks close to 5 30 in the eve, what it was not less than a movie scene and I got a firsthand experience. I saw a quarrel going on between a cab driver and a female passenger, where she was not ready to give the legal fare of around Rs. 220 maybe because she thought she could use her female power to not pay the driver his fees.

When the driver couldn't get his fees politely after requesting multiple times, he called people standing there to intervene to which she exclaimed that the driver was misbehaving with her and slapped him publicly. What of hell? Is this what we mean by women empowerment that it doesn't even care to differentiate between what is right and what is wrong.

What happened after the slap is much more interesting to me and raises a lot of questions. After two slaps to the driver face, the girl aged in her mid-twenty`s started dominating the driver, not ready to pay the bill, to which the driver replied with a tight slap. Ahh! I might be a little jarring to audiences, I know.

Not able to ***"mis-use women empowerment"*** to save her Rs. 220 bills, she had no other choice to flee the place as the matter worsened. She at last didn't pay her bill, the driver had to go back empty handed but gained appreciation in public to how he responded to the girls wicked act.

Well! Who was right here?

The girl who didn't pay the bill, *mis-used women empowerment* gifting tight slaps to the driver for demanding something legal.

Or the driver who went first the calm way, but to save his money requested but then to save his pride after being slapped handed over the *return gift* immediately.

Well men may support men here that he did the right thing by answering with slap, women may say that the driver didn't do the right thing. Conflict. The reason for me to write this is because, I want to highlight here that there is a dire need for an understanding of the clear meaning of Women empowerment by both men and women.

Let me ask all the women and girls, "have you ever been a victim of the gatekeepers, like patriarchal mindset or the culture anywhere in your life? At office, home or anywhere? It may be as small as not being allowed to go out with friends although your little bro was free to go. Or wear a certain type of clothe as *the culture* wanted you to wear?

Simplest can be, to be told to clean the house and cook food, while you saw your male counterpart, your brother could play and not help in household chores because simply he is a male and males don't work at home.

If the answer is yes, keep on reading, if the answer is no and you never faced discrimination, say a big "Thank you" to your elders for raising you up in a healthy environment.

Why every time a girl must cook? Cooking is a life skill, right? Are skills also a gender specific? Surprising and hats off to the gatekeepers.

Now similar question for men and boys too which might be a bit uncomfortable for many readers, but that will not refrain me from portraying the truth - "have you ever been a victim of women empowerment?"

If someone had asked me, if would say a definite and a big, big **yes**. Why, when, and how is a story for some other time but yes definitely, I have faced the negative effects of women empowerment that certainly exists and cripples our surroundings. And here I am not talking about not getting seat in a metro train when I am tired and young girls who ask the elderly to get up just because those are the seats reserved for females. Hahahah!

I will get back to this in detail in the last sections, "Era – The Finale | Towards Actions." But for now, let us go back to the ted talk which we were discussing.

Lily`s, goal was always a seat at the table like every one of us. We are grinding to grab a seat at the table, right? Be it a software engineer or that Doctor or that lawyer. Or you are aspiring to be an IPS. It's what women and we all are conditioned to believe success is by the so-called *Culture*, the gate keeper? When I was being considered for marriage, I was surprised at the first questions that the potential family asked, "the pay cheque." Oh! am I product with a price tag. I could keep hearing, phrases "o that guy with Rs. 25 L or that 36 L Package."

Isn't earning supposed to be a something personal unlike in marriage where it is quite public. I did face questions like how much money is there in your bank account? Moving on, when the chair doesn't fit, when it doesn't reach the table, when it's wobbly, when it's full of splinters, we don't have the luxury of fixing it or finding another one. But we try anyway.

Women specially take on that responsibility, and they shoulder that burden. She has been fortunate enough to sit at a few seats, at a few different tables. And what she learned is, when you get the seat, trying to fix the seat won't fix the problem.

Why? Because the *"table"* was never built for them in the first place. The solution?

Build better tables.

I would like to present to you a set of guidelines as lily describes which she very eloquently calls: "How to Build a Table that Doesn't Suck." Sounds very literal, right? Hahahha! Now, right off the bat, let me tell you, this assembly is going to take more than one person or group of people. It's going to take everyone. Are you ready? Should we dive in? Let's do it.

1. **Don't weaponize gratitude**. Now, don't get me wrong, gratitude is a great word. It's nice, it's fluffy, a solid eleven points in Scrabble. However, let's be clear. Although gratitude feels warm and fuzzy, it's not a form

of currency. Women are assigned 10 percent more work and spend more time on unrewarded, unrecognized, and non-promotable tasks.

What this means is all the things' men don't want to do are being handed to women, and a lot of those things include things that advance inclusivity, equity, and diversity in the workplace. So, hear me when I say, a woman shouldn't be grateful to sit at a table. **She should be "paid" to sit at a table.** Especially ones she helped build. And a woman's seat shouldn't be threatened if she doesn't seem "grateful" enough.

In other words, corporations, this step involves a woman doing a job and being paid in money, opportunity, and promotion, not just gratitude. And women -- yes, go ahead, live it up, live your life. And women she further exclaims, "a moment of real talk, trust me, I've been there, and I know it's so tough, but we must understand and remember that being grateful and being treated fairly are not mutually exclusive. I can be grateful but still know exactly what I deserve. And that's the way to do it."

2. **Invest in potential.** When investing in women, don't invest in the "extra" time slot. Invest in empowering something different. Invest in a new voice. Give them the support they actually need. Cultural change takes time and money. Heck, it took her grandfather 25 years to see that she was worthy of more. So, a true investment is one that *values potential over proof*.

Because so often that proof doesn't exist for women. Not because they aren't qualified, but because they haven't been given the opportunity. In other words, if you're trying to be inclusive, don't give someone new a seat made of straw until they prove they deserve a better one.

Don't hold something called a "prove it again" bias, which requires less privileged people to constantly keep proving themselves, even though men tend to get by on just their potential.

Give them a seat that they can thrive in, that they can do the job you hired them to do in. Allow them to contribute to the table, and they will make it better.

3. **Make space for Women.** it is pure common sense, you know, for every three men at a table, there's only one place setting for a woman. People are so used to more men showing up that they plan for it. There's an extra seat in the corner, there's a steak under the heat lamp. When more men show up, the table gets longer. But when that extra RSVP is a woman, more often than not she's encouraged to compete against the only other woman that was invited to the table.

Next time when you sit a table do watch out for the number of female vs male sitting, whether it be a team meeting, a get together, a group discussion in a college or serious business meet. You will realize and then there are some tagged professions that belong to men and those that belong to women.

Instead, we need to build multiple seats for multiple women, not just one or two, so that women are not sitting on top of each other's laps, fighting for one meal. We already know that more diverse teams perform better. A recent study shows that corporations that have more gender diversity on their executive teams, were 25 percent more likely to experience above average profitability. And more racially diverse companies had 36 percent more profit.

The Organization and particularly the learning & development team with which I currently work at the time of writing this piece, it has eleven members who are female, me being the only male. And what is normal is the team really thrives, there is nothing wrong in that. No politics, no comparison and we work in unison.

And as we move up the ladder, there are budding and enterprising females giving their professional and personal best. I consider myself fortunate enough to work in such an organization and also all-women learning team. Although I refrain from the clothes and make-up gossip, Hahaha!

But on a serious note, there is so much to learn from them as to how they manage their work and also the tasks that *gatekeeper culture* has mandated for them without a vivid appreciation and recognition.

So really, no matter how you look at it, it's time to build longer tables and more seats. And Lily wants to say something, and she wants to admit something, she wants to be vulnerable for a second. Because she has fallen victim to this so many times, and women, let me know if you've experienced this.

We have to get rid of the **scarcity mindset and champion each other**, you know, because we have learned what's the better win? "**Me**" sitting at a table or "**us**" sitting at a table? Don't be convinced to fight for one spot. Instead fight for multiple spots. Let her lead by example right now and say, *"I know there's many other women that are going to come on this stage, and I hope they all nail it, and I will be cheering you all on because we can all win. And I'm going to be your biggest cheerleader when you're up here."*

4. **It's time to upgrade the table talk:** Now, stories make the world go around. You thought it had something to do the solar system? Joke's on you, it's stories. Stories are how we understand ourselves, how we understand others and how we understand the world. And the most important stories are those we see in the media.

   Because we've seen time and time that they control the narrative and impact culture. For example, the most recent, the west Asia crisis, how Hamas, Isarael & Palestine being projected every now and then preceded by Canada India truss where the media and countries tried to control the narratives.

   Abduction by Hamas of more than two hundred nationals were subdued and defending of its own territory against terrorism was magnified as inhuman.

   Don't be a victim of narratives. Instead try to *"look beyond the obvious"* vividly discussed in the *"ERA 3- The Buddha Way and ERA 4 – Are we right?"* earlier, in this work.

   When it comes to genre, you can argue that certain genres have certain target demographics. When it comes to the world news, the target demographic is the world, and we know half of the world is female. Yet women and girls make up only a quarter of the people interviewed or that the news is even about in the first place.

   Instead, when it comes to issues that impact women, women not only need to be included in the coverage, but they also need to be driving those stories and dimensionalizing their own experience. Inviting everyone in on the table talk isn't just a nice gesture. It makes for better, more productive, smarter conversation with more than one point of view. And that's how you get better.

So, this all sounds like a lot of work. And it is. But Lily tells us why it's necessary and worth it. To be honest, this is about so much more than just women in the workplace. In fact, she could produce many more guidelines across many other industries. This is about creating a world where half of the population can thrive.

You see, because the work women do today can create a world where future generations of girls can have equitable access and opportunity. And here's the best part. Are you ready for it? Everyone reading today, all the men, the women, everyone in between, the big companies, the small ones, the media outlets, the people that snuck into the back, all of you, you can help create this future.

A future where women have longer tables and more seats that actually work instead of fighting for a seat at the old ones that don't. A future where everyone is seated at the table equally. And a future where being assigned female at birth is not a disappointment or a disadvantage, because girls are encouraged, empowered, and expected to do wonderful things. And together with Lily, I can't wait to make that a reality.

The Gangafication | Menstruation & Periods | Purification of Perception

All Right! Are we ready for the taboo talk?

Or should I ask *why* is it still a taboo talk? Yes, menstruation or better known as periods. The moment this topic comes into picture we start shying away, right? This might make you feel uncomfortable, but it can save millions of girls and can help preserve their mental and physical health as well.

And you know where I got this idea from to write about such a thoughtfully tabooed topic. I had never decided, nor I had the courage to write about periods but my visit to a temple in northeast which was further reinforced by a conversation with my mentor changed my perspective towards this "beautiful" natural phenomenon.

I was researching about the subjects that I could write on with Ms. Sangeeta Sharma, the Director of Modern Public School in a small town in Jharkhand, where I did my schooling from. She has been pivotal in shaping my thought process and what I am today and one of the most influential women after my mom. I asked her," What topics would you choose to write and *why* if you were about to draft a book?"

She is 64 Years old but sounds much younger like a 25-year-old beauty. I thought she would talk about education being an educationist or women empowerment but to my sheer surprise, she exclaimed. "The first thing that I would love to write will be about periods."

Imagine a 64-year-old director of a school talking to one of her ex-students i.e., me, about such a topic with great ease. I vividly remember her trying to explain the *why* behind her thought. She described how still we live in a hypocritical society and people just love *talking* rather than *doing*. And in this case, people even shy away from talking.

Let me ask you and it hardly matters whether you are a man or a woman reading this, aren't we all a result of periods that our mother`s went through? We all exist because our mothers underwent such a process of purification what I term here as *"The Gangafication."*

Then Ms. Sharma, went on to explain how it affects the mental and physical health of girls not being able to get any support for such an important aspect of their body's event. "There are still places in interiors where girls are kept separate during the cycle and are considered untouchables. We may have grown as shown but the reality sets in once you start such a topic among even the educated masses."

Who's the culprit? Let us explore this purification process together!

I remember while I was in this conversation with her, I discussed how once I had the luck of visiting one of the most pure and beautiful temples in Guwahati in Assam in the year 2022, for a training assignment. I love my country India for a number of reasons, one of the prominent being our **Culture, the true culture.** India is a diverse cultural combination, where every Indian celebrates a sizable number of festivals all year round. Each festival is unique in its way.

When I was in the temple, I heard it the very first time that the people were about to celebrate an upcoming festival then which was quite unique to me. *The celebration of periods or the menstruation.*

The process represents the transition from girlhood to womanhood and is one of the most important aspects of it. This transformation used to be marked by the elders claiming that the girl was now as fertile as nature. On the other hand, Menstruation has also become taboo over time, and myths arose from half-baked stories, most untrue.

A menstruation celebration, first moon party, or period party, celebrates menstruation. Distinct cultures and communities across the globe celebrate Menarche (first period). This practice is followed by Apache, Ojibwe, and Hupa tribal communities from various parts of North America, Ulithi tribe from South Pacific region, Japan, Africa, and India, among others.

For example, in 2020, Parents writer Christine Michel Carter researched the celebration of first moon parties in the Black community in the United States. Most girls get their first menstrual cycle between 12 and 13 years old, according to The American College of Obstetricians and Gynecologists. The age of menstruation onset is slightly younger for Black girls due to health disparities, increased material hardship, and levels of stress. For Black girls, the first moon party is a rite of passage that instills values, principles, and knowledge of a young girls' self.

Next, Apache Sunrise Dance Ceremony, is a celebration of menarche by the Apache tribal community in Arizona and Mexico region. The community members and leaders assist the family in conducting this ceremony. The community starts preparing for this ceremony months before. A day prior to the ceremony, the girl takes a sweat bath, meanwhile the male relatives and a healer make the items that will be required during the ceremony. In the evening, these items are presented to the girl.

The ceremony takes place over a period of four-days and in eight stages. During this ceremony, the girl wears the traditional Apache attire and dances, which signifies female strength. The friends and family also participate and sing traditional songs and the girl also receives a massage and the ceremonial blessing from the traditional healer and other people.

Festival of Ambubachi Tradition, belief, culture, and spirituality these four-terms are linked to a religious festival called "Ambubachi". In Sanskrit, 'Ambuvaci' is known as 'Goddess,' from which the local Assamese word 'Ambubachi' or

'Ambubosi' is derived. It means that water is emitted, which refers to the earth's swelling from the monsoon's onset.

This festival is popularized as a celebration of the menstruation time of Goddess 'Kamakhya' in some parts of India. However, it is seen as a menstruation of the entire mother earth. However, the goddess Kamakhya remains the focal point of the festivities. It is referred to as the Yoni or Genital Goddess (one of the leading 'Shakti Pith' where it is assumed that the genital organ of Sati has fallen). Usually, Ambubachi said on the seventh day of the month of Ashara, every year.

The temple of Kamakhya remained closed for three days during the 'Ambubachi mela.' Mother Earth is considered unclean for three days as traditional women's menstrual seclusion. The widespread belief is that the earth's holy mother is a fertile woman and is cultivable for the germination of seeds and the cultivation of crops that made her fertile. That is why the woman's womb is compared to 'Kshetra' for cultivation.

Ambubachi symbolizes this phenomenon of the ancient concept of agriculture. The Bodo community called this festival 'Amthi-sua'.

Menstruation is still stigmatized and shamed worldwide, as well as in India also. Many Hindu festivals and mythological concepts celebrate this significant event in a pubescent girl's life and social, behavioral pattern. The discussion is entirely based on my observation and the secondary data from different literature sources available in esteem journals and web pages. Most of these festivals and mythological stories indicate that the young girl had reached marriageable age, and the celebrations often promote a hetero-normative, patriarchal view of womanhood. This scenario played an essential role in the behavioral pattern of a girl towards her womanhood.

Menstruation is a natural physical activity that has been oblique in mythology, endowed with both positive and evil symbolisms, and has been the subject of a wide range of taboos and rites in all traditional societies for as long as records go back. Many misconceptions and cultural misunderstandings about Menstruation still exist today. Nevertheless, the menstruation festival has become a part of social and behavioral life that cannot be ignored.

The first period of a girl's life has a considerable influence. It is regarded as a sign of maturity towards womanhood. Even though Menstruation is still stigmatized and shamed worldwide, many Hindu rituals honor this as a cultural event, as the young girl reached marriageable age. Women's puberty is often celebrated as a sign that they can now marry and bear a man's children, reinforcing a patriarchal, hetero-normative view of womanhood.

Several Hindu festivals celebrated menstruation centuries before women found it empowering to talk about menses in front of men, much to the chagrin of their moms and grandmothers, and televised ads provided women with the confidence to normalize the monthly periods. The menstrual festival is a hinge of a girl's life from a period of rapid physical growth, sexual maturation, the activation of new desires and motives, as well as a wide range of social and affective changes and problems.

Girls' mental health influences the social, behavioral changes in this phase. More specifically, it is believed that pubertal maturation is linked to the activation of social and motivational tendencies, which regulate behavior and mood swings. Menstrual blood is described as sacred, a gift from the Gods, or a punishment for sin in these stories, but it is always magical and powerful. Menstruation's stigma harms women's health, sexuality, well-being, and social position and behavioural changes.

Self-consciousness and **hyper vigilance** connected with concerns about revealing one's menstrual status are two of the most common repercussions. Period stigma harms those who experience it, ranging from physical issues such as a shortage of sanitary supplies to verbal shaming of menstruation persons as 'unclean.' Significance of the study Festivals have an essential role in fostering social cohesiveness. However, menstruation and its related festivals are surrounding by social taboos and norms.

Menstruation ritual and women's psychological changes and behavioural patterns are related deeply. Some four-day festival commemorates the earth's fertility regeneration cycle, and this is similar to a girl's or woman's menstruation cycle. The Hindu Lower Assam Community is called 'Amoti' or 'Ameti.' In West Bengal, it is called 'Ambabati' respectively. Tuloni Biya Assam also has a unique tradition of public puberty celebrations, known as Tuloni Biya. Tuloni Biya is a ceremonial ritual celebrated seven days after a girl reaches puberty. Various rituals and ceremonies are organized in distinct parts of the state.

This ritual celebrates a girl's journey to womanhood. Raja Festival The word 'Raja' originates from 'Rajaswala' (meaning a menstruating woman). Contextually, this festival became more popular from the Middle Ages as the 'Raja Festival' in Orissa. This festival enjoys an agricultural break and worship ceremony for Bhudevi, Lord Jagannath's wife. 'Raja Festival' was held in mid-June. The first day is named 'Pahil Raja.' The second day is known as 'Mithuna Sankranti.' The third day is known as 'Bhu Daaha' or 'Basi Raja', and the fourth last day is celebrated as 'Vasumati Snana.'

These four days, women take a holiday from their daily schedule and wear new saree, alata (a red colored liquid spread across feet for decoration) and ornaments. This festival is like 'Ambubachi Mela'. The villagers organized a joyous celebration for three days to welcome the monsoon. According to common belief, menstruating women is a sign of fertility, and the festival is considered a menstruating span of the planet. Therefore, all agricultural activities remain suspended for these four days.

Notably, it is a festival of unmarried girls and potential mothers. There are some restrictions on these three days, especially in bathing, not to walk barefoot, not to scrap on the ground, and not to cook. Guru Panchami Brata 'Guru Panchami Brata' is seen on Shukla Paksha Panchami in the lunar month of Bhadrava, i.e., the day after Ganesh Chaturthi. Brata is practiced by married women who held upabasha and paid obedience to sapta rishis (seven sages) to eliminate 'rajaswala dosha' as women who consider Menstruation impure immoral their lives.

Ritual Kala Samskaram Festival Ritu Kala Samskara or Ritushuddhi is a Hindu ceremony conducted in South India when a girl passes through the menarche (first Menstruation). At this stage, a girl's family and friends donate a sari to her as part of the celebration. Nowadays this festival is becoming popular as 'Half-Saree Party' or 'Half-Sari Feature'. When the girl begins to menstruate, a separate room is arranged. Her relatives visit her with presents.

On the last day of her menses, her mother and other women in her family perform a 'Bath ceremony'. The girl dresses in new clothes and ornaments, and the 'Griha Pravesh' ceremony is organized. The festival of Keddasa, The Keddasa or Tulu festival is an ancient festival. This festival is associated with the annual fertility season (agriculture) of mother earth in Kerala and Karnataka. Mother Earth is expected to go through an annual transitional cycle or menstrual period.

After that, the world will bear fruit and crops. Manjal Neerattu Vizha's Festival 'Manjal Neerattu Vizha' is a three-day menstrual festival in Tamil Nadu. At this festival, the girl undergoes ritual seclusion, ritual bathing, and many other local rituals. A turmeric bath ceremony is organized when they first received Menstruation. Friends and family are invited to enjoy these occasions, and for the first time, offered the girl to present a saree as a mini version of marriage.

The Tradition of the Tantric Culture, The Temple of Devipur in Andhra Pradesh is an important centre of Devi Srivida in the Tantric tradition. Devipuram Guruji is synonymous with menstrual rites and restrictions. It is also essential that menstruating women are not allowed into the temple because it is believed that menstruating women will generate an imbalance in the temple's energy.

Festival of Thriputharattu Kerala is a region where the idea of Menstruation is being celebrated. Every month, the Murti (idol) of the goddess Parvati (Bhagavati) is believed to be menstruating. Therefore, her Murti has been transferred to a hidden room for three days. After the menstruation cycle is over, a female elephant is brought to the Pamba River for a ceremonial bath. The festival is known as the Thriputharattu Festival When the goddess bleeds.

Festival of Peddamanishi Pandaga 'Peddamanishi Pandaga' is celebrated in parts of Andhra Pradesh and Telangana. The first and last days of a woman's life are celebrated luxuriously. On the first day, the girls have 'Mangal shan' with five women in their family or relatives, except their mother. The girl is staying in a separate room. When menstruation is over, her family members have arranged a huge celebration known as the 'Peddamanishi Pandaga Festival'.

The Bauls are the religious community, blending elements of Hinduism and Islam, consisting of people who renounce the practices of Bengali society to survive by collecting money from singing in public places. The Bauls practiced a peculiar ritual to celebrate Menstruation. In Baul culture, having a friendship with a menstruating woman is a way to attain divine happiness and spiritual emancipation.

Worship of River and Menstruation: The rivers of India are considered holy places and as 'mother'. Since that, most of India's streams are considered impure for two months per year, and then this is implied as the menstrual cycle is going on. However, due to the purity of the Ganga, Yamuna and Saraswati rivers, there is no restriction on using their water.

Indian Mythology and Menstruation: All most all the part of India, Menstruation is considered dirty and impure. The origin of this **associated myth** dates back to the Vedic times. In the "Rig Veda," Lord Indra, the King of Heaven, killed Vritra with a thunderbolt but felt much guilt after the murder of Vritra because he was the son of a God. Lord Indra then rushed to the nearby woman to protect her.

The woman said she would be guilt on Indra's behalf if Lord Indra promised to bless her healthy offspring, and this guilt emerged as Menstruation.

Women, unlike men, do not become impure when they come into contact with filthy objects or persons, according to the Skanda Purana, since their impurities are wiped away during Menstruation. The 'Devi Bhagavata Purana' claims that a woman is forgiven of adultery when she goes through

Menstruation, whereas the 'Manusmriti' claims the same for mental adultery.

Having sex with a lady during her menses is thought to result in the birth of evil-minded nasty offspring, as Narakasura, who, despite being the son of Bhudevi and Varaha avatar of Lord Vishnu, had a predisposition to Asuric tendencies because he was conceived while Bhudevi was undergoing Menstruation, according to the 'Kalika Purana.'

Procreation celebrations are not limited to such old Hindu rites. Historian Jawhar Sircar believed that the cycle of creativity among human females and nature are linked somehow. According to the Egyptians thought, Menstruation was the real strength behind the Pharaohs, making them immortal. From the primitive era, Menstruation- festival and socio-cultural behavioural pattern of adolescence are interdependent.

Socio-cognitive functional changes with psychical development characterize adolescence, and culture plays a catalyst in this whole scenario. The researchers believe that the surge in reproductive hormones during puberty triggers motivational tendencies, such as appetitive motives in the arena of social objectives and rewards, which aid in social reorientation which reflects on the worship of the Mother Goddess through the menstrual festival.

The activation of these rituals has a favorable impact on the behavioural pattern in the curtail point of puberty. The experiences of pubertal development, both in terms of hormonal changes and contemporaneous social events, impacts teenage development and later conduct, which is celebrated through festivals and rituals. Given the compelling discoveries to date on the contributions of biological factors to teenage social behavior, future research extending this line of inquiry to individual differences in the relationship between puberty and social behavior will be exciting.

It is vital to investigate the range of pathways through this developmental age, just as it is essential to explain standard, mean-level developmental patterns of adolescent behaviour. As reflected via the festival, periods as a symbol of creativity and women have always been an essential component of society's culture.

On the other hand, Menstruation has been stigmatized for a long time, whereas in some places, it is honored as menstruating earth. In truth, while the event is credited with honoring menstruation women and the soil, it also reinforced and glorified the societal norm of not letting menstrual women and girls participate in household work.

Festivals commemorate the birth of Gods and Goddesses, as well as their victories over evil forces. Festivals are reflections of people's faith, social, and cultural lives. Hindu festivals, in particular, are intertwined with peoples' religious lives. The appreciation of nature's contribution to human life and humans' responsibility for maintaining nature's good health is another significant aspect of these festivals.

Moreover, what perplexed stated that, even though it was a celebration of menstruating earth, it was not acceptable to treat women and girls as usual when they had their periods. It was simply a physical function. Therefore, it was never discussed publicly.

On the contrary, such traditions are represented to empower women and promote menstruation health and happiness. Based on mythological context, women's blood is considered sacred in some cultures, and it is believed that it should be ritually separated. According to this logic, sacred blood only becomes ritually hazardous or 'unclean' when it comes into contact with nasty things, but it is always magical and powerful.

With its robust, deeply ingrained patriarchal foundations, ***period poverty*** creates significant impacts on menstruating women around the world. Shyness, fear, and anxiety not to get menstrual desire products during Menstruation create a negative psychological impact. Anyone who can use menstrual products needs the freedom to regulate their periods without shame, stigma, or fear. This is not only a health danger; it can also damage a girl's education, well-being, and, in some cases, her entire life.

Many of these beliefs and cultural misunderstandings still exist today, manifesting in a broad spectrum of unfavorable attitudes regarding Menstruation, which can have substantial and direct consequences for reproductive health.

After walking through all the historical and modern anecdotes, things will change only when **you** and **I** decide and commit ourselves to improving this antique problem plaguing our thoughts. We are now in the modern age and Iet us be modern in our thoughts and actions too.

Moving towards solutions:

1. **Normalize talking around periods with known and unknows also with females and males both.**
2. **Understand it as a normal biological process like breathing digestion and others.**
3. **Provide ample support to a girl or woman in need. Support must provide for psychological and physiological safety both.**
4. **Start questioning the myths around it.**
5. **Don't be a victim of the patriarchal mindset.**

Leadership Lessons from "शक्ति."

There is a lot that women go through that makes them unique. The time has come when we *stop telling* them what to do and instead *start learning* from them.

So here I present seven leadership lessons from women. This one comes from Tomas Chamorro-Premuzic and Cindy Gallop which I came across during my research. Although the majority of people at the top of organizations are men, studies show that it is actually women who have what it takes to effectively lead. So, rather than advising female executives to act more like men to get ahead, society would be better served by more male leaders trying to emulate women.

There are seven big lessons they can learn from a different sex. Although there is a great deal of public interest in ensuring more women become leaders, thereby reversing their under-representation in the ranks of power, too many suggested solutions are founded on the misconception that women ought to emulate men. The thinking is: "If men have most of the top roles, they must be doing something right, so why not get women to act like them?"

But this logic fails to account for the dismal performance of most leaders — who are overwhelmingly male. As we have argued before, the real problem is not a lack of competent females; it is too few obstacles for incompetent males, which explains the surplus of overconfident, narcissistic, and unethical people in charge.

As a consequence, gender differences in leadership effectiveness (what it takes to perform well) are uncoordinated with gender differences in leadership emergence (what it takes to make it to the top). Indeed, research shows that the prevalence of male senior leaders is not a product of superior leadership talent in men. Rather, large quantitative studies, including meta-analyses, indicate that gender differences in leadership talent are either nonexistent, or they actually favor women.

With this in mind, it would be more logical to flip the suggested remedy: instead of encouraging women to act like male leaders (many of whom are incompetent), we should be asking men in power to adopt some of the more effective leadership behaviors more commonly found in women. This would create a pool of better role models who could pave the way for both competent men and women to advance.

Here are some critical leadership lessons that most men can learn from the average woman.

1. **Don't lean in when you've got nothing to lean in about.** There is a trend of telling women to "lean in" to qualities like assertiveness, boldness, or confidence. In men, such qualities can manifest as self-promotion, taking credit for others' achievements, and acting in aggressive ways. Since there has never been a strong correlation between leaning in and being good at something — especially for men —a better option would be to stop falling for people who lean in when they lack the talents to back it up.

    In a logical world, we would promote people into leadership roles when they are competent rather than confident, vetting them for their expertise, record, and relevant leadership competencies (e.g., intelligence, curiosity, empathy, integrity, and coachability). Note that all these attributes are far better evaluated with science-based assessments than via the typical job interview.

2. **Know your own limitations.** We live in a world that celebrates self-belief, but it is far more important to have

self-awareness. And often there is a conflict between the two. For instance, awareness of your limitations (flaws and weaknesses) is incompatible with skyrocketing levels of self-belief, and the only reason to be utterly devoid of self-doubt and insecurities is delusion.

Although women are not as insecure as they are portrayed to be in the self-help literature (and much of the popular media), studies do show that they are less overconfident than men. This is good news because it enables them to understand how people see them and gives them the capacity to spot gaps between where they want to be and where they actually are.

People who see themselves in a more critical way than others do are better able to prepare, even if it means overpreparing, and that's a solid way to increase your competence and performance.

3. **Motivate through transformation.** Academic studies show that women are more likely to lead through inspiration, transforming people's attitudes and beliefs, and aligning people with meaning and purpose (rather than through carrots and sticks), than men are. Since transformational leadership is linked to higher levels of team engagement, performance, and productivity, it is a critical path to improving leaders' performance.

If men spent more time trying to win people's hearts and souls, leading with both EQ and IQ, as opposed to leaning more on the latter, and nurturing a change in beliefs rather than behaviors, they would be better leaders.

4. **Put your people ahead of yourself.** It's extremely hard to turn a group of people into a high-performing

team when your main focus is yourself. People who see leadership as a glorified career destination and individual accomplishment are too self-centered to foster their teams' wellbeing and unlock their subordinates' potential. Imagine a person who is only interested in being a leader because they are chasing a bigger paycheck, the corner office, a more senior title, or any form of status.

They will be inherently less interested in making others better; their only goal is to be more successful themselves. Because men are more self-focused than women, they are more likely to lead in a narcissistic and selfish way. If the average male leader wants to improve their performance, they would do well to adopt a less self-centered style of leadership.

5. **Don't command; empathize.** Throughout history, we have told women that they are too kind and caring to be leaders, but the notion that someone who is not kind and caring can lead effectively is at odds with reality. We are not living in medieval times. Twenty-first century leadership demands that leaders establish an emotional connection with their followers, and that is the only reason to expect leaders to avoid automation.

Indeed, while AI may hijack the technical and hard-skill elements of leadership, so long as we have humans at work, they will crave the validation, appreciation, and empathy that only humans — not machines — can provide. Men can learn a lot about how to do this effectively by watching and emulating women.

6. **Focus on elevating others.** Female leaders have been proven to be more likely to coach, mentor, and develop their direct reports than male leaders. They are true

talent agents, using feedback and direction to help people grow. This means being *less transactional* and *more strategic* in their relationship with employees, and it also includes the openness to hire people who are better than themselves, because their egos are less likely to stand in the way.

This enables them to unlock other people's potential and promote effective cooperation on their teams. While we gravitate towards leaders who are self-focused and self-centered, the likelihood that such individuals can turn a group of people into a high-performing team is low.

7. **Don't say you're "humbled." Be humble.** We have been asking for humble leaders for 20 years or so, but we keep gravitating toward ones who are overconfident and narcissistic (not female). There are well-established gender differences in humility, and they favor women. Not all women are humble, of course, but selecting leaders on humility would result in more female than male leaders.

   Humility is fundamentally a feminine trait. It is also one that is essential to being a great leader. Without humility it will be ridiculously hard for anyone in charge to acknowledge their mistakes, learn from experience, take into account other people's perspectives, and be willing to change and get better. The issue is not that men are unwilling or unable to display it, but that we dismiss them for leadership roles when they do. This must change, for humility is a critical driver of leadership effectiveness in both men and women.

Does reading this upset you?
Ask yourself why. If you're a man, does this make you feel that there's a campaign against males and toxic masculinity and that

angry feminism is on the rise? That reaction is getting in the way of your learning from women what you can do to make yourself more successful. If you're a woman — and/or a feminist — do you reject the idea that women are more likely to display feminine traits than men are? That's exactly the reason the average woman has more potential for leadership than the average person.

At the end of the day, the only controversial aspect of our views is the notion that increasing female representation in leadership would augment rather than reduce meritocracy. The best gender equality intervention is to focus on equality of talent and potential — and that only happens when we have gender-equal leadership to enable men to learn different leadership approaches from women as much as women have always been told to learn leadership approaches from men.

This article is a short cut. Men, these lessons accelerate your leadership development. Women, these are the reasons why you should have been leaders already and why you should demand what you deserve now.

ERA 6

Towards SOLUTIONS

- **Surprise for the Men, finally! Men get space here!**
- **"Stimulated" Language - Top must Know languages of this era.**

Surprise for the Men, finally! Men get space here!

Why not start this conversation by continuing a poem that you have read in the very beginning, I have curated for all of us, and particularly the most influential man on this earth for us, i.e., our father, and if you are a father, it should make you walk down the memory lane.

………………………..continued from the beginning.

May his honor never diminish, his eyes never be moist,
Have we ever saluted him?

If the mother's sacrifice was incredible,
the father would be incomparable,
Don't forget this, it's like this alone,
He is happy defeated by you, else the world burns and churns.
The question will not be wrong - where he buys such power from?

Then came the time as, the father had once explained to the father,
Respect for everyone, now he had to do marry his daughter to a groom,
Money raised, killed his own, every desire,
So, may he respect everyone and keep daughter's emotion,
Set land, property, and houses on fire-sale.
He had to make his little one glad.

Be it a son or a daughter, fed his own soul,
While their marriage and education were his only goal.
He gave up his life, so now let's ask him,
Where does so much power come from?

He didn't know that his hard work would pay off and off.
He had sown and spread, killing his dreams,

They would one day give him a toss,
They would become their own boss.

Did I make a mistake giving up my dreams? The father sighed,

In the confusion, this father recalled his father's words,
"This is the way world is, no one is with anyone forever."

Now let's go back to your youth,
the dream that was left unfulfilled, now stands to accomplish,
Laugh, smile, the game is for just four days,
How long will you think, there was no hair in those ages,
Nor now, this is the world since sages.

If a father does so much,
why not ask today *where he buys such power from?*

He who has not respected his father,
don't forget you will be the one, one day,
The only difference will be,
A father will no longer be able to see,

If he is around, then the day will come for you too,
If you want to live head held up high, take a sigh, and

Ask him once – *where he buys such power from?*

I hope the above poem might have taken you all for a ride.

Moving on, Masculinity: Is it still associated with man's power?
Let us have a look.

As patriarchy is the outcome of the past, we cannot easily get rid of this long-standing, stubborn fact. That's why the domination of men and the subordination of women is not a self-reproducing system. We accept that deep-rooted, male-controlled customs have contributed significantly to the acceptance of domestic violence too. But with the advent and significant modernization of eras, we have seen domestic and mental harassment not limited only to women, but men are too subjected to all kinds of cruelty.

And the best part is that men are not supposed to express their vulnerability. Why? To save masculinity from being perceived as weak.

From the moment we're born, our society begins teaching us about gender. We're given a "sex" at birth, either "male" or "female." Throughout childhood, we get taught about the roles, behaviours, and attributes that are considered appropriate for that female or male identity. The term "masculinity" refers to the roles, behaviours, and attributes that are associated with maleness and considered appropriate for men.

Similarly, the term "femininity" refers to a society's ideas about the roles, behaviours, and attributes that are considered appropriate for women and associated with effeminacy," softness," shyness," and the list goes on.

If we go back to mythology, we have a great showcase of masculinity, which can pave the way for how it can be healthy. Its concept has been multifaceted and complex, transcending its simplistic associations with strength and aggression as prevalent in multiple modern narratives.

Instead, mythological texts offer a more nuanced view of masculinity interwoven with virtues like wisdom, duty, compassion, and restraint. **Shiv,** often seen as the epitome of masculinity, embodies destruction and creation, asceticism, sensuality, fierceness, and tender-heartedness. He is a yogi who meditates on the snowy peaks of Mt. Kailash, signifying self-control, and introspection, and yet he is an enthusiastic husband of Parvati and the loving father of Ganesh and Kartikeya.

From him, we can learn the importance of our multi-faceted nature, finding strength not just in action but also in observation and emotional presence. Vishnu, the preserver, exemplifies responsibility and commitment. His numerous avatars, including Ram and Krishn, are illustrative of his desire to descend into the world to restore balance. Ram, the hero of the Ramayana, is often held as the paragon of virtue, embodying the principles of honour, loyalty, and righteousness. He shows that true masculinity involves upholding one's duties and making sacrifices for the greater good.

Krishn, on the other hand, represents a more playful and compassionate aspect of masculinity. His life story teaches the importance of intellect, diplomacy, and the embracing of life's pleasures without being enslaved by them, which perfectly resonates with Rudyard Kipling's poem titled *"If.."*

He says, "If you can dream and not make dreams your master, if you can think and not make thoughts your aim, if you can meet with triumph and disaster and treat those two imposters just the same, yours is the Earth and everything that isn't."

Furthermore, Krishn's role in the Mahabharat as a guide to Arjun emphasises the power of wisdom over brute force.

Hindu mythology's perspective on masculinity often challenges stereotypes. It pushes against the notion that to be masculine is to be violent or unfeeling. For instance, Hanuman is both immensely strong and a model of devotion and humility. His strength doesn't lead to arrogance but is in service to others, indicating that power should be coupled with selflessness and service.

Ardhnarishvar, a form of Shiv, shows one half of him as a fully developed woman. He is half male and half female. It shows that the masculine and feminine are equally divided among each of us, and there is interdependence between both energies. This serves as a powerful metaphor for the modern man to recognise the need for inner balance and the integration of what are traditionally considered feminine qualities—nurturing and intuition.

Today, when men are increasingly encouraged to defy traditional gender norms and to express a broader range of emotions and traits, mythological tales provide a rich source of wisdom, illustrating that strength comes in many forms, that leadership can be compassionate, wise, and inclusive, and that it is crucial for men to feel comfortable sharing their feelings and to seek support when necessary. The legendary warrior Arjun, for instance, experienced doubt and anxiety on the battlefield of Kurukshetra, yet he readily sought guidance from Krishn, his confidant and guide. Ram, too, turned to the sages Vishwamitra and Vasishta for wisdom.

These examples show that if divine figures and heroes can show emotional openness and seek assistance, so can you, me, and all modern men. We, together, can look to Hindu mythology not for rigid templates to copy but for inspiration to cultivate a well-rounded character.

Fast forwarding from mythology to the modern age, **colonialism** paved the way for the origin of masculinity by dividing gender roles because European women went to the colonies, as wives and servants within households controlled by men. We deal with these social ideas about masculinity and femininity every day. Though the very idea of masculinity dates back to around the 16th century, several types of masculinities have emerged, and since then, masculinity has been redefined due to political awareness, debates, and criticism.

In many parts of the world, men are dominant in different sectors like politics, economics, education, sports, and family.

Genuine gender equality is still a dreamer idea.

However, it doesn't mean that all men are powerful. But the fact that having power over political, economic, and social affairs is associated with masculinity. The roles, behaviours, and attributes that are associated with maleness and considered masculine usually bring greater social status, economic reward, and political power than those associated with femininity.

Even if the number of women taking on leadership roles in many levels of society is on the rise, from the government to private companies, the norm remains that leadership is seen as masculine and done mostly by men; that is, authority still has a male face. There are several Nepali women who have gone into politics or been promoted to senior positions in business, but they're often stigmatized for not showing womanly characteristics or being too manly.

Advertising is quite common in contemporary society. Many do not feel that its effect is beyond the normally considered province of economic transactions in the market. Advertisements can affect our values and perceptions of something. Some advertisements and posters represent hegemonic masculinity, which many people may not be aware of. They attempt to construct "hegemonic masculinity." For example, in a Nepali advertisement for Maruti Cement, Rajesh Hamal in his westernized attire is placed at the centre with both his arms visible, whereas other female actors in their simple traditional attires are squeezed into the crowd of other men.

Besides, in the posters of schools and colleges, girls are seen holding books, dancing, singing, or drawing, while boys are seen riding a horse, trekking, swimming, doing sports, and the like.

It isn't limited to actors and students. A female receptionist, not a male receptionist, is seen working in her office. A suited and booted male is seen sitting in his spinning chair in his well-furnished office. Such a publicity tendency may project men as "hegemonic masculine" males and females as "subordinate characters."

Some men tend to say firmly that they must demonstrate strength within marriage through physical discipline to correct their wives' behaviours and to adhere to static social roles. Hegemonic masculinity must be expanded to understand role entrapment, which is the function of conformity to gender expectations related to the pressure to follow hegemonic masculinity. Furthermore, in patriarchal societies, women aren't conceptualized as holding power, wielding power, or being powerful, unless it is in relation to aspects of the domestic or private domain, which is seen as the "natural" location for women.

So, a common reason behind domestic violence is family disputes with traditional expectations of men as well as men's attempts to express their masculinity. Masculine stereotypes include heterosexuality, strength, leadership, and dominance. The exhibition of such characteristics disempowers and weakens girls' morale by creating opposite qualities to function within.

Since women are subordinated by body-reflexive practices that are typified by an "obligatory heterosexuality" ingrained in hegemonic masculinity, men are entrapped in the patriarchal framework to follow hegemonic masculinity because of traditionally defined gender roles and societies' expectations of them.

Education, awareness, technology, and media are playing an instrumental role in transforming hegemonic masculinities into transformative or healthy masculinities. Nevertheless, some incidences or examples of hegemonic masculinities are still deeply rooted in Nepali patriarchal societies, ingrained in people's mindsets, and strongly grounded in everyday lived experiences. We, as grandparents, fathers, uncles, brothers, nephews, brothers-in-law, and sons-in-law, can play a critical role in establishing a fairer, more peaceful, and happier society around us.

"Stimulated" Language - Top must Know languages of this era.

Before we move on, it would be best if we try to understand the terms *"Stimulated Language"* and *"why"* it is important to know.

We have heard a lot that people wish to improve their communication skills. It is of utmost importance to know a *blanket skill* first before any other skill. It can supersede any other skill which certainly will help us all to make quantum changes in our impact in communication or any skill that we talk about.

Motivation isn't a power word anymore. Let me replace it with ***Stimulation - It is something that arouses interest, inspiration, or incitement to action.*** Isn't it something that we all are looking for?

To start our journey towards stimulation, the language of sports can be one of the easiest and the most impactful *stimulant* and *depolarizer*. To put it simply, I was enjoying a tea-break when India had few minutes back then scored 397 against the New Zealand recently in the semifinal match where we *WON* in the Cricket World cup 2023. During my walk to the tea vendor, four entirely different personalities asked me the exact same question as I was glued to my phone watching the live score even while walking.

"What's **Our** score?"

Without a second thought, I answered in the affirmative, "It is 397, and Virat Kohli, after gifting himself a birthday gift by the much-waited 49th ton earlier against the mighty South Africa, had then scored the 50th " The reactions of all those four were mostly the same: pride, a smile on the face, happiness, ecstatic, joyful, and a feeling of belongingness to the country.

Those four who asked were:

1. The tea vendor in his mid-forties
2. An aunty was returning from her office, whom I even didn't know. She was in her mid-fifty`s.
3. A young schoolchild in his early teens.
4. A polished senior guy who just got out of his shiny four-wheeler to have a sip of tea.

Fast-forwarding, let me take you through a time-travel of *grit, gumption, and glory* that will make you smile and feel proud. And that is not enough; it will *stimulate* you towards something, something bigger than you, a purpose, to think beyond yourself, and most importantly, to take action.

Life gave them a raw deal, but instead of wallowing in self-pity, these para-athletes aimed for the podium and made India proud in Hangzhou 2023. She shoots with her feet; he is paralyzed from the neck down, so he does it with his mouth. They are among India`s elite para-athletes who totted up 111 medals— 29 gold, thirty-one silver, and 51 bronze.

Meet the *super-humans—the* minimum word that I can use to suit their personalities. **Sheetal Devi,** the 16-year-old from

Loidhar village in Jammu and Kashmir's Kishtwar, was born without arms. As a child, she learned to write with her toes, but in archery, phew! You need a lioness's heart to even think about doing something like that. She has won three golds in mixed archery with her teammate Rakesh Kumar and is aiming for a Paris Paralympic gold in 2024. Do you have words for her grit? I honestly don't have any. The best I can do is to salute her efforts. Amazing indeed.

Next, do you find it difficult to get up early in the morning or to go running?

Well! Not for **Ankur Dhamma**, who won gold in the men's 1500m and 5000m T11 events in Hangzhou. He not only competes but also trains other para-athletes. This is special, right? But I have something more to offer in his story. When he was six, doctors told his parents that he would not be able to see again. So, he does all this magic as a 100% visually challenged runner by relying on a guide runner to point him in the right direction.

While you read the above lines, did you think about religion, gender, age, caste, etc.? I am sure not! This is the power of sports; it helps to get united, to de-polarize, and to think beyond the boundaries.

The Language of Sports

So, when was the last time you played? Played anything. I would love it if you could just pause for a bit and go down your memory lane a bit deeply about the last time you played something, cricket, badminton, kho-kho, kabaddi, or anything. And here I am particularly talking about something physical.

And now, if you can remember, can you also try to think about how it made you feel?

No bypassing allowed, please; I urge you all to seriously go down memory lane to feel that feeling of playing or watching the last time, however old or recent it might be.

If you have a cute smile on your lucky lips now, that is the impact I am talking about. We feel connected to the people with whom we play. We certainly were disconnected from or got disconnected from the gadgets while playing that allow us to *connect* in real life with our friends, the environment, the fresh air, and most importantly, *ourselves*.

While writing this, the Indian Men's Cricket team was 10-0 in the ICC Men's Cricket World Cup 2023 and has just thrashed New Zealand, who were virtually posed as the strongest team. The relentless efforts of the Indian team were on full display, and you know I was waiting for India to win the world to hand over the manuscript for the work in your hands right now to the publisher.

But writing now, post-World Cup win, we never lost. Ten wins out of 11 games, i.e., a 91%-win ratio against the entire best of the best teams, beating each and every squad convincingly with stellar performances by each individual. Technically, we might not have been able to lift the World Cup, but more importantly, the Indian cricket team has been far more successful in uplifting morale, status, and dominance.

Ask any team, even those who won the World Cup, and there will be one name: ***India.*** Isn't that great? I have never heard or seen our team play better than this.

India ranks a lowly 126 out of 150 countries in the 2023 Global Happiness Index, calculated on six wide-ranging parameters: GDP, life expectancy, generosity, social support, freedom, and corruption. But Team India's triumphs gave moments of collective happiness to millions that those wide-ranging parameters cannot capture. Life, in the end, is a few stories we remember and want to share.

Dear Rohit and Team,

You won our hearts, and we will be ready to go. Indiaaaaa... again, the moment boys are in the field. You gave us the chance to celebrate and enjoy waving in joy; you gave us a month and a lifetime full of memories that are incomparable. We will prepare with you for the next 2027 World Cup. Thank you for playing and making us play along with you.

Tailpiece: The radio cab had agreed to the ride but wasn't moving. He called the driver and said, "Can you please wait for a couple of minutes, sir?". "Just three more balls before the innings get over." It wasn't an Indian game. But as an Indian, the passenger understood. *"It's Okay. Take your time,"* he said.

Moving on, what I want to delve into is: no one questioned the religion of the person who took wickets and who scored runs, right? Why?

The answer to **"Why"** is the takeaway here? Sports are one of the *stimulating languages* that help us move beyond the obvious. Beyond the boundaries, beyond the layers of society, and beyond whatever polarises us. We are here as **India,** and this feeling is above everything else. Being a learning and development person, we in our organization are striving for gamification in our work, training methods, and learning.

As our champion, MS-Dhoni, said in one of his interviews, "We must cultivate some sports in our lives." At least, what sports can offer is that they will help us stay healthy.

Now the next thing if you say, ***"I don't get time for sports"*** sounds to me like, ***"I don't have time for me and my health."*** If this is so and you are okay with it, I don't mind. But

I am *not okay* with not being able to stall for myself. Isn't that what we work for, right?
It is time to do things that we want to do.

And by pursuing sports, I don't mean you necessarily win a medal for our country or go to a stadium to play. You just need to cultivate an environment around your surroundings that allows your body to get moving with any activity. Personally, I play. I play a lot and will keep on playing. As an author and an avid reader, people assume that I am always immersed in reading or writing. Yet my best ideas come during my play time.

So, what's next? Go! Get moving; if you are already playing, that is great; if not, do plan to cultivate some sporting days in your week; even if that means once a week, at least start.

Get set Go and experience the change within!

The Language of Sign

While Goa is known for the beach, the shore, and beer, giving you vibes of a holiday and a cool summer clothing line, I was delighted to read one good day about a move aimed at sensitizing schoolchildren about inclusivity. The Goa Board of Secondary and Higher Education has decided to introduce Indian Sign Language (ISL) as the seventh optional subject in high schools in the state.

The National Education Policy 2020 and the Prime Minister seek that ISL be propagated. I am so passionately pursuing communication strategies in new and impactful ways, what I call *the power communication* method. They would eliminate the communication barrier for the deaf as well as hearing students.

I also had the good fortune this November 2023 to attend the Global Diversity and Inclusion Summit in New Delhi with my colleagues, where Women and Child Development Minister Smriti Irani said that the guide on gender-inclusive communication and the Anganwadi protocol for divyang children will help empower children with special abilities and their families.

More than anyone's masterclass, what I was mesmerized by was the performance by artists. It was not just a normal performance. It was Indian classical dance, too, by specially abled children. Some of them were on wheelchairs, and some were deaf. Can you imagine how they would have prepared for this? I simply don't know, but what I know is that they mesmerized everyone with their accomplishments on beautiful tracks.

What I learned then was how to clap for them. Clap without a hint of sound to appreciate. We were asked to shake both our hands in the air, bringing them to the level of our shoulders. With special abilities, they were able to communicate, and not only that, but they could also display a breath-taking performance. That is why I call *language of sign* as *stimulated language* that can go beyond normal boundaries and help us communicate, creating inclusion.

You don't necessarily have to do a certification course in sign language to improve, but at the most fundamental level, what we can try is to be mindful of our own body language.

Have you observed the body language of eminent personalities? They have a lot to say via their bodies, and people do make perceptions even before they hit the microphone. Body language, or sign language, is indeed way more impactful than the actual words spoken and complements the speaker convincingly.

The Language of Compassion

Ours is a country known for its compassion. In an extraordinary showcase of gesture, what we mean by our culture was recently displayed by one of the organizers of a community Durga Puja in Kolkata's New Town. As reported in the Times of India Newspaper recently, to break the tradition by worshipping 8-year-old Nafisa as Goddess Durga during Kumari Pooja on Maha Ashtami to promote the message of communal harmony.

Amazing, isn't it?

While it is common to worship prepubescent girls on Durga Maha Ashtami, traditionally, only Brahmin girls are chosen as Kumaris. The decision to select Nafisa carries a message of ***inclusivity and communal harmony*** inspired by Swami Vivekananda's actions over a century ago. Let me proudly bring it out here.

In 1898, during his travels, Swami Vivekananda requested a Muslim sailor to allow him to worship his four-year-old daughter as Durga at the third Bhavani temple in Srinagar, a gesture that still resonates with people today.

He touched the little girl's feet as part of the ritual. His teachings have influenced people not only in India but are spread across the world. If Swami Ji could worship a Muslim girl more than a century ago, why can't we do it now? Now, if you think about the effect it had on her mother, It was more than expected. Nafisah's mother, Saba, who works as domestic help, was excited to be a part of the ritual. She said, "She was surprised and did not know how to react initially. We sat her down and explained the customs, and she agreed happily," said Ganguly, Nafisa's teacher.

Imagine a world where we move beyond the boundaries of religion. How beautiful the world would be! Do you think it is not possible? If it can be possible for one Nafisa and one Saba, if it can be possible for a city like Kolkata, why can't it be replicated across entire India and the world?

If you are wondering what the meaning of compassion is, Here it is.

Compassion is a social feeling that motivates people to go out of their way to relieve the physical, mental, or emotional pains of others and themselves. It is sensitivity to the emotional aspects of the suffering of others. Compassion involves "feeling for another" and is a precursor to empathy, the "feeling as another" capacity (as opposed to sympathy, the "feeling towards another"). Empathy has been talked about a lot. I personally go in this order.

Compassion >> Empathy >> ~~Sympathy~~

It involves allowing us to be moved by suffering to help alleviate and prevent it. It requires us to be:

"***A Man of Deeds*** rather than being A Man of Words."

An act of compassion is one that is intended to be helpful. Other virtues that harmonize with compassion include patience, wisdom, kindness, perseverance, warmth, and resolve.

It is time we become compassionate and learn the ***language of compassion.*** If the above story about Nafisa and Saba made you smile, you can certainly feel the beauty of the language, which has the potential to bring people closer. This language can help bring peace around us. Our great leaders like the Budha and Swami Vivekananda have always advocated for such language, and I strongly feel this language cannot be more desperately needed than it is now.

I strongly urge everyone reading to remove the ***lens of religion*** and acquire a ***lens of compassion.*** Also, it is more important than reading this to replicate this behaviour on the ground in your daily lives. And believe me, there is no harm, and it is very doable.

The Language of Smile
Did you smile today?

If not, why not start by looking at your own beautiful smile in the mirror or that smart phone in your pocket? Your smile is powerful. It can invite a lot of opportunities, solve wars, and save relationships. Are we living in an era where a simple smile has become so scarce that people believe in abusing rather than just smiling?

And, in which language do you smile? Could you connect to the smile of forty-one laborers stranded inside the Silkyara Tunnel in Uttarkashi? Experts of different nationalities and laborers from multiple districts in India had that one thing in common when they all safely came out.

What about that village, or about America and Africa? And what about Japan? Well! I can only smile in one language; if you come to know of some other language of smile, feel free to let me know!

But for now, it is one of the most precious stimulated languages that we should be practicing. Smiling more often reduces stress and improves your daily conduct. Even while talking to a person of a different nationality, the least you can do is simply smile, and you are there to go! The next time you are talking to someone, just reflect on who you are with that smile!

The Language of Nature
If you ask me, what's my super-secret sauce? Here is the answer. Earlier in our journey, we came across going close to nature. How does it speak?

Can we communicate with nature? The rain and that breeze and that sun with shadow, that mountain with flower valley. Even once we start to imagine the picture, it starts to have a promising effect on us, and we start to get seduced for the better. It straight away uplifts our moods. So why not experience the language of nature often? It helps to heal. My most fruitful and productive ideas have come from it, which has so much to offer. But we need to communicate with nature and understand. The greatest lesson of my life, I must say, is that I have started to connect, communicate, and learn from it. You know there is one thing that is perfect in the world, and that is *nature*. And best of all, it doesn't demand anything except your time and respect. So, I would urge all of you reading this to start practicing this wonderful, *stimulating language of nature*.

ERA – The Finale

Towards ACTIONS

So, if you have come this far, congratulations! You have invested your time in quiet and thoughtful moments.

Now it is time to get moving closer towards action soon. Some quick lines from my earlier work, which I love to re-iterate,
"Starting tasks is the first characteristic of intelligence; once started, Bringing tasks to completion is the second characteristic of intelligence."
Let us start where it all started.

TOWARDS *THE BETTER YOU*

The entire journey has been evolving towards a better me, and I hope it does the same for you.
What is right is right.
We have earlier seen in "ERA *5: The Shakti"* how a female tried to escape paying the cab bill by misusing women's empowerment, and we have also seen how males have since ages dominated and society is gripped by a patriarchal mindset.
Being right is

- o **Gender Neutral:** A male or a female, anyone could be right or wrong.

- **Age-independent:** Not necessarily; an older guy would always be right when compared to a younger guy.
- **Caste-independent:** One sect is not always right over any other sect because of the question "who" said it.

What is more important are the aspects of "why" and "what" rather than "who.."

Solution offered,
- **Primarily, accepting and normalizing that there exists a difference.**

- **Next, respecting that difference is key.**
- **The third is distancing ourselves from *Avidya*, ignorance, as discussed in "ERA-3:** *The Buddha Way."* **True education and knowledge are the keys to moving away from unawareness.**

Let us paint it pink.

This would be the final ride for all of us together on the journey here before we meet at my next job.

We have earlier dealt with *Chitra* and *Sid*'s true love story as to how they were separated and what happened after they married different personalities, which co-incidentally didn't turn out well for both of them.

So, what had happened before marriage? How and where did they both meet and fall in love? How and why did they part?

Some of the questions to be answered here in the section. The most important aspect to know would be how destiny played with them before bringing them together again and, of course, our learnings from the episode.

Why is this section called *"Let us paint it pink?"* Partly because it is a beautiful love story and partly because it is placed in the beautiful Pink City. Yes, you guessed it right.

Sid was on his way to the Pink City, Jaipur, for some official work along with his friend Nishant. Sid had a few research projects going on to be completed in Jaipur. He was supposed to meet a lady in Ajmer (a city near Jaipur) for the research work, but once Sid started his journey to Ajmer to meet the lady, she informed him that she had met some emergency and would not be able to meet him.

The cab driver asked, "Sir, is everything all right?" Sid, after a pause, told the cab driver, No problem, let us continue. It is just that instead of going to Ajmer City, let's move directly to Ajmer Sharif.

The cab driver answered in the affirmative, and the journey started. Sid, being an interactive and active learner, sat along with the driver in the front. His name was Ravi.

The journey began, and they started mingling about family and friends. Their personal favorites track one after the other and ghazals as they loved it. Soon they started their personal stuff. After getting cozy with the driver and going to the *friendship zone*, they discussed a variety of subjects like cricket, children, education, weather, rain, songs, ghazals, and what not!

Soon, Ravi asked, "What about marriage, sir?"

"A learning experience, Ravi," Sid replied. To which the driver followed up with a question, "Is everything all right?"

Sid: "Now, everything is all right, but earlier it wasn't."

"Why, sir, what happened?" asked Ravi.

Then Sid started by saying, "I was married to a girl with whom I am getting divorced, and before you ask me why, let me tell you upfront that the reason is parental abuse and a relationship with a past guy."

Then Ravi stopped the music being played in continuation, one after the other.

The environment in the cab suddenly got gloomy along with the weather as it started to rain fairly. Instead of the off talk, Sid started by sharing the only girl who had loved him, but he couldn't marry her for whatever reason. She was Chitra, the girl who used to live in Jaipur and shifted to Delhi, NCR, after parting ways with Sid in 2020. Sid had a great smile on his face while talking about her.

Ravi became very curious to know about Sid`s story, seeing his smile, as to how it started and ended. One thing is for sure: Sid had truly little idea that soon after his return to Delhi from his pink trip, destiny had some other plans for the story. But first, the beginning. Sid, in his own enticing language, stated by saying,

"It was a bright but pretty frosty night around mid-March 2018 in a guest house where I lived with a dozen officemates for official purposes. It was a big guest house with a roof-top balcony. I went to the same guest house for an official assignment, where he first met Chitra, though she had seen me earlier too."

"It was not first-sight love all together; it was just that we liked to talk to each other. Luckily, it was her birthday when we met, and it was also the caretaker's birthday, so I ordered a cake for both to make them happy and comfortable, as I had met both for the first time. Soon, after the sweet, it was again a long night for both of us, as we prepared the mid-night tea that kept us talking and sipping through our mugs till the early morning before we realized that it was now time to prepare to go for the individual official tasks."

"The wintry night, the pink breeze, or the sweetness of the tea that kept us glued together, or our destiny, with truly little idea of what was around the corner. All seemed lovely, pink, and rosy, but after a year or so, we parted with time, and everything seemed to be over."

In the *ERA 2: Challenge Your Mindset When The High Tea | The Love Story begins,* we see how Chitra and Sid were married to two different personalities after they parted ways.

Ravi became more interested, but before he could ask any further questions, it was time for Sid to be back at the hotel and then in Delhi with Nishant. Ravi and Sid both exchanged their phone numbers, as they had developed a good bond.

Fast forwarding: soon after a short span of two months, Sid called Ravi, the cab driver, and exclaimed in excitement before even saying hi or good morning!

"Do you remember Chitra?" Yes, sir, I replied to Ravi.

"She is back, and we are together now! This is nothing short of a miracle!" shouted Sid with joy.

"Wow! Congratulations sir! I am glad," said Ravi in return, along with questions of how, when, etc.

Before Ravi could know all the answers, Sid said that he would call later. Whether Sid called Ravi back or not is a story for another time, but I have an answer to the "how" and "when" of Sid and Chitra coming together even after getting into the wrong marriages right next!

The leap of faith—friends are *badass!*

Sid once suffered mental torture from his better half, or not so better half, *Maya Singh*. *He* was devastated and was trying to recover from the mental agony of police cases, harassment, and abuses. After regaining a bit of strength, he confided in one of his faithful friends, Ankit. They two together sat at around 10:30 in the night at their *Adda* (a most sought-after place to meet for close friends). Both were really tense about the situation and didn't see a ray of hope.

Ankit, during the discussion, asked a question: "What have you thought about your next marriage and future now?"

To which Sid exclaimed a powerful line that he didn't know would change his life forever.

Sid exclaimed!

> "All the life we strive for different goals and plans, but not this time."

"I am going to give life the opportunity to offer me what it can."

It was indeed a strong statement, but Ankit quite amusingly started to smile and laugh like anything. It agitated Sid, who said, "I am undergoing life's hell, and you are laughing at me?"

Ankit: "I have good news for you!"

Sid: "Really, nothing is good these days! But yeah, anyways, please at least stop that laugh and tell me the news."

Ankit made an unbelievable statement, which Sid could not believe. "You know Chitra is getting divorced."
Friends are badass!!!

"What? I mean, are you kidding me? This is not a suitable time to joke, for sure!" said Sid.

And Ankit kept laughing, partly because he was happy for Sid and Chitra and partly because he could taste a miracle. "Yes." Finally, Ankit broke his laughter, and he stopped Sid from calling Chitra suddenly after disappearing from her life two years ago.

But Sid, being Sid, called and somehow connected to Chitra and requested to meet the same night. Chitra, to her sheer surprise, was taken aback and was decision-less with the thoughts of how to meet Sid, as someone else's wife, with health deteriorating, devasting life, and more.

But somehow destiny had planned this before they could think, and they met the next morning after Sid waited for her the entire night close by her home. Even in the morning, Chitra was skeptical about meeting Sid in the first place, as it was something startling beyond her imagination. But she gathered strength and then met Sid.

They both could never imagine that they would meet again, and that too in such a devasting situation, each with a failed marriage and a victim of domestic violence. Soon they shared what had happened to each other, and then, as we had read earlier, it was: first, Sid weds Maya, and second,

Chitra weds Rajveer, which would soon become Sid vs. Maya in the court cases, and then Chitra vs. Rajveer.

They started out their own battle, and then the ray of hope of Chitra married Sid now. Whether it came to be true or not? It may be in the next piece of work after a year, but yes, learning is offered right here!

The Modern Marriage and Divorce

I don't know who needs to hear this, but since it is significantly important, I need to bring it out here.

After getting a close taste of multiple successful marriages along with unsuccessful ones around me, including my own, I was bewildered by a few important questions.

What does it take for a marriage to be successful or unsuccessful? What do we need to do ourselves, as parents or in society, to make marriages successful? What is the right age for marriage? Why is religion given importance in marriage? When should a couple think of getting divorced? Does marriage give rise to domestic violence? Why are there numerous examples of failed marriages, be they arranged or by choice—the love marriage? How are the old ones at home placed after marriage? Does the groom's parent become insecure about a new girl coming into her son's life? Does the bride lose independence after getting married?

I asked these questions to my mentor, Mrs. Sangeeta Sharma, whom you had met earlier in the journey.

She had some interesting anecdotes to share from her own marriage. Those will be a good starting point for us all.

She is currently sixty-four at the time of writing, and she was married back in her 20s. Her father was a learned scholar too. She wanted to study to become an IPS officer, being from an educated family. Though what she actually did is an inspiration for us, She was married in a good-to-go family, but it required her to cover as a new bride, and such olden rituals were to be followed.

Within a few weeks of her marriage, it perplexed and tensed her like any other new bride after not being able to adjust to a pristine environment. She called her brother and father and explained her situation. She shared with me the reply that she received, which made her traverse her journey from being a young, bright student to a new bride who was supposed to follow patriarchal and outdated customs, and then to becoming the principal and director of a prestigious institution.

Her father said, "Anyone can thrive in favorable situations; now is the time to utilize and put into action your education and show us how you navigate adverse situations with your intellect and what you have earned." You need to create a **balance**. **That is all life is all about.**"

Although she is so humble to accept the fact that little did she understand the statement then, smilingly she told me that this statement actually helped and changed her action for the better.

She explained what she has observed: what happens now is that if a girl tells the same story, which happens very often these days, then the parents go one step further and ask her to come back to her paternal home or to not follow everything that is being told by the in-laws. And in turn, the bride is further propelled in the wrong direction.

Then there are another set of parents and brides who teach and learn the art of balancing, respectively.

This takes me to the inference that I would love to share.

Firstly, in the former case, the word comes as "compromising," and in the latter, a healthier version, "balance."

Secondly, there has been a significant development of two entirely opposite shades of society. There are those who are ready to embrace a bit of discomfort and gain relationships, and then there are those who don't want any change or discomfort post-marriage and are ready to continue convenience at the cost of relationships. Here, I am talking from both the boy's and the girl's perspectives, as well as their parents too.

Now I am not looking here to advocate for who is right or wrong, but one thing is for sure: both are different from each other.

Thirdly, there is a "change" in everyone`s life post-marriage, be it a boy or a girl, parents, in-laws from either side, siblings, etc., and so on. And the problem is not the marriage, but the unwillingness to accept the change.

Next up, to what degree is change acceptable? Or to be better put, is the change ethical with good intent?

The Last up, Patience. Cmon guys you got married and it is a big event of life to navigate. It will take some time. Patience has seen a downward trend in the Youngsters and sometimes in the aged too. It is not the generation that has lost patience. It is the time, the ERA that we live in, has stolen the priceless art of patience.

Imagine if Mrs. Sangeeta`s parents hadn't counselled her well, would she go on to create a balance in married life and educate thousands of youngsters now?

I don't think so.

I don't know whether I have been lucky or unlucky to witness diverse types of marriages around me including mine, but that gave me different perspectives to look at it.

1. I saw, Chitra *weds* Rajveer which soon became Chitra *V/s* Rajveer in civil court.
2. I observed Sid weds Maya, which similarly traversed to Sid *V/s Maya*.
3. I could see Parul *weds* Himank, which will soon become Parul V/s Himank.
4. I discussed, Payal *weds* Piyush, which is going the same way.

But don't worry guys, I have good examples too. Hahaha! Marriage is not that bad. Don't change your plans to get married if you are planning to get your partner soon. Your better halves would kill me!!

1. Ankit weds Swati, which remains as it is, and they already have a baby and are going great.
2. Then there is, Rashmi weds, Shashank, a second marriage and even going better.

And there are many more examples, but what I can say best is that marriage is trusted social institution that has served since ages in different forms. If we blame marriage, it is like a situation where a Honda make car gets damaged in between the journey and we say that entire automobile industry is sick.

Now knowing when to leave that car to save yourself from further damage which can cost you your life is equally important. You know what I mean right?

I mean there is nothing wrong in it. Right?

Earlier we talked about *ethical change* post marriage. Let's us quickly explore what worked and what not and what are the stats that can guarantee a blessed marital life.

In the first case, Chitra and Rajveer, soon after the marriage, Raj started physically abusing her and went for unethical demands coupled with physical violence. In the second Sid and Maya, it was the girl now, Maya who started mentally assaulting her in-laws for money and tortured her husband to part away from parents so that she could live a life without responsibility. And why did Maya take revenge from Sid and his family?

Because before her marriage she was in love with some else of a different caste which her parents didn't like, so they found the answer in Sid, hurried for marriage, matched all the stats supposed for a successful marriage namely:

1. Similar caste
2. Arranged Marriage
3. Source of income
4. Nuclear family
5. Metro city
6. Good Looks (with the hope that *kids born out of them would be charming enough that would suit their "KHANDAAN"*)

But even the stats couldn't keep the marriage alive.

Now one thing is evident here, *suffering is not limited to one gender,* although historically females have been subjected to more atrocities. Next for Parul and Himank and the last Payal weds Piyush, it was the in-law's pressure and non-acceptance of new norms of the bride that would soon cost them their marriage.

What's the common thread here in these unsuccessful marriages?

If you closely observe, you will find it linked to at least one or multiple of the five inferences that I have put across before few lines. Reasons could be many, but the trigger and the bigger picture would crystalize down to those.

So, how about successful marriages and re-marriages? When to say *No means No*? and when is the time to go after divorce? What is the mantra? Have we normalized divorce or still a taboo talk? We want the children to suffer but don't want a divorcee tag, right? The re-marriage of Rashmi and Shashank mentioned earlier, had an interesting element to it, Rashmi had a kid too from her first marriage, yet Shashank *accepted* both and are living happily. You see the keyword here, ACCEPTANCE.

Well! Just a marriage isn't working anymore!

Marriage with *trust* and *commitment* have always worked and will always keep on doing so.

So, here are some true bites for each one of us, and then a beautiful poem awaits for you next:

- **Males:**

I know you work hard to get money and care for your family. You faced the pressure of studying, then building a good career that too was under the *pressure of getting good "Rishtaas,"* while you were also navigating your teenage hormonal imbalances. On one side, you had and still have that peer pressure to *look good* and *earn good piloting in* the competitive world. You are one of those who went away from home to build a career, from a king-size bed to a single room without a bed. You learned to cook, and some days you didn't cook because your wallet balance showed a low.

You lost many of your friends and girlfriends too, with some close ones becoming distant ones, and you realized life is tough out there. You were taunted, for the way you looked, how much you earned, and how much that Mr. Sharma's kid earned. You were also compared with those who went abroad and were demeaned to the extent that your struggles looked as if you were a failure.

Cmon! I cheer up for you; you have come a long way! Give yourself a pat on the back. It was YOU who still stood tall after all these. But...but... but...

This doesn't entitle you to forget the struggle your parents went through, including your better half's. Why? Because for them, you both were kids, and their education, food, and stubbornness were their responsibilities, which they never denied.

Then comes your *wife*, who went through the same struggles as you did, and do you know what? They had to bear some of them that were tagged to her because she happened to be a *she*. You had the pressure to look good, but that was a bit higher for her; otherwise, she would not get a good life partner. She was awarded the responsibility to cook because *something is socially meant for girls,* though you could go out and play. Yes, it's true that she has already suffered from patriarchy since childhood.

While you could go out of the city to study, she was denied because she was, *and* the world didn't want her to flee. Freedom was awarded to you once you were born male, but she got little chance to taste it, which is the reason she gets irritated when you deny her something. You were born with a taste of freedom; she had to fight to get even a sight. She has already said "**no**" a thousand times for things she demanded. While you were misbalancing and balancing your hormones in your teens, she was struggling when puberty hit her, and a monthly pain found the most consistent partner of her body before you entered her life.

She has gone a bit beyond your struggle, so please don't let her struggle anymore. She married you with the hope that now would be the time to get relieved of her pain, only to shortly discover after marriage that her dream was all in vain. You are a father figure to her, and you know she confides in you. Yet, many of us have let her re-invigorate the pain that she has already gone through.

You demand money; why? Can't you earn yourself? Or you want a *car* from her parents. Is that the level of education you got that you even didn't mind begging for? Wow! And did you call yourselves men? Then you say, "No." It was not me who demanded. Really, then who is supposed to drive that car and keep all the money? That is the level of maturity you learned from your elders? Would you blame your elders, society, or someone else for such a *great* act?

A man is one who cares, loves, earns, and takes a stand not between his parents or wife but between what is *wrong* and what is *right*.

The next time you want to be a man, stand for what is right; otherwise, the woman knows how to fight; don't take her as someone light.

And if you are the one who always stands up for what is right, then give yourselves a pat on the back, for you are the man in sight!

- **Females:**

We know you have borne a lot; for those, the words cannot fulfill! You have been the garden, the delight to show us the light. You have been the epitome of sacrifice, and you will be the one who shows us light. You have the power that no one has. Take a look around; everyone waits for your sight. Your childhood had been *special*, for you had to bear that we had to bear none, the *she* worked, the guardrails for you, you had to fight.

You waited for your turn always; you sat behind so that those males could take the main seats at home, yet you came so far that none of us could match. You are seen as an inspiration that we look forward to, all thanks to your dedication and the excellent work you do.

You loved someone but couldn't reveal what society would say, you hindered your own zeal so that your parents could lay high. Some took your advantage, and your heart was broken. You learned how not to choke. You are grown up now and understand the world—the *why, what, and how!*

Despite all the hurdles, you built a woman much upwards and onwards than men; you are the gender by which we know nature; you are the one who decides our future. You are the ones whose name's rivers are known by; sometimes down and sideways, you learned how to keep the head held high!

But..But..But..
That doesn't entitle you to enter into a fight; the question is not who is wrong or who is right. No one is always right, and not everybody lies. The man in your life started as a father, then came a man who committed to you for the rest of his life. We understand that you had to leave your home, friends, and regular sights to come to a new home. Isn't the home yours now?

Elders are elders; we think how tough it is now, but those very elders taught us the meaning of life. The new members look forward to you as a friend, spouse, mother, and whatnot. They have a dream together with you: your mother was once the same, a new bride at the home that you call yours. The new becomes your home now that marriage has happened, so why the worry of a new place? Life has given you a beautiful new beginning, yet you are entangled in the past.

Your husband, too, underwent a lot that many matches cannot! See how beautiful the world is together; dream, not the freedom that makes everyone cry. Freedom and responsibility are two sides of the same coin. Get to the family; why not have them join?

Believe me, if you are lucky to have them, then there are people who beg for them; at least someone is there to see you when you return home; someone cares where you go; and those who care when you are low.

Marriage is a beautiful thing that has made several kings. Lament not what happened and will happen; time is all yours to make it happen. Yes, it is true that people can live together happily and soundly and laugh with each other on the ground. If you think you left your family for him, he did the same by committing to share his life and his dream. The world is beautiful if we make it work; otherwise, hell is near to making it worse.

Ok, so now you stood for what is right, and you were domesticated, until you offered a fight? Pat yourselves up. You are a hero; you know to stand; the fight is not YOU vs. ME, but what is wrong and right? Coming back from a marital home, moving out of marriage—is it all right? Yes, it is if it offers you a new life. You are not a puppet; you need to have a life. For anything demanded that doesn't seem right, do offer a tough fight. Taking a stand for what is correct is a sign of bravery, not a dessert. You are a human too; with dreams, you are not the one supposed to scream.

You are not fighting with your better halves or the in-laws; you are fighting with your own better versions.

It is always the right you vs. wrong you, you know, and if you don't, hesitate not to ask for help from someone who seems fit to go!

Freedom is not free of responsibility; freedom is not snatched at any cost; true freedom is when you are genuinely happy inside and out. And if the definition sounds like baggage, please don't get into marriage!

- **Parents and in-laws:**

I understand you lived your lives; you struggled for our education and meals at night. You cared for us, those sleepless nights, and the prayers you offered for us to get well soon! You did your best to care for us. We can't just say thanks for what you did for us, nor can we repay the debt. But one thing is for sure: we want you to be happy and healthy, and long live your dreams and reality. Yes, we want to care for you.

You were not alone; we tried our part, though we could do little, but we withstood the worst of life. It is hard out there, I know, but I was in the same world as you. Nothing changed in the modern age; life was tough and is getting tougher now. With all the wishes you had, we were blessed with whatever we could have.

You got us married to someone new, selecting among the many and drilling down to a few. Wishing us good luck and a new life.

But...but...but...

Does that entitle you to our freedom too? You expect from us, so we do. There is a new bride who needs time; she can't live the way you want her to; she is not a bird in a zoo. She is a human with her own ways of living; there must be some good; let us see what she is giving. Relax; she has just been married the way you were without any knowledge. Yes, it is true that you had to do a lot, but yes, it is also true that the new world demands that we do a lot more.

Freedom is what we need, the way you needed it at your early age. Don't tell us to plan for the future; please let us young people live. Past and future keep us entangled; did we learn to live in the present? Nature's pace is the best; why not trust nature and let it unfold the rest?

You can't control whom we should like; we are humans, different from animals, with our own thoughts; mistakes know no age; you may have had many let us make ours; something can't be taught; it has to be learned along the way.

Understand the gap; yours was a different time, and now it is mine. The world has changed; we need to hop on the ride, or else we will be left behind.

If you want life the way you want, why did you give it life? This is not to be debated; there is no right or wrong; just change the perspective.

And if you are the one who supported the kiddo in every decision and dream, you are the God that we refer to before we enter the temple and become mean. You have been the peak figure for us, whether mother, father, or in-laws. We understand it was tough, but it is nowhere different now!

The world has changed; that's the only difference now. Our lives can't be complete without you; you are the one who helped us become what we are now!

- **Siblings:**

Yes, you have always been together, the night before and thereafter. Elder or younger, you have been like one, sharing meals, clothes, and whatnot! Those fights you know you didn't mean, yet it was a beautiful part that made you both dream.

You know I got married now, a new person in my life. My life has changed, and so will everyone's. I wonder why the fights—you were the one, the most excited for it, yet you can't take it.

Ok, so you now got married; it is nothing new, and for the better, it has to happen some day or later. You are a boy or a girl; remember, we had our share of pains, as have the new ones in our lives. So worried are you for your own life? What would have happened if the elders thought like us? Is that why our parents were laborious?

Siblings, if you are reading this, you are lucky; at least you have a sibling and a family. Ask those who have no one to care for.

- **Those four people in society:**

I hope no one from this audience will read this piece. So why bother with them?

For us, let us try not to be in this category ever and respect the privacy of all around us the way we want our lives to be private.

1 Minute Course towards the Better You

1. **Smile! You have come a long way!**

2. **Get Close Nature! Get a home-based plant in your room.**
   Want it to be sent from me? Sure, contact me at the tap of scan below, with your address, and I promise I will get it delivered for you, the only ask will be to post a picture with the plant and this book together. And if it can reach me, I will just love it.

3. **Share the knowledge and mindset that you developed during this journey. How? Why not pass this piece to someone close to you.**
   Post your picture with the book at

4. **Incorporate Buddhas Teaching in your life. The first one:**

   "It is better to conquer yourself, than to win a thousand battles."

5. **Sit for 2 to 5 minutes in silence to practice mindfulness and calm yourselves down and focus on breathing and reflect internally.**

6. **If not already said today, say *"I love you"* & *"thank you"* to your better halves, parents, and the people you love. You actually need to "say" it.**

7. **Think of those one or two learnings (apart from the ones I have suggested) that you can apply right from today.**
   You know, we can't learn driving a car by a book, it can of course show us the way. But life will get better only by action and practice.

8. **Think of that ONE NOT SO GOOD HABIT that you will counter today and stop it. And actually, take action.**

9. **Think of that ONE HABIT that you will start to develop from NOW Onwards. And actually, take action.**

10. **ACT Now and get moving!**

    Congrats! You are a better YOU Now!

About the author

Rahul Thakur is the successful author of two books that inspire and motivate professionals and students, with a special attention to female education, to learn to become a better version of themselves. He intends to leave his audience healthier and happier. Not only make his audience *feel better* but, most importantly, *get better*.

As a learning and development professional and strategist, Rahul has made it his mission to support the education of curious learners of any age. He does this through his flagship training programmes and engaging conversations, which teach us how to reboot our mindset to become our best selves.

He has helped a number of businesses, professionals, and students become creative. His signature programmes draw from his own experiential learning and encourage us to take the next step and carve out resilient paths. His books and training programmes have influenced thousands to move ahead on the career ladder and step up. He personally assists needy youngsters with a desire to succeed through learning and execution.

Rahul currently works with a US health care organization and is a guest lecturer at various prestigious colleges in India. He is so fond of sports, music, and travel that you will find him always engaged with his hobbies, which form the centre of his conversations.

He holds a master's degree in HR and is a certified cognitive behavioural therapist. Rahul lives in Delhi, NCR, with his mom and dad.

You can connect with Rahul at:

Scan the QR code to get connected.

Why not continue our journey with a beautiful poem right here.. before we meet in our next.

Title: *"Mom, why you are the way you are?"*

This question comes from my soul every time.
Come on, you tell me today.
Mom, why you are the way you are?

When I wasn't even born,
You started to care, how did you dare,
Your voice used to come when I was in the womb,
The question was there then, when will I meet this fairy sound?

When my eyes opened on the planet,
I heard your first voice,
Though, It wasn't my choice,
The question was still there,
Compelled with my childish voice tottering, couldn't ask then,
Come on, tell me today, mother, why you are the way you are?

Hunger satiated, I was the first every time with your hands,
You didn't get even get to touch your share of food, in the stands,
You made excuse *"Today there is some work"*, when I asked,
You said you have a lot to do, you are tasked!
You gave me the share of cool breeze in the summers first,
You starved and satiated my thirst,
You didn't utter a single word!

When my body was feverish,
You meditated on temples, mosques, and churches.
Begged for me to get well soon.

Didn't worry about yourself even then,

Being Goddess Saraswati, gifted me voice, art, and education,
So why can't I ask this question?
Come on, tell me today, mother, why you are the way you are?

Fought like *"Rani Bai"* against the world,
Whenever *they* pointed a finger, no one felt sorry,
Address for the triumph, even then you handed over to me!

Everyone wondered how he did that,
What didn't they know, it was your blessing,
Even back then, I was surprised, troubled by questions,
You know I have blessing in disguise!

Beauty, fame, strength first you handed over to me,
Improved my appearance, spoiling your own,
The questions again troubled me, you acted ignorant,
When I asked, you showed me the mirror,
You said, "It's a matter of age.
In this era, everyone has to dissipate!

"Don't let the conscience move, don't let the head bow,
Whenever the heat comes on you, my blessings will show,
You will win, wrote it with my heart signed by the great
I have done whatever little I could for your sake!"

"I will live forever, in your voice, art and education,
You will always everywhere find my mention,"
I was relieved to hear this, but why did you say so -
We were happy together; do you ever plan to go?
Cmon! Tell me today, why you are the way you are!

Unlucky are those, who does not know the meaning of a mother,

When "*she*" could not come on her own, *"Raani"* came as the avatar of a mother!
Smile, courage, and love handed over so why to bother?

If she is still with you, Ask her once more,
Mom, why you are the way you are?

Bibliography

1. https://thesouthfirst.com/news/team-chandrayaan-3-meet-the-women-behind-the-successful-mission-thats-put-india-on-the-map/
2. https://www.thehindu.com/sci-tech/technology/navic-and-its-integration-into-iphone-15-explained/article67311882.ece
3. https://www.thehindu.com/news/national/karnataka/amazon-web-services-ties-up-with-isro/article67303869.ece
4. https://centralvista.gov.in/
5. https://centralvista.gov.in/evolution-central-vista.php
6. The Times Of India: 27th Aug, 2023
7. https://en.wikipedia.org/wiki/Vikram_Sarabhai#:~:text=Vikram%20Ambalal%20Sarabhai%20(12%20August,develop%20nuclear%20power%20in%20India.
8. https://en.wikipedia.org/wiki/Space_exploration
9. https://en.wikipedia.org/wiki/ISRO
10. https://en.wikipedia.org/wiki/Kolar_Gold_Fields
11. https://en.wikipedia.org/wiki/Hindu_cosmology
12. https://www.viralfactsindia.com/sanskrit-slokas-with-meaning-in-hindi-on-vidya-education/
13. Page 4: https://en.wiktionary.org/wiki/Shakti#:~:text=From%20Sanskrit%20%E0%A4%B6%E0%A4%95%E0%A5%8D%E0%A4%A4%E0%A4%BF%20(%C5%9B%C3%A1kti%2C%20%E2%80%9Cpower%2C%20energy%E2%80%9D).
14. Page 5: https://en.wikipedia.org/wiki/Shakti
15. Page 8: https://www.highclap.com/i-love-my-india-lyrics-pardes/
16. Page 12: https://www.camelmountain.com/blogs/stories/analyzing-

travel-far-enough-you-meet-yourself-quote-from-david-mitchell
17. The Time of India, Sept 13, 2023. Page 24
18. https://en.wikipedia.org/wiki/Forrest_Gump#:~:text=The%20film%20follows%20several%20decades,the%2020th%2Dcentury%20United%20States.
19. https://screenrant.com/best-quotes-forrest-gump-movie/#quot-my-mama-always-said-life-was-like-a-box-of-chocolates-quot
20. https://www.educationtimes.com/article/campus-beat-college-life/99733719/reducing-neet-pg-percentile-will-cut-seat-wastage-claims-govt
21. https://timesofindia.indiatimes.com/city/allahabad/a-life-takes-a-u-turn-from-busted-tyres-to-halls-of-justice/articleshow/103895805.cms?from=mdr
22. https://www.artic.edu/swami-vivekananda-and-his-1893-speech
23. https://www.un.org/en/observances/yoga-day
24. https://en.wikipedia.org/wiki/Vedanta
25. https://en.wikipedia.org/wiki/Bhakti_yoga
26. https://en.wikipedia.org/wiki/Uniform_Civil_Code
27. https://en.wikipedia.org/wiki/Secularism
28. https://www.quora.com/Are-Muslim-men-recommended-to-be-obedient-to-their-mothers
29. https://en.wikipedia.org/wiki/Baba_Farid
30. https://en.wikipedia.org/wiki/Women_in_the_Guru_Granth_Sahib
31. https://www.womansday.com/life/inspirational-stories/g29199258/bible-verses-about-women/
32. https://www.un.org/en/observances/yoga-day
33. https://en.wikipedia.org/wiki/List_of_military_unit_mottoes_by_country
34. https://en.wikipedia.org/wiki/Sare_Jahan_se_Accha

35. https://en.wikipedia.org/wiki/Women_in_Hinduism
36. https://nuawoman.com/blog/menstruation-festival-in-india/
37. https://indianexpress.com/article/cities/mumbai/around-town-week-long-festival-of-maasika-mahotsav-celebrates-menstruation-8619852/
38. https://en.wikipedia.org/wiki/English_Education_Act_1835
39. http://www.columbia.edu/itc/mealac/pritchett/00generallinks/macaulay/txt_minute_education_1835.html
40. https://vediconcepts.com/how-many-gurukuls-were-there-in-india-before-british-rule/
41. .https://vediconcepts.com/macaulayism-in-india/
42. https://vediconcepts.com/contact/
43. http://www.thesundayindian.com/en/story/macaulay-pioneer-of-indias-modernization/304/46935/
44. https://vediconcepts.com/gurukul-education-system/
45. https://en.wikipedia.org/wiki/Student-centered_learning
46. https://en.wikipedia.org/wiki/Education
47. https://en.wikipedia.org/wiki/Education_policy
48. https://en.wikipedia.org/wiki/History_of_Buddhism
49. https://en.wikipedia.org/wiki/Compassion
50. https://www.dictionary.com/browse/stimulation
51. https://timesofindia.indiatimes.com/india/grit-gumption-glory/articleshow/104996158.cms?from=mdr
52. https://timesofindia.indiatimes.com/blogs/toi-edit-page/why-purush-and-prakriti-are-gender-neutral/
53. https://timesofindia.indiatimes.com/city/nagpur/a-temple-of-sita-without-any-idol-of-lord-ram/articleshow/105133446.cms
54. https://www.youtube.com/watch?v=9EBkS2kE7uk
55. https://en.wikipedia.org/wiki/Menstruation_celebration#:~:text=It%20is%20a%20four%2Dday,three%20days%20of%20the%20festival.
56. https://www.historyjournal.net/article/97/3-2-6-548.pdf

57. https://en.wikipedia.org/wiki/Kamakhya_Temple
58. https://hbr.org/2020/04/7-leadership-lessons-men-can-learn-from-women
59. https://en.wikipedia.org/wiki/Sustainability#:~:text=%22Sustainability%20means%20meeting%20our%20own,to%20meet%20their%20own%20needs.
60. https://timesofindia.indiatimes.com/india/meet-the-unstoppable-21-under-21/articleshow/104200027.cms?from=mdr
61. https://timesofindia.indiatimes.com/india/to-meet-sustainable-development-goals-260-institutes-to-offer-courses-in-climate-change/articleshow/105193600.cms?from=mdr
62. https://timesofindia.indiatimes.com/blogs/toi-edit-page/the-buddhas-wisdom-can-help-to-heal-the-mind/
63. The Buddha & His Dhamma, By Dr. B.R Ambedkar.
64. https://timesofindia.indiatimes.com/blogs/toi-edit-page/mythology-inspires-a-bold-vision-of-masculinity/
65. https://thehimalayantimes.com/opinion/masculinity-is-it-still-associated-with-mans-power
66. https://timesofindia.indiatimes.com/sports/cricket/icc-world-cup/news/thank-you-for-the-memories/articleshow/105336515.cms?from=mdr

www.ingramcontent.com/pod-product-compliance
Lightning Source LLC
LaVergne TN
LVHW061539070526
838199LV00077B/6839